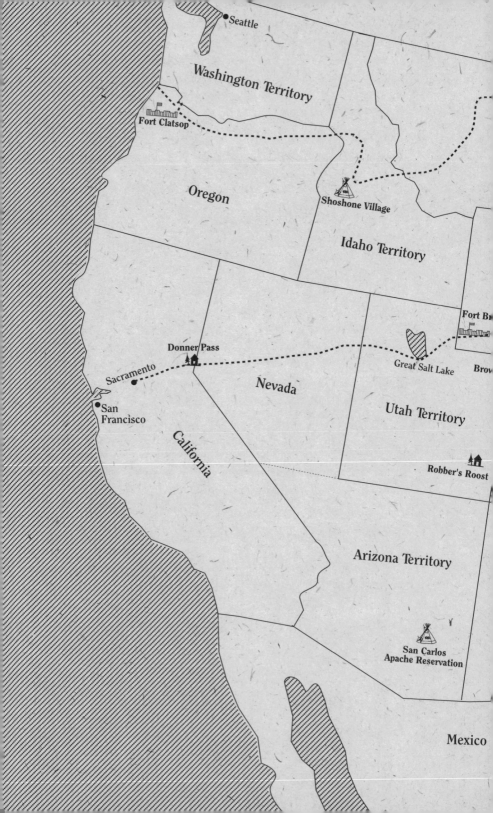

Best of
Dee Brown's West

BOOKS BY DEE BROWN

NON-FICTION

Grierson's Raid — 1954
The Gentle Tamers: Women of the Old Wild West — 1958
The Bold Cavaliers: Morgan's 2nd Kentucky Cavalry Raiders — 1959
Fort Phil Kearny: An American Saga — 1962
The Galvanized Yankees — 1963
The Year of the Century: 1876 – 1966
Bury My Heart at Wounded Knee: An Indian History of the American West — 1970
Andrew Jackson and the Battle of New Orleans — 1972
Tales of the Warrior Ants — 1973
The Westerners — 1974
Hear That Lonesome Whistle Blow: Railroads in the West — 1977
The American Spa: Hot Springs, Arkansas — 1982
Wondrous Times on the Frontier — 1991
When the Century was Young (A Writer's Notebook) — 1993
The American West — 1994

WITH MARTIN F. SCHMITT

Fighting Indians of the West — 1948
Trail Driving Days — 1952
The Settlers' West — 1955

WITH MORT KUNSTLER

Images of the Old West — 1996

EDITED BY DEE BROWN

Pawnee, Blackfoot and Cheyenne — 1961

FICTION

Wave High the Banner — 1942
Yellowhorse: A Novel of the Cavalry in the West — 1956
Cavalry Scout — 1958
They Went Thataway — 1960 (republished as Pardon My Pandemonium — 1984)
The Girl from Fort Wicked — 1964
Showdown at Little Big Horn — 1964
Action at Beecher Island — 1967
Tepee Tales of the American Indian — 1979
Creek Mary's Blood — 1980
Killdeer Mountain — 1983
Conspiracy of Knaves — 1987

Best of Dee Brown's West

AN ANTHOLOGY

DEE BROWN

Edited by STAN BANASH

Clear Light Publishers
Santa Fe, New Mexico

Copyright © 1998 by Dee Brown and Stanley D. Banash

Clear Light Publishers, 823 Don Diego, Santa Fe, N.M. 87501
First Edition
10 9 8 7 6 5 4 3 2

Library of Congress Cataloging-in-Publication Data

Brown, Dee Alexander.
    Best of Dee Brown's West: an anthology / edited by
Stan "Tex" Banash.
        p.   cm.
    Includes index.
    ISBN: 0-940666-76-6 (cloth) — ISBN: 0-940666-77-4 (pbk.)
    1. West (U.S.)—History. 2. Frontier and pioneer life—West
(U.S.) 3. Indians of North America—West (U.S.)—History.
I. Banash, Stan, 1940– . II. Title
F591.B863 1996
978—dc20   96-6237
                                                           CIP

Printed in the United States.
Typographical Design/Production: Vicki S. Elliott

Articles comprising the chapters in this publication appeared in *American History
Illustrated, Civil War Times Illustrated, Southern Magazine*, and *True West*.

Contents

Editor's Acknowledgments

The preparation of editorial and visual material for this book involved a number of people to whom I am grateful, but it is dedicated to only one: Laura Fanucchi, who was there in 1990 when it all began, in Little Rock, Arkansas. Initially, Peter Matson, Sterling Lord Literistic, is deserving of thanks for providing contractual assistance as Dee Brown's literary agent. Among those whose cooperation is appreciated for granting reprint rights are: Cynthia Cooper, permissions coordinator, Cowles History Group; John Joerschke, editor, Western Publications; and Alan Leveritt, publisher, General Publishing Company. I wish to thank Mimi Babochay, Mary "Roxi" Crawford, and Christine Pachota, who provided computerized expertise in preparation of select visuals. Gratitude also is extended to Fred Egloff, Bruce Herrick, Tom Joyce, Art Sowin, and Tom A. Swinford for suggesting titles of books that should be included in the reading list. Special credit goes to Clear Light Publishers staff: Sara Held, my editor, who guided me and offered advice, recommendations, and support; publishers Harmon Houghton, who had confidence in this project from our first meeting, and Marcia Keegan, who, with graphic artist Vicki Elliott, provided creative design and layout guidance; and Ellen Goldberg, who "rode herd" on me, making certain I tied up loose ends. Chip Carlson, Cathie and Sam Moscato, and Dorothy and Bob Wolf provided valuable investigative assistance.

Many thanks to the reference staff at the Park Ridge Public Library in Illinois, who helped me clear up obscure historical details regarding names and dates. Similar gratitude is extended to the Buffalo

Historical Society, New York, and to Northwestern University Library
for verifying additional reading sources. I am indebted to the many
archivists who were helpful in guiding me to photographs I sought or
made suggestions that might enhance the book's visual content:
Mario Einaudi, photo archives, Arizona Historical Society; Elizabeth Holmes, associate registrar, Buffalo Bill Historical Center; Linda
Ziemer, prints and photographs, Chicago Historical Society; Montana
Historical Society Photograph Archives; Rose Wilson, public affairs,
and Tom Durant, historical photo archivist, National Park Service;
John Carter, curator of photographic collections, Nebraska State
Historical Society; Chester Cowen, photo archivist, Oklahoma His-
torical Society; Karen Runkel, slide librarian, Oregon Tourism Com-
mittee; and William Sweeney, market analyst–publications designer,
Legislative Administration Committee, the State of Oregon; Sheri
Penney, manager of marketing communications, Pinkerton, Inc.;
Charles Brown, head of reference, St. Louis Mercantile Association
Library; and Linda Laws, curator of arts, Woolaroc Museum. And,
finally, a highly regarded special thank you to my friend, Dee Brown,
who paved the way for me by writing these articles over a period of
years and who laid the groundwork for so many other popular historians whose interest in the American West was kindled through him.

STAN "TEX" BANASH

Foreword
by Dee Brown

*I*t would be false modesty on my part to deny that I am gratified that an editor and publisher have seen fit to bring back into print a number of periodical articles that were published some years ago. Seeing them here all together, I am reminded again of the longevity of Americana, particularly Western Americana. Attitudes and writing styles may change through the years, but the basic elements — the events, the human beings, the tales, the myths, continue to entrance us as readers.

So great has been the recent interest in certain personae of the American West that print and film media, eager to supply the demand, have tended to turn some parts of our heritage into clichés. Splendid books have been written and numerous first-rate movie and television films produced about Little Big Horn, George Armstrong Custer, Sitting Bull, Geronimo, the Earp Brothers, Crazy Horse, Wild Bill Hickok, Red Cloud, Billy the Kid, Calamity Jane. Perhaps I've left out two or three others who are continually being warmed over and turned into fluff. The point I'm trying to make is — the Old West is being constricted into a handful of characters and incidents to the detriment of hundreds of other persons and events that are as colorful, or more so, than the dozen or so that the popular media continue repetitiously to thrust upon us.

Of course if one of us sacrifices a year of research and writing to tell a tale about a virtually unknown but immensely fascinating fur trader, or a valiant hot-blooded woman engaged in the cattle business, the media may scorn the results unless Calamity Jane and one of the Earps are included in the narrative. But after all, until a speculative pioneer writer chose to write for the first time about Wyatt Earp and another about Calamity Jane, no one before then had heard of Wyatt or Calamity. As J. Frank Dobie used to say, writers should not rake over old bones.

Old newspapers are not old bones, and one of my good friends in Illinois has recently spent a year going through nineteenth-century files via microfilm with all the delight and success of a true treasure hunter in search of something new. He has proved that untold riches, fresh as biscuits from the oven, still lie waiting for earnest prospectors working with typewriters and word processors.

Readers in search of imaginative accounts of the American West would do well to consult publications of the regional presses, the privately owned as well as university presses. Unlike the nabobs of the giant commercial publishing world, they dare to take chances, to step off the overtrodden paths that continue to lead us to too many thrice-told tales. Louis L'Amour once remarked that the best sources he could find for invigorating his fiction were small local publications, like the British chapbooks of yore, printed locally by someone with a burning desire to tell a true and wondrous tale.

When I look over the magazine pieces that Stan Banash has chosen for this collection, I see a few "big names" there, but at the time I wrote these pieces the incidents and characters had not become the stereotypes that they are today. Publishers who were then in the literary marts of trade had scarcely heard of those names. I am pleased to see included — thanks to long-ago editors willing to take chances on the unfamiliar — quite a few pieces about events and people off the beaten track. Some still are off the track, but I haven't lost my faith in the rewards of venturing into undiscovered country.

DEE BROWN

Introduction

*L*ife in the Old West was more difficult than often depicted, less exciting than some might want, and not as romantic as others might believe. But the West has a special place in American annals. Dee Brown, for almost fifty-five of his nearly eighty-nine years, delighted and informed readers with his writings about the "true history" of the Old West. His more than twenty-five fiction and non-fiction books, for the most part, emphasized the 1860–1890 era; his shorter pieces, however, covered a period that exceeded a century. It is the latter that piqued my interest, for in these works he reported on some of the most intriguing, controversial, and compelling episodes of American history.

The topics he explored concerned real people, places, and events. Sometimes subjects were suggested by editors, and other times he pursued them directly. Regardless of the selection process, Brown wrote with commitment, candor, accurate detail, and sincere feeling. He now claims to have written all he can about the American West; his work is complete. (In fact, he was reluctant to write a foreword to this book, believing it was akin to asking the guest speaker to introduce himself.) He told me that it is for others to write about new discoveries of diaries and personal accounts, to espouse and document new theories, and to pursue detailed research.

Brown's philosophy and approach to writing about the West can best be summed up with an excerpt from his introduction to *The American West,* published in 1994. He noted that "today it is fashionable to mock the myths and folklore of the American West. Yet if we trace the origin of almost any myth and tale we will usually find an actual event, a real setting, an original conception, a living human being. We must accept the fact that the Old West was simply a place of magic and wonders. Myths and folktales form the basis of almost every enduring saga in the literature of the American West. They are the comfort and joy of screen and television scriptwriters. But let us be wise enough to learn the true history so that we can recognize a myth when we see one." Brown understood the era because he immersed himself deeply in the people and their culture and lives by seeking out letters, diaries, and other personal accounts and reminiscences.

My first introduction to the writing of Dee Brown occurred as it may have for so many other people with the publication in 1970 of *Bury My Heart at Wounded Knee*. This work, which compassionately detailed the repetitive injustices perpetrated on Indians by the U.S. Government, caused many of us to look at Indians in a different light. In fact, the book, subtitled *An Indian History of the American West*, was selected recently as one of the New York Public Library's "Books of the Century." Although Brown had written seventeen books earlier, several in conjunction with the late Martin F. Schmitt, he remained known only to a gradually widening circle of historians, western history students, and others with an avid interest in the subject. He credits TV personality Dick Cavett with propelling the book to the forefront of bestsellers by quoting passages on his show. *Bury My Heart at Wounded Knee*, more than any other book of its kind, significantly touched the emotions of many readers including my own, compelling me to write Brown and express my sympathetic thoughts. He answered my inquiry with genuine interest and sincerity and seemed to value my views. I began reading his other books, and we exchanged more correspondence.

It wasn't until 1990, however, that I telephoned Dee Brown to inquire about visiting with him in Little Rock. He graciously consented and received me with cordial hospitality. During my visit he reminded me of the approaching 100th anniversary of the massacre at Wounded Knee, South Dakota, on December 29. I had heard about South Dakota's harsh winters, but vowed that I would be a part of this significant commemorative event. Brown did not feel able to join me due to his age and the severe weather he would be likely to encounter. It turned out to be extremely cold. I observed the midday outdoor ceremonies in -25 degree temperature. At an afternoon indoor powwow, I delivered a short greeting from Dee Brown, and offered additional remarks of my own on his behalf. My attendance and participation seemed to cement a bond with him that has grown stronger each year. More conversations, visits, and letters led me to collect and study his writings, which yielded fresh insights about the West each time I returned to them. One of the most compelling features of his writing, for me, is the compassion that he evokes for the people of the West, regardless of their role in the settlement of the American frontier.

Brown, who was raised on the edge of the Plains and whose grandmother's father hunted with Davy Crockett, once confided to me that he often viewed the horizons of the rolling western landscapes as if he were atop a horse. There is no question that Brown maintains a kindred spirit with those who played a role in the settlement of the West.

Two years ago, he explained in an interview with Dale Walker for *Louis L'Amour Western Magazine* that he sees the nineteenth-century as "an era of romance, adventure, and courage; the era of steamboats, the first railroads, the madness and glory of the Civil War and the Indian wars; of cattle drives, the cowboy, the settlers on the Plains, the miners in the mountains, the first American ballads and ragtime; of religious fervor and the first truly American pieces of literature. With all its dangers and evils and the brevity of lives, it was a special time. No other century in any other part of the world appeals to me as does the nineteenth-century in America."

In this anthology are the people and events of the 1800s Brown felt merited further examination. Most of them are not the "superstars" whose legends frequently outgrew fact, but their contributions were equally great and in many cases greater than those whose exploits are recounted most often in books, television, and film. Dee Brown writes of the lives and the events in which these people participated in substantial, thoroughly researched articles that supplement some of his other published material. He strips away familiar stereotypes and romanticized images to show the West as it really was. Readers will find in this book a historical time capsule of chronological material encompassing the westward movement of immigrants who used river transportation in the late 1700s to the massacre at Wounded Knee slightly more than 100 years later. It is a trail of adventure, lore, and mystery evoking both sorrow and joy, while providing a macroscopic view of westward migration, development, and transformation.

The passing of the American frontier reflects the fatalism that each of us faces. But while the development of the frontier had ended by 1900, the roles of participants and their spirit continue through Dee Brown and other writers who follow his example in passing on the real history of the American West.

STAN BANASH

Prologue
Writing Western
by Dee Brown

I have been exploring and reading and writing about the American West for sixty years and never really paused to ask myself *Why?* until this moment. It is perilous to analyze anything that is dear to one, but I'll chance it and do a bit of retrospective musing.

In my teen-age days of reading, I was torn between *Tarzan of the Apes* and anything about the Old West. For this teen-aged reader, Zane Grey was the greatest novelist of all time. Edgar Rice Burroughs was entertaining, but compared to Grey he was only a novice. The West and its people were real, the adventures occurred in country that I knew, and no matter how desperate a situation might seem, I knew that in the West there was hope.

Attitudes and preferences change with age and exposure. Before I was twenty I believed that Meriwether Lewis and William Clark were the greatest writers of prose. They are still high on my list. Their journey through uncharted lands to the Pacific is Old West mythology that truly happened.

Some uninformed people believe that the Old West is all mythology. They need to read more Western history, the documented kind. When Jedediah Smith was attacked by a grizzly that tore off half his scalp and an ear, he asked a fellow trapper, James Clyman, to stitch them back on with a needle and thread.

When the Nez Perce tribe decided to escape persecution by fleeing to Canada, 230 warriors burdened with more than 400 women and children outfought and outmaneuvered 2,000 soldiers for 1,800 miles.

When John Colter ignored a Blackfoot warning to stay out of their trapping streams, he was captured, stripped naked, and told that if he could outrun the swiftest of the Blackfoot runners, he could save his own life. Colter outran his pursuers for seven days, until he reached Manual Lisa's fort. His feet were torn, bleeding, and filled with thorns.

When Janette Riker's father and brothers disappeared on a buffalo hunt, leaving her alone in an isolated covered wagon late in the season, she decided not to pray for death, but to build a small weather-proof shelter against the descending winter. She survived three months of blizzards, and when the spring thaw came she was rescued by a hunting party of American Indians who took her to the fort at Walla Walla.

These are all documented myths of the Old West. How do they compare with the Old World deeds of Beowulf, King Arthur, Robin Hood, Samson, or El Cid? Their stories are all myths, not nearly as well documented as some of our myths of the Old West.

One of the gratifying elements of stories about the West are the interrelationships of people and places. Jedediah Smith went west from New York state because he read what Lewis and Clark had written, and at twenty-one he resolved to see everything they had seen, and more. George Catlin risked his life to record on canvas the different tribes in the Plains and Rockies. When Catlin held an exhibit in Boston, Francis Parkman was so overwhelmed by the paintings that he traveled into the West and wrote *The Oregon Trail.* John Colter was one of the young men enlisted for the journey by Lewis and Clark, and he was the first to return to the West, as a trapper, even before he reached home. Had the Nez Perce not shared smoked salmon and camas root with the starving members of the Lewis and Clark expedition, shown them a route to the sea, and taken care of their horses, the explorers might never have reached the Pacific or returned to St. Louis.

It is a challenge to a fiction writer's talents to base a tale upon a myth of the American West. The facts are already too dramatic, the characters almost too heroic or too villainous to be believable. A. B. Guthrie learned how to do it. Ernest Haycox, Henry Wilson Allen writing as Will Henry, and Clay Fisher came close. And half a dozen writers working today are nearing there.

People ask: Has everything already been told? Is there anything left to write about the American West? Most of the occurrences have been reported, but many not too well. A considerable number of diaries and collections of letters surely are still to be found in the attic trunks or in libraries. Much is yet to be written about women and children in the West. There are still dark mysteries to be pondered, such as the manner of dying of George Custer and Meriwether Lewis. And every generation must rewrite its history and literature from the angles of its own prism.

As long as the literature of the American West attracts devoted readers, there will be writers somewhere around working hard to improve the product.

PART I

The Early Frontier

A flatboat carries several families and their livestock down the Ohio River. Many of these travelers fell prey to the river pirates lurking along the shores. Engraving from a drawing by Alfred R. Waud. Courtesy of St. Louis Mercantile Library Association.

1

The Pirates of the Ohio

*"These legendary brigands and cutthroats made opening the
trans-Allegheny west a colorful, but deadly, business."*

*I*n the years following the Revolutionary War, many Americans
began venturing westward from the more settled seaboard
states. The principal route to the lands beyond the Alleghe-
nies was the Ohio River, and 1788 saw the first big surge of
emigration upon its waters.

Among those who decided to go west that year were Robert
Finley and his son James. They had heard glowing accounts of "this
terrestrial paradise, this new Canaan flowing with milk and honey"
which bordered the banks of the lower Ohio. With several other
families, the Finleys boarded flatboats on the Monongahela near
Uniontown, Pennsylvania, and began the long journey that would
take them down the Ohio. "I felt as though I were taking leave of the
world," young James Finley wrote afterward. The Finleys were in fact
leaving their known world, and in preparation for the unknown the
boats were strongly manned and armed. After they left the familiar
bounds of Pennsylvania, a twenty-four hour watch was rigidly
maintained.

"Just below the mouth of the Great Scioto, where the town of
Portsmouth now stands," said James Finley, "a long and desperate
effort was made to get some of the boats to land by a white man, who

feigned to be in great distress; but the fate of William Orr and his family were too fresh in the minds of the adventurers to be thus decoyed. A few months previous to the time of which I am writing, this gentleman and his whole family were murdered by being lured ashore by a similar stratagem."

Finley assumed that his readers would know that the real purpose of the decoyers was not to murder the unfortunate Orrs, but to obtain their rich store of goods. This incident was typical of early Ohio River piracy, and throughout the thirty years or so that it flourished one of the most common devices used to entrap unwitting emigrants was to pretend distress, to make travelers believe that help was needed by a fellow human being.

In the years which followed the Finley incident, piracy moved farther down river, keeping always to the outer edges of settlement. The outlaws formed gangs in order to overcome any strong resistance offered by prospective victims. By the beginning of the 19th century they were so well organized that they developed their own network of spies to report on approaching boats laden with rich cargoes, and, after the owners were murdered, they had their own crews of boatmen to carry the captured goods down the Mississippi River to markets for conversion into money.

＝＝｝＞◆＜｛＝

The vessels which the pirates preyed upon in that pre-steam era were flatboats and keelboats. Emigrating families used flatboats varying in length from twenty to sixty feet, and in width from ten to twenty feet. The hulls were of heavy hardwood timbers which rose three or four feet above the water line and afforded some protection from armed attacks. Like the covered wagons of the western plains, flatboats were households in motion, carrying the family members, their furniture, dishes, food, powder kegs, weapons, tools, and even their livestock. As it was almost impossible to pull them against a river current, the owners usually demolished the boats when they reached their destinations and used the lumber in building a home. Flatboats with ark-like houses built upon their decks were called broadhorns; they were also known as Ohio-boats and Kentucky-boats. Three men usually were needed to handle one of these boats, which were steered by sweeps as long as the vessels themselves.

Keelboats were used for transporting goods both up and down the river — salt, whiskey, flour, gunpowder, bacon, glass, nails, cotton, corn, furs, livestock, tobacco. A heavy timber placed at the bottom to protect against snags and other obstructions gave these boats their name. Keelboats were longer and narrower than flatboats, were fitted with masts and sails, and were manned by tough, experienced crews of three to six men. River pirates preferred to attack flatboats, but would take on a keelboat if they believed its cargo to be unusually valuable.

In 1822 — more than thirty years after the flood of emigration began down the Ohio — Charles and John Webb set out upon this river journey to the West. The Webbs were young brothers bound for St. Louis in hopes of making their fortunes. After working their passage to Louisville, they made a similar arrangement there with Jonathan Lumley, proprietor of a cargo-carrying flatboat. Lumley was taking corn, provisions, and whiskey down to the Mississippi. Very likely a pirate spy noted the richness of the goods aboard, and before the boat left Louisville had marked it for capture farther downstream.

"I was playing on my flute as our boat was nearing Cave-in-Rock," Charles Webb said afterward, "and when within full view of the high rocky bluff, at the base of which is the entrance of the cave, we observed a woman on top of the bluff hailing us by waving a white cloth, whereupon our captain, as we called Mr. Lumley, ordered us to pull in shore, within easy speaking distance, so as to learn what was wanted."

A man appeared from the entrance of the cave and shouted to the boatmen that he and his family were short of rations, and would gladly buy bacon and other provisions. Furthermore, he said, a woman and a boy were stranded there and needed passage to the mouth of Cumberland River.

It may seem strange to modern Americans, who live in an age of swift communications, that neither Lumley nor the Webbs were suspicious of this combined appeal to their sympathy, chivalry, and money-making instincts. After all, it was the same sort of decoy described by James Finley some thirty years earlier. For years river pirates had been operating in that area; many travelers had been robbed and murdered. Yet it was possible that none of the men on Lumley's flatboat recognized the danger they were in. They swung the boat toward the river bank and tied up about two hundred yards below the cave. Lumley, John Webb, and two others on board stepped ashore and walked up to the entrance of the cave.

"After waiting for more than an hour, and none of our men returning," Charles Webb recalled afterward, "I asked my remaining companions to go up to the cave and see what was detaining them." Left alone on the boat, Webb watched a bank of storm clouds obscure the setting sun. "I began to feel uneasy, and to add to my uneasiness, a large dog which we had on board began howling most dismally. Presently by the dim sunlight, I saw three men approaching the boat from the cave."

At first young Webb thought the men were his companions returning. They were river pirates, however, and came aboard with drawn pistols. Webb realized immediately that resistance was useless. While the outlaws were binding his arms behind his back, he asked what had happened to his friends. The outlaws informed him that his friends were all right, that the captain was in the process of selling the boat and its cargo and would soon return. At the same time, however, they were searching Webb's pockets. They took all his money and his beloved flute, then blindfolded him and lifted him into a small skiff that someone had brought alongside the flatboat. Thoroughly alarmed now, Webb demanded to know what had happened to his brother, and pled with his captors to let both of them go because they had no interest in the boat or its cargo.

"The fewer questions you ask," one of the men replied, "the better it'll be for you by a damned sight."

Webb sensed that the skiff was in motion. A few minutes later it jammed against another small boat, and he could hear the men conversing in low tones. One of them leaned closer and told him they were going to turn him loose in the middle of the Ohio. The pirate warned Webb to keep quiet until morning, and then he slacked the cords that bound the boy's arms. "You can work 'em loose when we're gone, say in about an hour, but not sooner, or you may get into trouble. And don't never come back here to ask any questions, or you'll fare worse and do nobody any good."

A few years earlier Charles Webb undoubtedly would have been slain, his body weighted with stones and dropped into the river to disappear forever. By the 1820's, however, the freebooters had either become more merciful, or Webb's youth and naiveté may have appealed to some spark of humanity in the men who held him in their power. Webb's story is probably the only known account of an Ohio River traveler captured by pirates who survived and made record of it.

After he was left alone in the drifting skiff for what he believed to be an hour, Webb managed to free his arms and remove the blindfold. The pirates had left no paddles in the boat, and the storm clouds which he had observed at sundown now darkened the night sky so that he could see only dim outlines of the river bank. A thunderstorm swept over the river, and waves began washing into the small boat. "I know if the downpour continued for many minutes my skiff would fill and sink. There was but one way to bail out — to use one of my thick leather shoes as a scoop. I worked manfully while the rain lasted, which, fortunately, was not for more than an hour."

About daylight Webb sighted a forested island ahead and smoke rising from a cabin back in the trees. Using his hands as paddles, he succeeded in reaching the island, soon found the cabin, and was made welcome by the family who lived there. The islanders were not surprised at his story; they had often heard of robberies committed by river pirates around Cave-in-Rock. They gave young Webb a boat paddle and advised him to proceed down to the mouth of the Cumberland, where there were small settlements of law-abiding citizens who might help him search for his missing brother.

In the village of Salem, Kentucky, Webb found a judge who in-formed him that a man named James Ford was suspected of being the leader of the river pirates. Ford, however, was such a clever operator that he left no evidence of his guilt. The judge was sufficiently in-terested in the matter to lend Webb a horse to ride to the farm of Colonel Arthur Love, who lived near Ford's home and might be able to help in determining the fate of John Webb and the other boatmen.

On the way to Colonel Love's place, Charles Webb was thrown from the borrowed horse, the fall badly injuring his ankle. From that moment on Webb's adventures took on the quality of one of Huckle-berry Finn's complicated entanglements during his journey down the Mississippi. While Webb lay beside the muddy road, a young girl found him, insisted that he ride her horse to her nearby home, and when they arrived there she told him that her name was Cassandra Ford, daughter of James Ford. Her father, she told Webb, was away from home much of the time. Then she showed him a flute that her father had recently given her. Of course it was Webb's flute, which the pirates had stolen from him on the flatboat.

As curious as Huckleberry Finn would have been to see what was going to happen next, Charles Webb remained in the river pirate's home until Ford returned. The outlaw was a tall, powerfully built man of about 50 with penetrating steel-gray eyes, and his manner re-minded Webb of "a good-natured, rather than a surly, bulldog." Ford questioned young Webb at length, but he made the boy welcome and eased his ankle pain with hot toddies. A day or so later, several piratical characters called at the house, and Webb recognized one as the man who had set him adrift in the skiff. After the man left, Cassandra Ford slipped into Webb's room to warn him that her Sfather had been told who he was. Fearing that his life might be in danger, she helped him escape.

———⟫●⟪———

Like most accounts of river piracy, the full story of the Webb broth-ers has been embellished in the usual manner of folklore, so that it is difficult to separate fact from fiction. According to legend, after

Charles Webb escaped he remained nearby, determined to learn the fate of his brother and the other men on the boat. Upon learning that the pirates had released his brother, Charles boldly returned to Ford's house, convinced him that he knew nothing of his piratical activities, and not long afterward married Cassandra.

James Ford's gang was the last of a series of outlaws who preyed on Ohio River traffic, and the fact that the Webbs survived is an indication that piracy had become much less cold-blooded in its later days. From the time of James Finley's account in 1788 to the beginnings of the 19th century, most river pirates were nameless figures who killed with brutish savagery. They struck without warning, vanished before the victims were missed, and seldom left any survivors who might identify them.

One of the earliest of the freebooters to be known by name was Colonel Fluger, sometimes recorded as Pfluger or simply Plug. Colonel Plug's base of operations was a hundred-mile stretch of river which twisted like a corkscrew between the mouths of the Green and the Tennessee. His tiny band consisted of a partner known as Nine-Eyes, his wife, and sometimes a pair of villainous roustabouts picked up on the spur of the moment. The colonel always chose boats manned by inexperienced emigrants and would use the old trick of hailing from the riverbank. He usually had a good story about being a stranded traveler lost in the wilderness. Once aboard a boat, the colonel waited until darkness came and then contrived to pick the oakum caulking from the boat's seams. By careful timing he usually managed to sink the boat near a place where his small band could assist in salvaging the goods aboard, and often the owners of the boat did not know they had been stripped of everything until after the pirates had vanished into the darkness of the Kentucky forests.

The colonel liked to vary his methods. Sometimes he would pose as a pilot who could steer a boat through a particularly dangerous passage, such as the Louisville rapids. Once at the steering oar, Colonel Plug was certain to guide the boat upon a large snag near where his confederates would quickly come to the rescue and help carry off the plunder.

One evening the colonel happened to observe a boat pull in to the river bank. The passengers, weary of water travel, all went ashore to cook their dinners and perhaps sleep on land for a change. In the gathering darkness, Colonel Plug crept aboard the boat and crawled into the narrow space between the steering deck and the bottom planks. Next morning when the boat started moving, the colonel began pulling out oakum caulking, but this time he either worked too fast or the cracks between the planks were too wide. The water poured in like a flood, sinking the boat so quickly that the passengers barely escaped with their lives. As for the colonel, it was his final act of piracy. Trapped below deck, he drowned.

The legendary half-horse, half-alligator known as Mike Fink is sometimes linked with the Ohio River pirates, and although he is known to have plundered farms along the river for their crops and livestock, there is little evidence that he and his crew raided other boats. Mike Fink was a roistering boatman himself, and tradition has it that he and his men once tangled with a band of river pirates purely because they loved a good fight. Dressed in his red flannel shirt, blue jerkin, linsey trousers, moccasins, and coonskin cap, and displaying a sheathed hunting knife in his belt, Mike Fink swaggered his way up and down the Ohio. He was a bully and a braggart; he would as soon shoot a man in the heel as look at him; he once cured his wife of looking at other men by forcing her to lie down in a pile of leaves while he set fire to it.

"That'll larn you," Mike told her when she jumped in the river to extinguish her burning clothes, "to be winkin' at them fellers in the other boat."

If Mike Fink had wanted to be a pirate, no one could have stopped him. His coarseness of manner and his code of conduct were typical of that violent era on the river, but he was probably too restless to stay in one place long enough to lay traps for passing cargoes.

One of the first outlaws to organize a large band of river pirates was Samuel Mason. Using the name Wilson, he established a tavern in 1797 at Cave-in-Rock, a natural cavern on the Illinois bank of the river about twenty miles below Old Shawneetown. It was the same place where some twenty years later, Charles Webb was captured by James Ford's gang. Mason posted a sign outside the cave: *Wilson's Liquor Vault and House of Entertainment.* According to an early chronicler of Kentucky "it soon became infamous for its licentiousness and blasphemy."

Cave-in-Rock, for many years the headquarters for both river and land pirates, was an ideal location for outlawry. From its entrance, which was screened by shrubbery and trees, one could see boats far up and down the river. The forty-foot-wide cavern extended back into solid limestone for more than fifty yards. At its rear was a hole in the roof which could serve as a chimney or as an emergency exit or entrance. There was also a small upper cave which could be entered through a small opening. When pirates were not inhabiting the cave, passing travelers often used it as a temporary shelter.

Eventually so many boats were reported missing between Shawneetown and the mouth of the Cumberland that suspicions of piracy along that stretch of river began to grow. Cave-in-Rock appeared to be the obvious headquarters, and a group of volunteer militiamen was organized upriver to put an end to the piracy. The expedition tracked down some of the pirates, and in a sharp fight killed or captured several of them. Mason escaped, however, and continued his career as a land pirate along the Natchez Trace. When the governor of Mississippi offered $500 for his capture, two of his confederates turned traitor, killed Mason, and carried his head into Natchez to collect the money. The reward was paid, but immediately thereafter the two bounty hunters were arrested for their previous crimes. Following their conviction and execution, the reward money was returned to the treasury of Mississippi.

⟞⟝◆⟞⟝

Punishment for river piracy was harsh. If murder was not involved, convicted pirates usually got off with the loss of one or both their ears. When an English traveler, Thomas Ashe, was journeying down the Ohio in 1806 he was warned to be on the lookout for outlaws along the river, and especially to be wary of river town inns operated by them. Ashe asked how it would be possible to recognize these dangerous men. Look for an *absence of ears*, he was told.

Although Ashe was inclined to exaggerate, he did have an opportunity to visit Cave-in-Rock after Mason's band was dispersed, and he recorded his impressions of the place. "The interior walls are smooth rock stained by fire and marked with names of persons and dates, and other remarks etched by former inhabitants. . . . The walls bear many hieroglyphs well executed in the Indian manner." During his exploration of the cave, Ashe said that he found human skeletons, two of which appeared to be of recent times, the others belonging to a remote period of the past. "Two of the skulls were beaten in, and several bones were fractured and broken, from which I inferred that murder had been committed."

Ruthless though the Mason gang may have been, none of its regular members ever quite matched the terrible evil of a pair of brothers who joined them briefly during their rule of the lower river. Micajah and Wiley Harpe came out of the North Carolina hill country in the late 1790's, roving westward across Tennessee and Kentucky, robbing and murdering as though in a rage against all mankind. Accompanying them were three women. By the time they reached the edge of the Bluegrass country in 1799, the Harpes were already legends of terror. Micajah, a brawny six-footer with bushy black hair, was called Big Harpe. Wiley, a scrawny, narrow-faced man, also black-haired, was Little Harpe. The law finally caught them at Stanford, Kentucky, and all five were thrown into jail. At the time of their capture, the three women were pregnant. A few weeks later the Harpe brothers escaped, leaving their women behind to stand trial.

In the chivalrous spirit of the time, the three mothers with their newly born children were acquitted on the promise that they would return to their homes in the East. As soon as they were out of sight of Stanford, the women changed their course back to the west, seeking Big Harpe and Little Harpe. The Harpes were easy to follow; once again they were laying a trail of bloody murder behind them, a trail that led straight to Cave-in-Rock.

After they joined the Mason gang, the Harpes injected a new

viciousness into river piracy. Instead of simply murdering their victims, they tortured them. The Harpes seemed to be more interested in refinement of cruelty than in booty taken from captured boats. So brutal were their methods, their use of knives to mutilate and dismember, that even the hardened criminals of Cave-in-Rock began to look upon them as monsters.

One day after the capture and robbery of a flatboat, with attendant murders, the Harpes took the lone survivor and a horse up to the top of a rock cliff near the cave. The Mason gang remained on the river bank below, too busy sorting out their plunder to notice the absence of the Harpes. Suddenly from the rim of the cliff came a crashing of brush and a horrifying scream. The pirates looked up to see a horse with a naked rider plunging down to smash into crushed bones and flesh upon the rocky edge of the river. A few moments later the Harpes appeared from above, laughing at the startled pirates, their eyes burning with sadistic pleasure. This was too much for the Mason gang. Perhaps some of them feared the bloodlust of the Harpes would eventually turn against them. At any rate they drove them from the cave that night — Big Harpe, Little Harpe, and their women and children.

During the next few months the Harpes went on a rampage of murder through western Kentucky, killing any human being who happened to cross them — men, women, even one of their own helpless children. At last the infuriated settlers caught Big Harpe. His head was cut off and mounted at a crossroads, a place which to this day is known as Harpe's Head. Little Harpe escaped, fled to Mississippi, and eventually persuaded the fugitive Samuel Mason to let him rejoin the transplanted Cave-in-Rock gang. Ironically Little Harpe was one of the two men who later murdered Mason and took his head into Natchez for a $500 reward. As we have seen, that was the end of the road for Little Wiley Harpe.

For the next twenty years along the lower Ohio, pirates came and went. By 1822, the year Charles Webb was captured by James Ford's gang, the land was becoming settled, with towns and villages all along the river. Pirates were forced to become more sophisticated in their methods if they expected to avoid capture and punishment. James Ford was a prototype of the modern crime syndicate boss in that he maintained a respectable front, engaged in legal businesses, influenced politicians, and cherished his family. Behind all this he apparently was involved in pirate operations on the river, managed a ferry where travelers vanished without a trace, and had an interest in inns where travelers also disappeared. Rumors were prevalent that his operations extended to a liaison with John Murrell, notorious land pirate of the Natchez Trace. Ford's death was also curiously modern; he was lured into a trap and executed by gunshot, probably by some of his own associates.

Several years before Ford's death, organized river piracy on the Ohio River had virtually ended. The coming of steamboats, better communications, growth of population, and law and order, had doomed the practice. Reminders of that violent era, however, lingered long afterward. The Kaskaskia (Illinois) *Free Press* of July 23, 1832, published a notice of two runaway slaves, "one of whom Ben plays on the violin, with both ears cut off close to his head, which he lost for robbing a boat on the Ohio River."

2

The Great Adventure

"To explore the river Missouri from its mouth to its source . . . and seek the best water communication thence to the Pacific Ocean," President Thomas Jefferson sent two young army officers, Meriwether Lewis and William Clark, off into the unknown West. This is their story, the story of the great adventure."

It has been said that the most enduring works of literature are stories of journeys in which the chief interest of the narrative centers around the adventures of the hero. If this be true, there is no greater adventure story in American history than the expedition of Meriwether Lewis and William Clark, a journey filled with danger, mystery, romance, and suspense. Instead of one hero it contains several, but there was only one heroine — a Shoshone Indian girl, Sacagawea.

The journey began on the rainy afternoon of May 14, 1804, a few miles north of St. Louis at Wood River opposite the mouth of the Missouri. In addition to Lewis and Clark the permanent party consisted of fourteen soldiers from the U.S. Army, nine carefully chosen young frontiersmen from Kentucky, two French boatmen, Captain Clark's Negro servant (York), a civilian interpreter (George Drouilliard), Captain Lewis' Newfoundland dog (Scannon), and two horses to be used for towing, hunting, and other chores. Additional soldiers and river men would accompany them as far as the Mandan villages where the expedition was to camp for the first winter.

In 1804 St. Louis was a village of fewer than a thousand people, but a considerable number came to see the three small boats set out "under a gentle breeze up the Missouri River." This casual departure was the result of months of planning, the outcome of a long-delayed project of President Thomas Jefferson who in January 1803 had sent a secret message to Congress asking for $2,500 to finance an expedition up the Missouri. Although the territory to be explored did not then belong to the United States, Congress had complied with the request.

Linked in Jefferson's mind with this bold journey was a burning ambition to secure for his country at least part of the vast and unknown land beyond the Mississippi. In the spring of 1803 opportunity came suddenly and unexpectedly when Napoleon Bonaparte, badly in need of money to finance his wars, offered to sell Louisiana Territory. Jefferson of course leaped at the opportunity. For fifteen million dollars he doubled the land area of the United States, acquiring more than half a billion acres for less than three cents an acre. Even before the transaction was completed, he began devoting much of his energies to thorough and detailed planning for an exploring expedition. Although the Rocky Mountains marked the westward limits of Louisiana Territory, Jefferson was more determined than ever that Lewis and Clark should "explore the whole line, even to the Western Ocean." Both Great Britain and Russia claimed the Oregon country, but neither had bothered to establish colonies there.

⟞⟩⊕⟨⟝

When Jefferson took office as President in 1801, he summoned Captain Meriwether Lewis from the Army to serve as his private secretary, and when he began planning the expedition he named Lewis the leader. Lewis in turn chose William Clark as his partner in discovery, to bear equal rank and responsibility. All three men had known each other for years, having grown up around Charlottesville, Virginia. Clark was a brother of George Rogers Clark and had served with General Anthony Wayne on several Indian-fighting excursions.

In 1804 Lewis was 30, Clark was 34, and they complemented each other well. Lewis was an introvert, preferring solitude; his mind was restless, always inquiring. At times he was moody, more often melancholy than exhilarated. Clark was a red-haired extrovert — genial, optimistic, practical. Both men were highly intelligent and resourceful, perhaps near geniuses, and were as attuned to the frontier wilderness as modern-day astronauts are to outer space.

When the two explorers started out on that May day near St. Louis, they had no maps or charts beyond the Mandan villages 1,600 miles upriver. What knowledge there was of the far Rockies was more myth than fact — legends of solid salt mountains hundreds of miles long, of live mammoths wandering the deep canyons, of fierce Indians who killed without warning. All food staples and manufactured goods that thirty men would need for two years had to be carried in three small boats. They packed everything with care; for instance, they wrapped gunpowder in thin sheets of lead which kept the powder dry and then could be melted to make bullets. Each bale of supplies contained small packets of every article carried, so that if a bale were lost the entire supply of any one item would not be lost.

Almost a year before the journey began, Jefferson prepared a letter of instructions so detailed that there could be no doubt as to the objectives of the mission. Lewis and Clark were to ascend the Missouri River, cross the Rockies, and descend to the Pacific by the most practicable river route. They were to make a thorough survey of a possible water route to the Pacific; they were to study and cultivate friendships with Indians encountered and estimate the possibilities of establishing commerce with them. They were to observe and record all that was noteworthy concerning animals, plants, minerals, soils, and climates. They were to map the sources and courses of rivers, and determine the latitude and longitude of important landmarks.

For the first few days of the journey upriver, progress was slow and monotonous. The 55-foot keelboat was equipped with a square sail and twenty-two oars; the two pirogues had six or seven oars, so that there was plenty of work for all. As would be the pattern for much of

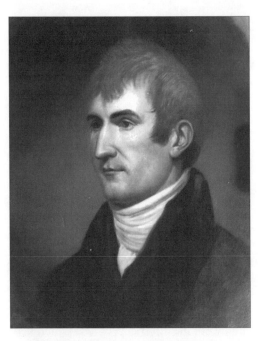

*Meriwether Lewis.
From the portrait by
Charles Willson Peale.
Courtesy of Independence
National Historical Park
Collection.*

*William Clark.
From the portrait by
Charles Willson Peale.
Courtesy of Independence
National Historical Park
Collection.*

the journey, Lewis spent a great deal of his time ashore with his dog Scannon, walking and exploring while the boats made their average progress of nine miles per day. Clark remained with the boats, making certain that everything proceeded according to schedule.

On May 24 at La Charrette trading post, they met some fur traders headed downstream. The news the traders brought from upriver was not good. Sioux Indians had stopped them before they reached the Mandan villages and had exacted tribute, stolen their horses and goods, and then refused to let them proceed. The whole venture had been a disaster. Lewis and Clark took some comfort in the fact that they were better manned and armed than the defeated fur traders. The keelboat carried a new weapon — an airgun which did not need to be loaded, wadded, and primed, but could be fired as fast as a man could drop in bullets and was almost as powerful as a Kentucky rifle. For defense they had ingeniously placed their lockers along the boat's gunwales so that the lids could be quickly raised as shields against arrows.

When they left La Charrette, they passed the last cabin inhabited by a white man, none other than the aging Daniel Boone who always preferred to be in the vanguard of civilization. From now until their return from the Pacific, the members of Lewis and Clark's Corps of Discovery would be the vanguard.

Fighting river currents, summer heat, drenching thunderstorms, and mosquitoes, they reached the sandy mouth of the Platte on July 21. Ten days later, 22-year-old Sergeant Charles Floyd wrote in his diary: "I am verry Sick and Has been for Somtime but have Recovered my helth again." Young Floyd was much sicker than he realized, but the excitement of the expedition's first council with Indians took his mind off his ailment.

The Indians were of the Oto, Omaha, and Missouri tribes. Clark ordered "every man on his Guard & ready for any thing," but he and Lewis kept the meetings on a friendly footing, showing their respect for the Indians but quietly informing them that they were now under protection of a new White Father at Washington who wished them to keep the peace and would soon send them "traders to supply them with all necessities." They named the camp where the councils were held "Councile Bluff, a verry proper place for a Trading establishment." Some years afterward Council Bluffs, Iowa, would be established in the area.

"Serjeant Floyd is taken verry bad all at once with a bilious colic," Clark recorded on August 19. "We attempt to relieve him without success." Medical historians believe that Floyd was suffering from acute appendicitis, and none of the medicines carried by the explorers could have saved him. He died the next day "with a great deal of composure." They buried the young Kentuckian on a high bluff and named a nearby river in his honor.

To replace Floyd as sergeant, the enlisted men were authorized to hold an election. They chose Patrick Gass, a swarthy, black-haired 33-year-old Irishman from Chambersburg, Pennsylvania — a master of carpentry and profanity. Gass was now fourth in command. Sergeant John Ordway, a lanky, loose-jointed New England Yankee, was third in command.

———⟫•⟪———

By late August they were well into the Plains country with its abundance of game, many species of which were unfamiliar to any of the travelers. On August 25 Privates George Shannon and Reuben Field went ashore to hunt. They brought in five deer and a buck elk. Next day, Shannon was assigned the daily duty of driving the two horses along the bank. That night he failed to return to the boats. Although Shannon was only 19, he was one of the resourceful Kentuckians and no immediate alarm was felt for his safety. A few days later, Clark sent out a searching party, but they could find no trace of Shannon or the horses. John Colter, another of the Kentuckians, made a futile independent search. On September 11 the men of the forward boat sighted the half-starved Shannon on the river bank. For twenty-two days Shannon had believed the boats were ahead of him, and he had been desperately trying to overtake them while actually they were always behind him. George Shannon was the best educated of the enlisted men, a handsome, blue-eyed, black-haired youth, and a fine conversationalist, but he had little sense of orientation. Before the expedition was ended he would be lost again.

As they approached the country of the hostile Sioux, Lewis busied himself ashore, collecting and describing animals that he had never seen before — barking squirrels and odd species of goats and foxes. The barking squirrels were prairie dogs; the strange goats and foxes were antelopes and coyotes.

On September 24 five Indians hailed them from the river bank. Clark anchored the boats well out in the river. With George Drouilliard assisting, the explorers soon learned by sign language that the Indians were Teton Sioux. Since leaving St. Louis, Lewis and Clark had been expecting trouble when they met these proud and arrogant Indians, "the pirates of the Missouri." The explorers were prepared for them, and had no intention of being stopped. Learning that more than a thousand Sioux were camped nearby, they arranged for a council next day with the chief, Black Buffalo. If there had to be a showdown, they wanted to settle it and be on their way.

———⟫●⟨———

At sunrise the next morning they had the flag of the United States flying from a staff on the south side of the river (opposite the later site of Pierre, South Dakota). By noon the council was under way. "Captain Lewis," Clark wrote, "proceeded to deliver a speech which we were obliged to curtail for want of a good interpreter." Perhaps Lewis' phrases were too complex for translation into sign language. He solved the dilemma temporarily by passing out medals and presents to Black Buffalo and the other chiefs. The Indians accepted the red coats, cocked hats, feathers, and tobacco enthusiastically, but made it clear that these were not enough. If the white explorers wanted to continue farther upriver, they would have to make the Sioux a present of one of the pirogues with all its contents.

Lewis pretended not to understand. He invited the top five chiefs to come aboard the keelboat, graciously presented each of his guests with a quarter of a glass of whiskey, and demonstrated the power of the airgun. The Indians, however, were not interested in the boat or its weapons; they demanded more whiskey, one of them sucking at an empty bottle and making violent gestures. To divert them, Clark displayed presents in one of the pirogues and asked the chiefs to go ashore with him to help distribute them to their people. As they pulled into the bank, three warriors seized the pirogue's cable as though to take possession of it, and others had their bows strung and arrows out of their quivers as though preparing for an attack. At the same time one of the chiefs on board staggered against Clark, muttering insolently. "His gestures were of such a personal nature," Clark later wrote, "I felt myself compelled to draw my sword."

For a few moments the fate of the expedition hung in the balance. Lewis, who was on the keelboat, reacted quickly, ordering the men to arms and manning the swivel guns for action. He sent twelve infantrymen hurrying ashore, and when they arrived with rifles cocked, Black Buffalo backed down before the display of firmness, and all hostility seemed to vanish. The chief asked Clark to permit him and three other chiefs to be taken aboard the keelboat for the night. They wanted to ride up to their village next morning and show the wonders of the boat to their people. Clark was dubious, but Lewis thought it might be a conciliatory gesture to take them aboard. That night was a long one for Captain Clark. Distrusting the motives of his guests, he kept himself awake until dawn.

⸺⸺►●◄⸺⸺

Next morning, Indians lined the banks of the Missouri for four miles, and Black Buffalo seemed to enjoy having his people see him riding aboard the white men's keelboat. When they reached the tepee village, Lewis went ashore with the chiefs, handed out more presents, and tried to communicate with his hosts through George Drouilliard and Peter Cruzat, one of the French boatmen who knew a few words of Sioux.

In contrast to the previous day's hostility, the Sioux were so hospitable that the explorers remained at the village for two days and nights, being entertained with music and dancing, and dining on "some of the most Delicate parts of the Dog." On September 28, however, when they made ready to resume their journey, the Sioux chiefs came aboard and strongly objected.

"They said we might return back with what we had or remain with them," Sergeant Ordway wrote, "but we could not go up the Missouri any further. About 200 Indians were there on the bank. Some had firearms. Some had spears. Some had a kind of cutlash, and the rest had bows and steel or iron pointed arrows."

Lewis asked the chiefs to leave the boat. When they refused to go, he ordered his men to battle stations. Clark took a burning fuse from the gunner and stood ready to fire one of the swivel guns point-blank into the warriors on shore. Trying to save face, Black Buffalo stood his ground and demanded a farewell present of tobacco. Lewis, who had become very angry, raised his sword as though to cut the mooring rope. The warriors on shore readied their weapons. For the second time, the expedition's fate was in doubt. It was Clark who eased the tension; he tossed a twist of tobacco to Black Buffalo, and the chiefs departed with dignity. "We then set off under a gentle breeze," Sergeant Ordway noted tersely. That night for the first time in four days Captains Lewis and Clark slept. They had outbluffed the Sioux, and the word that these explorers could not be intimidated preceded them up the muddy river.

<hr/>

By October 8 the Arickaree village at the mouth of Grand River had heard all about them, and received them like conquering heroes. "All things arranged for peace or war," Clark noted, but the meeting turned out to be quite friendly. Another rumor the village had heard concerned a black man with curly hair. This was York, of course, and he enjoyed the attention given him by the Arickarees. "Those Indians were much astonished at my Servent," Clark wrote. "They never saw a black man before; all flocked around him & examined him from top to toe." The Indians believed that York's black skin was paint; some of the women boldly approached him and tried to rub it off.

"By way of amusement he told them that he had once been a wild animal and caught and tamed by his master; and to convince them showed them feats of strength which added to his looks made him more terrible than we wished him to be."

In Clark's opinion the Arickaree women were handsomer and more amorous than the Sioux women. "Our men found no difficulty in producing companions for the night by means of the interpreters," he noted. But they could not linger long among the Arickarees. The autumn days were growing shorter, the nights colder, and they had to press on to reach the Mandan villages before snow began to fall.

It was October 27 when they reached the first village. Around the confluence of Knife River and the Missouri were five Indian villages — two Mandan, two Minnetaree, and one Anahami. These Indians lived in log houses instead of skin tepees; the buildings were solidly constructed and the villages were surrounded by ditches and embankments for protection against the Sioux. The chiefs were friendly and accustomed to dealing with French and British fur traders. When the explorers arrived, French trader René Jessaume was in one of the villages. Jessaume was a rogue, but he could speak Mandan and thus eased the communications problem for Lewis and Clark so that they were able to make friends quickly with the principal chiefs.

Shahaka, a fat, good-natured, talkative chief, was the most cordial. Like many Mandans he was light-skinned, and was sometimes called Big White. Shahaka offered to share his winter corn supply with the explorers. "If we eat, you shall eat," he said. "If we starve, you must starve also." He taught Captain Clark how to kill buffalo with bow and arrows so that the expedition's ammunition supply could be conserved.

As the explorers visited from village to village, they searched out a good location for their winter camp, to be called Fort Mandan. On November 2 they began felling trees to build cabins, and the winter's work was begun. In a way, Fort Mandan was comparable to a satellite platform of the space age, a launching site for a further adventure into the unknown. (The map which the explorers carried showed only a blank space west of the Mandan villages to the Pacific.)

During the winter they built canoes to take them to the Rocky Mountains. They jerked (smoked, sliced, and dried) large quantities of meat. They replaced their worn clothing with apparel made of animal skins. They gathered intelligence from visiting Indians and traders. Clark was in charge of the fort and its construction; he modeled it after the triangular stockades he had seen Anthony Wayne build in the East, adding a blacksmith shop and a smoke-house. Lewis dealt with the Indians, made scientific observations, and wrote reports to be sent back to President Jefferson in the spring. He also made a point of interviewing all visitors.

As it turned out, the most important visitors to the Mandan villages that winter were an insignificant trader and his "wife." Toussaint Charbonneau was a Canadian who collected young Indian "wives." Sacagawea (Bird Woman) was his latest acquisition, a frail sixteen-year-old Shoshone girl who had been captured by the Minnetarees. When the pair arrived on November 11, Sacagawea was pregnant. During her confinement Lewis and Clark became well acquainted with her, Clark officiating at the birth of her child. "This was the first child which this woman had boarn," he recorded on February 11, 1805, "and as is common in such cases her labour was tedious and the pain violent; Mr. Jessaume informed me that he had frequently administered a small portion of the rattle of the rattle-snake, which he assured me had never failed to produce the desired effect, that of hastening the birth of the child . . . he administered two rings of it to the woman broken in small pieces . . . added to a small quantity of water. Whether this medicine was truly the cause or not I shall not undertake to determine, but . . . she had not taken it more than ten minutes before she brought forth."

From Sacagawea the explorers learned that they would have to abandon their boats at the source of the Missouri. To cross the Rockies they would need horses, and the only source of horses was the Shoshones — the Bird Woman's people. Both Lewis and Clark quickly realized how important she had become to the success of their mission. She could speak Shoshone and interpret for them; and she would know something of the country they would have to cross. But to obtain her they would also have to take her lazy rascal of a husband, Charbonneau. "We called him in and spoke to him on the subject," Clark wrote on March 17. "He agreed to our terms."

By early April wild geese were flying north and ice was breaking up in the Missouri. They packed nine boxes of specimens and reports for President Jefferson, and on April 7 started them back to St. Louis on the keelboat with a reduced crew of eight men.

On that same day, Lewis, Clark, and the remaining thirty-one men boarded their six canoes and two pirogues (one painted red, the other white) and resumed the westward journey. With them went Charbonneau, Sacagawea, and her six-weeks-old son Baptiste, whom Clark nicknamed Pomp.

"We were now about to penetrate a country at least two thousand miles in width," Lewis wrote, "on which the foot of civilized man had never trodden; the good or evil it had in store for us was for experiment yet to determine, and these little vessels contained every article by which we were to expect to subsist or defend ourselves. However, as the state of mind in which we are, generally gives the colouring to events, when the imagination is suffered to wander into futurity, the picture which now presented itself to me was a most pleasing one. Entertaining as I do, the most confident hope of succeeding in a voyage which had formed a darling project of mine for the last ten years, I could but esteem this moment of my departure as among the most happy of my life. The party are in excellent health and spirits, zealously attached to the enterprise, and anxious to proceed; not a whisper or murmur of discontent to be heard among them, but all act in unison, and with the most perfect harmony."

From now on they would be as completely out of communication with the civilized world as 20th century spacemen circling the backside of the moon. They could receive no messages nor send any.

Each day the Missouri grew more difficult of ascent, its current running rough and swift. To keep the little boats afloat, the men often had to leap out and swim or wade alongside. "We to be sure had a hard time of it," Private Joe Whitehouse of Fairfax County, Virginia, noted in his diary. "Obliged to walk on shore & haul the towing line and 9/10 of the time barefooted." Prickly pears were a painful annoyance to those who worked on shore, Lewis observing that they could penetrate deerskin moccasins, and Clark recording one night that he pulled seventeen thorns from his feet.

⟡

They reached the mouth of the Yellowstone on April 26, and for the next two weeks every member of the party was busily working with the boats, going on hunting parties, making short exploratory trips, recording river measurements, or collecting specimens of the abundant flora and fauna.

On May 14 a freak accident almost brought disaster to the expedition. The day was pleasant with breeze enough to use sail on the two pirogues. Charbonneau, who as yet had no opportunity to be of service as an interpreter, had asked permission to replace Drouilliard at the helm of the white pirogue. Peter Cruzat, the half-breed Omaha-Frenchman, was in the bow. Also aboard were Sacagawea, her child, and a crew of four men. Just before sunset, Captain Clark, who usually waited until all boats were anchored before going ashore, joined Lewis on the riverbank. The white pirogue with Charbonneau at the helm was still out about three hundred yards when a gust of wind struck without warning.

As the boat turned, the inexperienced Charbonneau "instead of putting her before the wind luffed her up into it." The sudden force tore the square-sail out of the hands of the man who was attending it. As Lewis and Clark watched with dismay, the wind "instantly upset the pirogue and would have turned her completely topsaturva had it not been for the resistance made by the awning against the water." Across the wind-churned river they could hear Charbonneau calling on le Bon Dieu to save him. Cruzat was shouting at Charbonneau, threatening to shoot him instantly if he did not take hold of the rudder and do his duty, or at very least to start bailing water.

The scene would have been a comic one except that the pirogue carried papers, instruments, medicines, and a considerable amount of merchandise intended as presents for the Shoshones in exchange for use of their horses. "We discharged our guns with the hope of attracting the attention of the crew," Clark later wrote, "and ordered the sail to be taken in but such was their consternation and confusion at the instant that they did not hear us." Lewis removed his coat, and was about to plunge into the river for a three-hundred-yard swim in rough water, but Cruzat, who was an expert boatman, had regained control of the situation. He cut the sail loose, and as all hands bailed frantically, began rowing ashore.

Sacagawea meanwhile had strapped her child to her back and was efficiently retrieving from the river everything floating within reach. Lewis gave her full credit: "The Indian woman to whom I ascribed equal fortitude and resolution, with any person on board at the time of the accident, caught and preserved most of the light articles which were washed overboard."

Everything had to be unpacked and laid out to dry. An inventory showed that the river had claimed some gunpowder, a few culinary articles, and a collection of garden seeds. Cruzat was delighted to find that his precious fiddle was still intact. Lewis was so relieved that no lives or indispensable articles had been lost that he suggested they console themselves with a drink of grog for each man around.

Every day now wild game was plentiful enough that they could save their dried meat for the crossing of the Rockies. Lewis' Newfoundland dog, Scannon, became an accomplished hunter; his specialty was trapping antelope, deer, and wild geese in the water and then bringing them ashore. He also outran and brought down a goat. On May 19, however, a beaver took revenge upon Scannon. One of the men shot the beaver and Scannon swam out to retrieve it. "The beaver bit him through the hind leg and cut the artery," Lewis recorded. "It was with great difficulty that I could stop the blood; I fear it will yet prove fatal to him." Lewis had grown very fond of his shaggy, bearlike companion, and tended him as carefully as a wounded child. A week later Scannon was ashore again with his master.

For days Lewis had been climbing hills along the river, his eyes searching westward, hoping to see the great Shining Mountains of which he had heard so many tales. On May 26 he saw the high range for the first time "covered with snow and the sun shone on it in such a manner as to give me the most plain and satisfactory view. While I viewed these mountains I felt a secret pleasure in finding myself so near the head of the heretofore conceived boundless Missouri; but when I reflected on the difficulties which this snowy barrier would most probably throw in my way to the Pacific and the sufferings and hardships of myself and party in them, it in some measure counterbalanced the joy I had felt in the first moments in which I gazed on them."

On June 2 the forward boat discovered that the "boundless Missouri" divided into two forks. Which stream was the tributary, and which was the Missouri that was supposed to take them to the headwaters of the Columbia? If they chose the wrong fork, they might go hundreds of miles off their course. They made camp, and Clark took a reconnoitering party up the south branch, while Lewis led another up the north branch.

Six days later they were reunited at the base camp, both captains in agreement that the south fork was the main stream of the Missouri. Almost to a man, however, the other members of the party believed the opposite. The north branch was muddy like the Missouri River they had been following for so many months, while the south branch was clear and swift. Cruzat insisted that the north fork was the "true genuine Missouri," but the captains pointed out that they were nearing the Rockies and that mountain water should run clear. Lewis was so sure that the north branch was a tributary that he named it Maria's River for his cousin Maria Wood, although its muddy waters "but illy comport with the pure celestial virtues and amiable qualifications of that lovely fair one." (Clark had already named the Judith River in honor of his fiancée.)

If the south branch was the Missouri and the stories they had heard from Indians were reliable, they should find a few miles farther west a giant waterfall thundering out of the mountains. Lewis volunteered to take five men and proceed beyond the forty miles Clark had explored on his reconnaissance. While the base camp was waiting to hear from him, they could caulk the boats and cache the red pirogue with its heavy blacksmith's tools, as well as some gunpowder and provisions for use on the return journey.

<hr/>

Lewis with Drouilliard, Silas Goodrich, George Gibson, and Joe Field left the base camp on June 11. Before noon Lewis became very ill with dysentery, but cured himself by making a brew from chokecherry twigs and drinking two pints of it every hour until he was relieved of pain. Two days later, they heard the distant roar of a waterfall. "The grandest sight I ever beheld," Lewis wrote exultantly. The water foamed over masses of rocks, throwing up spray in which the sun formed a perfect rainbow. Like most men of action — even to this day of lunar explorers — he wished for the pen of a literary master "that I might be enabled to give to the enlightened world some just idea of this truly magnificent and sublimely grand object." Not only was it a beautiful scene, it restored Lewis' confidence in his sense of geography. They were on the correct route to the source of the Missouri.

Next morning he sent Joe Field back to inform Clark to bring the boats up and be prepared to portage. While he and his men were waiting for the others to arrive they explored, fished, and hunted. Lewis had seen grizzly bears along the way, but did not believe the animals were as formidable or dangerous as the Indians represented them to be. He changed his mind when a huge grizzly caught him in the open and chased him eighty yards to the river, where Lewis managed to drive him away with a spear. "I must confess I do not like the gentlemen," he wrote respectfully, "and had rather fight two Indians than one bear."

On June 16 the boats were hauled up by ropes as close to the falls as a camp could be made, and Clark set out to survey an overland portage route. For the next several days, everything seemed to go wrong. Sacagawea fell ill, and none of the medicines given her proved beneficial. As she grew weaker, the captains feared for her life and that of her baby, and they worried about her loss as a negotiator with the Shoshones "on whom we depend for horses to assist us in our portage from the Missouri to the Columbia River." Lewis, who was a great believer in natural remedies, dosed her with barks, herbs, and water from a sulfur spring. In a few days Sacagawea regained her strength. Charbonneau, however, now began threatening to turn back and take her with him, and he had to be dealt with diplomatically.

Meanwhile a series of accidents plagued the portaging operations. To ease the burden of transporting their heavy baggage over sixteen miles of rough country, they cut wheels from cross-sections of a cottonwood and hewed out axles and tongues to form crude wagons. The soft cottonwood axles collapsed and the willow replacements were no better. Someone at last thought of cutting up the hardwood mast of the white pirogue which they had cached with all nonessential cargo. To crown their misfortunes a violent hailstorm caught the wagon party in the open, splinters of ice beating blood from the men before they could reach cover. Even on July 4, when they paused briefly to celebrate, there was a note of despair in Lewis' notation that the dram of grog doled out to each man was the last alcohol they had. Cruzat got out his fiddle, however, and "they danced very merrily until 9 in the evening when a heavy shower of rain put an end to that amusement."

—————

After almost a month's delay getting around the Great Falls, they at last resumed their journey. On July 20 they sighted signal smokes ahead, but none of the party could interpret their meaning. The explorers were hopeful that they might be Shoshone smokes, and ordered white flags hoisted in the boats to indicate they were on a mission of peace instead of war.

Their next geographical dilemma came a few days later when the Missouri divided into three forks, each of about the same size. As they had done at the confluence of the Marias, the captains explored a short distance up each stream, and then decided that the branch from the southwest was most likely to take them to the Rockies. In honor of the President they named that branch the Jefferson River; the other two were named the Madison and Gallatin for members of Jefferson's cabinet.

On July 30 the expedition began moving up the Jefferson River. In a short time Sacagawea became very excited. She recognized some of the landmarks along the stream, and then suddenly she saw the very campsite where the Minnetarees had attacked her people and captured her as she tried to escape by wading the river at a shoal. At last the expedition had reached Shoshone country.

But where were the Shoshones and their horses? Almost every day they found recent evidence of their presence, but the Indians seemed to be deliberately avoiding them (as indeed they were, out of fear of these strange bearded men). On August 3 Lewis and Clark both went ashore with scouting parties to try to establish communication with the Shoshones. During their scattered searches, George Shannon became separated from the others and failed to report to camp the night of the 6th. "We had the trumpet sounded and fired several guns but he did not join us. . . . This is the same man who was separated from us 15 days as we came up the Missouri and subsisted nine days of that time on grapes alone." Reuben Field went in search of Shannon but could find no trace of him. Two days later, however, Shannon caught up with the expedition; he had taken the wrong fork of a stream but fortunately discovered his error in time to retrace his steps.

———◦≫◦≪◦———

On August 10 the land parties found horse tracks only a few hours old. Sacagawea assured them that they were in the heart of her people's country, and pointed out a hill that she remembered from childhood; it was shaped like a beaver's head and was so called by the Shoshones.

Realizing that summer weather would soon end and that time was running out for a crossing of the snow-topped Rockies, the captains redoubled their efforts to find the Shoshones. On the morning of the 11th Lewis chose three men to accompany him — John Shields, the reliable Kentucky blacksmith; Hugh McNeal, veteran soldier; and George Drouilliard, who knew Indian sign language. When they came out upon a sagebrush flat with cliffs in the background, Lewis sent Drouilliard and Shields out as flankers. "After having marched in this order for about five miles I discovered an Indian on horseback about two miles distant coming down the plain towards us." Lewis lifted his spy-glass. The Indian was wearing a different costume from any they had seen before, and Lewis was sure that he was a Shoshone.

For the next few minutes, the four explorers and the Indian approached each other cautiously, Lewis and Drouilliard making peace signs. The Indian halted. Lewis, McNeal, and the two flankers moved forward to within a hundred yards, and then Lewis signaled the flankers to halt. Failing to see the signal, Shields continued advancing. Evidently suspecting that Shields was trying to get behind him, the Indian wheeled his horse, lashed it into a gallop, and disappeared behind a screen of willows. Lewis was bitterly disappointed. "I now called the men to me and could not forbare upbraiding them a little for their want of attention and imprudence on this occasion." The captain's comments, especially to John Shields, must have been unprintable, but he took the same men out again the next day.

On August 13 they found Shoshones at last, virtually capturing three women. With Drouilliard's help, Lewis managed to convince the women that no harm would come to them. "After they became composed, I informed them by signs that I wished them to conduct us to their camp, that we were anxious to become acquainted with the chiefs and warriors of their nation."

As they followed the obedient women down a trail toward the river, the explorers sighted the Shoshone chiefs and warriors much sooner than they had expected. Mounted and with weapons ready, about sixty warriors came galloping in a wild charge to rescue their women.

Was this to be the end of the journey, the end of Meriwether Lewis, the end of Thomas Jefferson's dream? All that Lewis could think of to do was to drop his gun and pull a small American flag from his pack. Facing into the charging warriors, he unfurled the Stars and Stripes, and as he strode forward to meet their fury, he began waving the banner back and forth above his head.

In those few minutes when Meriwether Lewis and his three scouting companions awaited the onrush of mounted Shoshone warriors, they must have prayed for the sudden appearance of Sacagawea to save them from sudden death. Sacagawea, however, was miles away on the river with Captain Clark. It was another Shoshone woman who tipped the balance for them, one of the three they had met and treated with kindness. She shouted to the chief that the strangers were friendly white men, and to prove it she held up the presents they had given her.

Dismounting in a single leap, the chief ran forward and embraced Lewis. Pressing his paint-smeared face against the captain's cheek, he said in Shoshone: "I am pleased! I am much rejoiced!"

From that moment on, the meeting became a gay celebration, and when Sacagawea arrived later to rejoin her people, the singing and dancing were performed all over again. By a remarkable coincidence the chief, whose name was Cameahwait, turned out to be Sacagawea's brother. This of course mightily improved the explorers' chances for obtaining horses to make the crossing of the Rockies.

To further impress the Shoshones the explorers demonstrated their airgun; Scannon went through his tricks; York demonstrated his feats of strength; and some of the men prepared a feast of hominy — a food unknown to these Indians. Cruzat got out his fiddle, and the men entertained the Indians with jig dancing.

Trading for horses, however, proved to be a long, drawn-out affair. To obtain the first four animals they had to barter a uniform coat, two pairs of leggings, a few handkerchiefs, four knives, and an old checkered shirt. When it became apparent that Cameahwait's band was unwilling to spare any more mounts, parties were sent to neighboring villages in hopes of finding others. Sacagawea's knowledge of the language and her suggestions to the explorers as to how to proceed proved invaluable in these negotiations.

⟶▸●◂⟵

During this enforced delay Captain Clark and Sergeant Gass, using Shoshone guides, made tentative surveys for a route across the mountains. What they observed and what they heard from the Shoshones offered little encouragement. One old man told them the mountains were inaccessible to man or horse, the rivers so filled with rocks and foam that no boat could float upon them, the country so bare of game or edible plants that no Shoshone ever tried to pass across it. The old Shoshone did admit, however, that an occasional Nez Percé crossed from the other side, and Clark was certain that if the Nez Percé could cross, then so could the Corps of Discovery. But horses would be absolutely essential.

Back at the Shoshone village, Lewis marked his 31st birthday on August 18. "I had in all human probability existed about half the period which I am to remain in this Sublunary world," he noted philosophically. "I had as yet done but little, very little, indeed, to further the happiness of the human race, or to advance the information of the succeeding generations. I viewed with regret the many hours I have spent in indolence, and now sorely feel the want of that information which those hours would have given me had they been judiciously expended." Resolving to live for mankind in the future as he had lived for himself in the past, Lewis closed his notebook for the day.

During the next few days he was so busily engaged in caching the expedition's canoes for use on the return journey and in cajoling the Shoshones into more horse trading that he had no time for further sober reflections. At last on August 29 the expedition was ready to start the most difficult part of its journey. With twenty-eight horses, one mule, and six Shoshone guides, they started marching toward the Bitterroot Valley. Sacagawea, Charbonneau, and Pomp were still with them. The young Shoshone woman wanted to go on to see the Great Ocean, and every man in the party welcomed her presence.

Captain Clark had almost fallen in love with her. He nicknamed her Janey and was constantly defending her from the boorish treatment given her by Charbonneau. "No woman ever accompanies a war party of Indians," Clark said, and he was convinced that the presence of Sacagawea saved them from attack more than once.

The nights were extremely cold now, the trail almost impassable and so precipitous that Joe Whitehouse described it as being "nearly as steep as the roof of a house." Sergeant Gass noted with his usual conciseness: "Fatiguing beyond description." During the night of September 3 snow fell upon their camp. "Our moccasins froze," Sergeant Ordway wrote. "We have nothing but a little parched corn to eat. The air on the mountains very chilly and cold. Our fingers ached."

Late that day in a valley now known as Ross's Hole they came upon a large encampment of Flathead Indians. The presence of Sacagawea and the Shoshone guides insured a friendly council, and as the Flatheads owned an abundance of mustangs, the two captains had no difficulty bargaining for eleven additional mounts.

⟨⟩⟨⟩

A week later they started across the Bitterroot Range, following part of the present-day Lolo Trail. By September 14 all their flour and corn was gone, and they could find almost no wild game or fish anywhere along the route. They slaughtered a young horse, and then for several days lived on berries, wolf meat, and crayfish. To keep from starving they had to break out their supply of candles and bear's oil. For water they used snow from the drifts which grew deeper day by day. On September 18 Clark pushed ahead with six men in a desperate search for food. Two days later they met a wandering band of Nez Perce Indians, who were hospitable enough to supply the explorers with dried salmon and camas-root flour. Clark sent Reuben Field back with rations enough to sustain Lewis and the main party.

At last they crossed the Rockies into the valley of the Clearwater, and were now outside the limits of U.S. territory. The cold, the hard going, the deficient diet had taken their toll. Almost every man was suffering from dysentery. During the last few miles of descent, some fell exhausted beside the trail and had to be carried into camp on pack horses. Lewis was completely debilitated. Although Clark escaped serious illness, he was thrown by one of the Indian ponies, injuring his hip. He took over Lewis' usual surgeon's duties and as soon as a rest camp was made beside the Clearwater he began dosing everybody with salts, tartar emetic, and jalap. Surprisingly they all recovered, but for three or four days the Corps of Discovery was defenseless, and no one was able to start building the canoes which they hoped would take them to the Pacific Ocean.

As soon as enough men were able to work they cut down five large pine trees, hollowed out the trunks by burning, and shaped them into dugouts of sufficient size to carry all members of the party and their remaining supplies. What to do with their thirty-eight horses, which they would need again on their return journey, was a major problem. They solved it by trusting the Nez Percés, giving them presents, and promising them more on their return. Remembering that the horses were property of the U.S. Army, Lewis had them branded. (The branding iron containing the words "U.S. Capt. M. Lewis" was later lost; almost a century afterward it was recovered on an island in the Columbia River.)

⟞⟝⟞⟝

They spent the month of October in a race to reach the Pacific before winter overtook them. The swift current of the Clearwater swirled the explorers through rapids that came near drowning the crew of one dugout. After surviving one of the roughest of these passages, the terrified Shoshone guides deserted without even asking for their promised payment in trade goods.

When the Clearwater took them into the Snake, the captains were sure they had reached the long-sought Columbia River. "The campsite that night was opposite the present cities of Clarkston and Lewiston on the Washington-Idaho border.) Although they were not as close to the Pacific as they had hoped, the river abounded with fish, and thus they were able to supplement their meager diet. Almost daily they met different bands of Indians, and in an effort to conserve their diminishing supplies of trade goods, they tried exchanging entertainment for food. Cruzat played his fiddle, the men sang and danced, York performed his feats of strength, and the captains exhibited the airgun, telescope, compass, and magnifying glass. Sometimes the Indians showed their appreciation with gifts of meat.

All their salt was gone now and the tasteless fish diet grew so monotonous that they eagerly accepted stews of dog meat from their Indian hosts. By the time they reached the Columbia River (October 16) they were trading for dogs to be used as meat as casually as they would have traded for wild game had any been available. After refusing to eat dog meat at first, Sergeant Gass finally admitted: "When well cooked tastes very well." Lewis declared that dog meat was far superior to horse meat. "While we lived principally on the flesh of this animal," he said, "we were much more healthy, strong and more flesbey than we had been since we left the Buffaloe country." Through all this time of short rations, no one ever considered sacrificing Scannon the Newfoundland. Every man in the party would have looked upon such an act as cannibalism.

———

When they reached Celilo Falls on October 22 they had to portage around the 20-foot drop of foaming water. Friendly Indians gave their assistance, and a chief warned Clark that the next tribe down river was hostile and would attack them. "We therefore examined all the arms," Clark noted tersely. "Increased the ammunition to 100 rounds."

Instead of attacking the explorers, however, the tribe watched with amazement as these mad, bearded strangers navigated the Narrows of the Dalles, which Clark described as an "agitated gut swelling, boiling & whorling in every direction."

A week later after a rough portage through the Cascades they noticed increasing signs that they were nearing the Pacific. Sea otters appeared in the broadening river; some of the Indians wore seashells in their noses; others carried articles made of copper and brass, and woven cloth. Then they met an Indian wearing a sailor's pea-jacket and round hat. He spoke a little English. "Son of a pitch" was one of his exclamations, and the explorers knew that American ships must occasionally touch ashore somewhere near.

The morning of November 7 was cloudy and foggy with a drizzle of rain. Gradually the air cleared, and then they saw "the object of all our labours, the reward of all our anxieties." Captain Clark quickly scribbled in his logbook: "Ocean in view! O! the joy."

They had hoped to find a ship, perhaps arrange passage back to the East Coast, but all they could find were traces of campfires where ships' traders had been. "They have all sailed away," Sergeant Gass noted with disappointment. With winter coming on, the thought of retracing the four thousand miles to St. Louis was something to be put out of their minds.

<hr>

After exploring the shores and inlets of the Columbia they chose a site on high ground about three miles up a small tributary. (It is now called Lewis and Clark River.) Here from an abundant stand of spruce and fir they began building winter quarters. For the friendly Clatsop Indians who lived nearby, they named it Fort Clatsop. Cold rains fell almost every day, hindering construction. It was Christmas Eve when the last slab of roofing was in place on two solid parallel buildings surrounded by a high picket wall. Next morning Lewis and Clark were awakened by a salvo of guns fired by the men, "followed by a song as a compliment to us on the return of Christmas." It was their second Christmas away from civilization, and everybody exchanged a few simple gifts, Clark noting that he received a pair of fleece hosiery from Lewis and two dozen white weasel tails from Sacagawea.

There was little to do at Fort Clatsop except hunt and fish, keep a sharp lookout for a visiting ship, and wait for springtime and the return journey. "Not any occurrences today worthy of notice," was a repetitive phrase in the daily log. A detail of men was assigned the tedious task of boiling sea water to replace the exhausted salt supply; they produced twenty gallons of salt by the end of February. Indian

Lewis and Clark at Celilo Falls on the Columbia River. From the mural in the Oregon State Capitol, Salem. Courtesy of Legislative Administration Committee, State of Oregon.

girls provided the major amusement, but most of the tribes along the coast had been corrupted by visiting traders and seamen, and many of the women were diseased. As Sergeant Gass said, they were also "much inclined to venery." Lewis in his role as official surgeon was continually warning the men to avoid infection, but before winter was over he had to administer several doses of mercury, the standard remedy of the day for venereal disease.

The incessant rain and dampness not only depressed the spirits of the men but put them to bed with colds and rheumatism. William Bratton, the awkward, oversized Kentucky gunsmith, came very near dying of an ailment which modern medical men believe was a severe abdominal infection combined with sacroiliac sprain. Lewis gave him purges, laudanum, and liniment, but Bratton grew weaker and weaker through the winter, and late in March when the Corps of Discovery packed up for the start home it was evident that Private Bratton would have to be carried to the boats. If he was not recovered by the time they reached the portages, a horse would have to be found for him.

On March 23, 1806, the day of departure, the hated rain delayed their start until noon. That first day they made only sixteen of the 4,100 miles that stood between them and St. Louis.

Until they reached the Dalles they could use their boats, but from that point to the east side of the Bitterroot Range they would have to follow overland trails. A few horses now became vital necessities. Bratton was barely able to stand, and it was impossible to carry all their baggage in back packs.

When they began bartering for mounts, their carefully hoarded trade goods disappeared rapidly. They had to give up their swords, knives, tiny twists of tobacco, even their badly worn clothing. As they climbed up into the country of sparse game, they also had to trade again for dog meat, and the Cascade Indians drove hard bargains. On April 11 two Shahala tribesmen attempted to steal back a dog they had just sold to John Shields, who took after them with a knife. In the midst of the altercation another member of the tribe had the audacity to kidnap Scannon.

Scannon's disappearance brought the entire expedition to a sudden halt. "This tribe of villains," Lewis said indignantly, "stole my dog." He sent three men in hot pursuit "with orders if they made the least resistance or difficulty in surrendering the dog to fire on them." The rescue mission was successful; when the Shahalas saw the angry explorers running after them they released Scannon and fled.

———◦———

On May 5 the expedition was back at the mouth of the Clearwater, and a week later ran into heavy snows. From their own observations and information given by Indians, it soon became evident that they would have to camp for two or three weeks until warmer weather cleared the snow-blocked passes of the higher ranges. The big problem now was obtaining enough food to see them through the enforced delay. By chance Clark discovered a bartering system that would later be used by a multitude of frontier doctors. In exchange for dosages of cream of tartar and flour of sulphur which seemed to cure numerous Indian ailments, he received edible roots, dogs, and a little dried meat.

For some reason, however, none of the medicine benefited Private Bratton, and the men were wondering how he could ever cross the Bitterroots. His good friend, John Shields, suggested a cure he had seen the Pacific Coast Indians use during the winter. After securing Bratton's permission, they made a crude sweat bath, supporting him over a deep hole filled with hot coals, covering him with blankets, and pouring water over the coals. After each sweating they doused the patient in cold water. The result was miraculous. In twenty-four hours Bratton was able to walk again; in a week he was almost completely cured. During this time Sacagawea's baby also became ill with high fever and a swollen throat. Clark dosed the child with medicines, but they brought no relief. Again it was a primitive remedy, a poultice of wild onions, which apparently cured Pomp of his illness.

When they found the Nez Percés with whom they had left their horses the previous autumn, they learned that the animals had been put to use during the winter and were scattered along the Clearwater.

During the long encampment, however, the honest Indians rounded up all but two of the horses, and on June 10 the expedition began retracing its hard journey over the Bitterroots.

After a bad start in which they lost their way, they began again with three Nez Percé guides. German-born John Potts, one of the Regular soldiers, cut his leg accidentally with a butchering knife and almost bled to death. John Colter's mount rolled down a rocky cliff into a creek and came near drowning the young Kentuckian. As they struggled through deep snow the horses became gaunt for want of forage. A cache of food which they had prudently stored on the trail kept the men alive until at last they were on the downslope. Lewis sent a hunting party hurrying ahead, and when the main body reached Lolo Hot Springs a freshly butchered deer was waiting for them. Once again they had conquered the Bitterroots.

At a place called Travelers' Rest, where they had camped on the way west, they stopped for two days to plan the most daring adventure of the expedition. It was comparable to a modern-day separation of a spacecraft into two, and then three different orbits. Afterwards if all went well the three parties would rejoin at two successive rendezvous points and then speed for home.

Captain Lewis would take nine men, search out a more direct route to the Great Falls and then turn northward to explore the Marias River. His purpose was to determine its limits of navigation for use in future fur transport. At the same time Captain Clark would lead the rest of the party down the Jefferson. On reaching the Three Forks, Clark's party would again divide, one party traveling in the previously cached boats down the Missouri to join Lewis' circuiting group, the other continuing eastward to explore several hundred miles of the unknown Yellowstone. The Yellowstone's juncture with the Missouri was the point of final rendezvous for the entire Corps of Discovery. In a wild country of unmeasured distances this plan was a series of risky operations indeed.

Lewis' party reached Great Falls July 11. There he left Patrick Gass and six men, and with George Drouilliard and Joseph and Reuben Field started on horseback for the Marias valley. His return date was set for August 5; if he was not back by September 1, Sergeant Gass was to abandon hope and hasten on to join Captain Clark at the mouth of the Yellowstone. Lewis was going into hostile Blackfoot country, and he must have had a premonition of trouble.

For two weeks his exploring party managed to avoid contact with Indians, but on the very day they turned back toward the Missouri, July 26, they ran into a band of eight Piegan Blackfeet. Lewis and Drouilliard communicated with them in sign language. They smoked a pipe together, and the Indians invited the explorers to camp with them for the night. Lewis decided the safest thing to do was to accept, but he assigned each man a guard watch. At dawn he was awakened by a loud shout from Drouilliard: "Damn you, let go my gun!" As Lewis came quickly awake, Drouilliard was scuffling with one Indian for his gun, and Reuben Field was stabbing another would-be thief to death with a knife. When Lewis whirled to pick up his own rifle, he saw another Blackfoot running away with it. The rest of the Indians were driving off the explorers' horses.

Meanwhile the Field brothers had caught the man carrying Lewis' rifle and forced him to drop it. The explorers now gave chase after their horses, Lewis shouting that he would fire on the Indians if they did not give up the animals. "One of them jumped behind a rock and spoke to the other who turned and stopped at a distance of 30 steps from me and I shot him through the belly. He fell to his knees and on his right elbow from which position he partly raised himself and fired on me . . . being bareheaded I felt the wind of his bullet very distinctly."

Certain that the surviving Indians, who vanished into the woods, would return with reinforcements, the explorers hastily saddled their horses and started for the Missouri River. "If attacked," Lewis instructed his men, "the bridles of our horses should be tied together and we would stand and defend them, or sell our lives as dear as we could." By two o'clock in the morning of the following day they had put almost a hundred miles between them and the Blackfoot camp.

———◦►●◄◦———

Next morning they heard the sound of rifle shots, and not long after they reached the river they "had the unspeakable satisfaction to see our canoes coming down." It was the boat party from Clark's group who had already passed Sergeant Gass's men at the falls.

On the way to meet Clark at the mouth of the Yellowstone, Lewis had one more brush with death. While hunting along the shore he was accidentally shot by Peter Cruzat who mistook the captain for an elk. It was a buttocks wound — not dangerous but causing Lewis a great deal of inconvenience. He had to lie on his belly in one of the pirogues for a considerable distance down the Missouri.

On August 12, almost exactly as planned and without the loss of a man, the separate parties of Lewis and Clark rejoined. In contrast to Lewis' dangerous adventures, Clark had experienced only routine incidents on his voyage down the Yellowstone.

Two days later they were back at their old winter camp in the Mandan villages. Along the way they met two young men from Illinois, Joseph Dickson and Forest Hancock, traveling westward. John Colter was so intrigued by their plans for a trapping expedition into the Rockies that he secured the captains' permission to join the venture.

After persuading Chief Shahaka to return with them to see President Jefferson, and saying farewell to Sacagawea and Charbonneau, the explorers set out for St. Louis. Now that their mission was accomplished, all energies were bent toward reaching their home base at the best possible speed. Poling and rowing with the current, they made a rapid descent, traveling as far as seventy-five miles on some days.

———◦►●◄◦———

On September 21 they reached St. Charles, startling the villagers by firing off their rifles and then going ashore for a celebration. Next morning they stopped at Fort Belle Fontaine near the mouth of the Missouri. Here they received free haircuts, and tidied themselves up as best they could for the reception which was awaiting them in St. Louis where the news of their safe return had created much excitement.

At high noon of September 23, 1806 — after a journey of two years, four months and nine days — they reached St. Louis and fired off their guns as a salute to the town. "We were met by all the village," Clark said, "and received a hearty welcome from its inhabitants."

He made only three more entries in his daily log:

September 24 — I slept but little last night. However we rose early and commenced writing our letters. Captain Lewis wrote one to the President.

September 25 — Payed some visits of form to the gentlemen of St. Louis. In the evening a dinner & Ball.

September 26 — A fine morning. We commenced writing &c.

The great adventure had ended.

POSTSCRIPT

The success of Lewis and Clark's remarkable journey had a profound effect upon the people of the United States, strengthening their national convictions and sustaining them through the dark days of the War of 1812. William Clark was named governor of Missouri Territory and lived out his life as a great man in St. Louis. Meriwether Lewis became governor of Louisiana Territory, but in 1809 while journeying overland to Washington he died mysteriously on the Natchez Trace. Some historians say he was murdered; others say he committed suicide. Sacagawea's later life is also controversial. Legend holds that she lived until 1884 and died on the Shoshone Reservation in Wyoming. More probably she died in 1812 on the upper Missouri. Her son Baptiste, or Pomp, was educated at Clark's expense, toured Europe, learned four languages, became a western guide and trader, and eventually returned to his mother's people in

Wyoming, dying there in 1885. Mystery also surrounds the fate of York. Clark gave him his freedom, and he either died of cholera in Tennessee or returned to the West to become a chief among the Crow Indians.

John Ordway took up farming on his land claim in Missouri, but most of the other men sold theirs. John Colter won fame by discovering what is now Yellowstone Park, which was called Colter's Hell by the fur trappers. George Drouilliard and John Potts, who also returned to the West, were killed by the Blackfeet. George Shannon lost a leg in an Indian fight, returned East to study law, and became a judge in Missouri. William Bratton and Patrick Gass soldiered through the War of 1812, the latter losing an eye during his service. Bratton settled in Indiana and fathered ten children; Gass did not marry until he was 60 but produced eight children. He was almost 90 when the Civil War began, but tried to enlist. The old sergeant was the last survivor of the Corps of Discovery.

3

Intrigue on the Natchez Trace

"Meriwether Lewis was a master explorer, but he took a wrong turn when he went to Mrs. Grinder's Place."

On an upland ridge between the Tennessee and Duck rivers, the old Natchez Trace crosses Tennessee State Highway 20. At this point on the west side of the Trace is a clearing broken by an occasional giant oak, a persimmon, a dogwood. At one end of the clearing is a broken column of marble standing upon a granite pedestal. This is the Meriwether Lewis monument.

Sometime during the dark hours preceding daylight of October 11, 1809, this peaceful little park was the scene of violence and horror and possible madness. Here died Meriwether Lewis, an American hero aged 35, killed either by his own hand or by a person or persons unknown. The tragedy has become one of the enduring mysteries of history.

Remarkably, even after a century and a half, there are still people in this area who hold strong opinions on the event. Through six or seven generations of families, oral tradition has turned the death of Meriwether Lewis into continuing legend.

Lewis was a Virginian, an army officer chosen by President Thomas Jefferson in 1801 to serve as his secretary. Both men grew up in the Blue Ridge foothills of Albemarle County. They were imbued with a similar Southern heritage, an awareness of the importance of land, and a fascination with the unknown territory beyond the frontier. The aging President saw in Lewis the son he had always wanted.

Soon after Jefferson acquired the vast Louisiana Territory in 1803, he set Lewis to planning an expedition to the Pacific Ocean. With William Clark, a friend of his army years, Lewis completed his epic journey of exploration in 1806. A hero to the nation, he was named governor of the Louisiana Territory and was soon embroiled in political contentions. His keenest desire was to arrange the journals of the great Lewis and Clark expedition for publication before spurious accounts were rushed into print to satisfy the demands of the public. Petty chores of office, however, interfered with his efforts. Adding to his frustrations were the actions of Washington bureaucrats who, even in that early time, were a bane to officials in the field. The bureaucrats refused to approve vouchers for necessary expenditures and questioned Lewis' integrity.

Finally, Lewis decided to journey to Washington to present his official records directly to his accusers and, more important, to deliver the journals of the Lewis and Clark expedition to his publishers in Philadelphia. He left St. Louis by boat on September 4, 1809, accompanied by his free servant, John Pernier, sometimes described as a Creole. Pernier had once worked for President Jefferson in Washington. Lewis' papers and other baggage were packed in four trunks. Not much is known about the boat, but it was probably a flatboat manned by a small crew, with a shelter at one end. Lewis' intention was to float down the Mississippi to New Orleans and continue by sail to the east coast.

As it usually is in early September, the weather along the river was exceedingly hot and humid. Before reaching Fort Pickering at Chickasaw Bluffs (present-day Memphis), Lewis fell ill, probably of malaria. Entries in his journal contain almost daily references to "bilious fever" and "pills of opium and tartar." It is worth noting here that during the expedition to the Pacific, Lewis served as medical officer. He was well supplied with laudanum, an opium-based medicine that is habit forming and can eventually cause mental deterioration. When he arrived at Fort Pickering on September 15, he was evidently in such a condition that the fort's commander, Captain Gilbert Russell, decided to detain him there "until he recovered, or some friend might arrive in whose hands he could depart in safety."

On the following day, Lewis was sufficiently recovered to write — in his style of haphazard spelling and colloquial grammar — a shaky letter to President James Madison informing him of his safe arrival at Fort Pickering and mentioning his physical exhaustion. "My apprehension from the heat of the lower country," he wrote, "and my fear of the original papers relative to my voyage to the Pacific ocean falling into the hands of the British has induced me to change my mind and proceed by land through the state of Tennissee to the City of Washington."

Rumors of an approaching war with Britain were certainly in circulation along the river, but there may have been more behind the change of plans than Lewis cared to put down in writing. Only three years earlier, Aaron Burr and General James Wilkinson had plotted with the Spanish government to establish a separate nation from the Mississippi valley into the Southwest. Wilkinson had concealed his treasonable activities by betraying Burr, and was now back in New Orleans commanding American troops. He possessed the power to stop anyone entering or leaving the mouth of the Mississippi. Wilkinson preceded Lewis as governor of the Louisiana Territory, and while in office he secretly accepted payments from the Spanish government. It is possible that Lewis discovered this treachery, and if so, he may have feared Wilkinson more than the British.

⟞⟩⊶⊰⟝

Three days after Lewis reached Fort Pickering, a government Indian agent, James Neelly, arrived there en route to Nashville by way of the Chickasaw Agency. Although Lewis knew the country around Fort Pickering (he had commanded the post in 1797), he must have welcomed the opportunity to travel with Neelly. They set out for the agency on September 29, with two trunks carrying Lewis' precious papers strapped to a pack horse; Lewis' other two trunks were left stored in the fort. The traveling party consisted of Lewis and Pernier, Neelly and his servant, and an unspecified number of Chickasaw Indians. The only source of information about the behavior of Lewis over the next 11 days comes from James Neelly, who may not have been a trustworthy man.

"On our arrival at the Chickasaw nation," Neelly later wrote to Thomas Jefferson, "I discovered that he [Lewis] appeared at times deranged in mind. We rested there ten days and came on. One days Journey after crossing Tennessee River where we encamped we lost two of our horses. I remained behind to hunt them & the Governor proceeded on, with a promise to wait for me at the first houses he came to that was inhabited by white people; he reached the house of Mr. Grinder about sun set. . . ." One of the odd actions of Neelly was sending his servant forward with Lewis and Pernier. Most men would have kept at least one assistant to aid in the onerous search for strayed horses.

The remainder of Neelly's letter contains information given him by Priscilla Grinder, who is history's sole source for the last hours of Meriwether Lewis' life. Priscilla Knight Grinder and her husband Robert came to Tennessee from Stokes County, North Carolina; they built a cabin that became known as Grinder's Stand, an informal sort of inn for travelers between Natchez and Nashville on the Natchez Trace. Priscilla Grinder told her story to Neelly, and a few months later to ornithologist Alexander Wilson, and many years later to an anonymous school teacher. It is mainly from their reports that historians have pieced together the circumstances of Lewis' death.

Neelly's letter, written only a week after Lewis died, states that Robert Grinder was not at home and that Mrs. Grinder "discovering the governor to be deranged, gave him up the house and slept in one near it." He added that the two servants spent the night in a stable loft some distance from the other house. At about 3 o'clock in the morning, Mrs. Grinder heard two pistol shots from the main house. She awakened the servants, but too late to save Lewis. "He had shot himself in the head with one pistol & a little below the Breast with the other — when his servant came in he says; I have done the business my good Servant give me some water. He gave him water, he survived but a short time."

⸺⋙●⋘⸺

Perhaps these were all the details that Priscilla Grinder could bring herself to tell James Neely so soon after the tragedy. Or perhaps Neely saw no reason to send a detailed account to Jefferson. He did recognize the importance of the contents of Lewis' trunks, and arranged for them to be forwarded to Washington.

About seven months after Lewis died, a Scottish-born ornithologist, Alexander Wilson, arrived at Grinder's Stand. Wilson was a friend of Lewis', who had given him specimens of birds brought back from the expedition to the Pacific. While stopping at Nashville on a journey to St. Louis, Wilson decided to venture down the Natchez Trace to learn something about his friend's death.

"In the same room where he expired," Wilson later wrote, "I took down from Mrs. Grinder the particulars of that melancholy event."

Apparently, Mrs. Grinder was willing to tell Wilson many details that are lacking in Neely's report. Governor Lewis, she said, arrived at Grinder's Stand along about sundown and asked for a night's lodging. He was wearing a traveler's duster, blue and white striped. When she asked if he was journeying alone, he replied that his servants were following close behind. He removed his saddle, brought it into the inn, and asked for spirits, but drank very little.

As soon as the servants arrived with the pack horses, Lewis asked Pernier for some gunpowder, saying he was certain he had some in a canister, but Mrs. Grinder was unable to hear Pernier's reply. After the servants went to the stables, Lewis began walking back and forth. "Sometimes he would seem as if he were walking up to me," Mrs. Grinder told Wilson, "and would suddenly wheel round, and walk back as fast as he could."

When she called him to supper, he sat down at the table, but ate only a few mouthfuls before he sprang up and began talking to himself in a violent manner, his face flushing. Calming himself,

Lewis lighted his pipe, drew a chair to the door, and sat down, remarking to Mrs. Grinder in a kindly tone of voice: "Madam, this is a very pleasant evening." Finishing his pipe, he arose and began pacing back and forth again. Refilling his pipe, he sat down to look toward the dying light in the west. "What a sweet evening it is," he said.

Although Mrs. Grinder prepared a bed for him, Lewis told her he preferred to sleep on the floor, and he called Pernier to bring his bearskins and buffalo robe. Mrs. Grinder went to the nearby kitchen-house to sleep with her children, leaving the main cabin to Lewis.

Disturbed by Lewis' strange behavior, Priscilla Grinder was unable to sleep. As the kitchen-house was only a few paces from the cabin, she could hear him walking back and forth and talking to himself "like a lawyer," she said. Sometime before sunrise she heard a pistol shot and something falling on the floor, followed by the words "O Lord!" Then she heard a second pistol fired.

A few minutes later Lewis was at her door, calling out: "O madam! Give me some water, and heal my wounds."

Why Priscilla Grinder did not respond to Lewis' cry for help has puzzled historians of the American frontier, who believe most frontier women would have done so. Years later, the Grinders' slave girl, Melindy, said she was with Priscilla and the children and that the sound of gunshots and Lewis' strange behavior made them all afraid to unbar the door.

Through chinks in the logs, Priscilla Grinder saw a shadowy figure stagger back from the door and fall against a stump between the kitchen-house and the cabin. He then crawled for some distance to a tree, where he raised himself and sat for about a minute before making his way back into the cabin.

Mrs. Grinder did not, or could not, recall how much time passed before Lewis once again returned to her door. He did not ask for water or help this time, but moved on to the well, where she heard him scraping the bucket with a gourd for water. "It appeared that this cooling element was denied the dying man!" Alexander Wilson wrote. "As soon as day broke and not before — the terror of the woman having permitted him to remain for two hours in this most deplorable situation — she sent two of her children to the barn, her husband not being at home, to bring the servants."

They found Lewis lying on the bed in the cabin, still conscious. A piece of his forehead was blown away, exposing the brain "without having bled much." Lewis uncovered his side and showed them where another bullet had entered. He begged them to take his rifle and blow out his brains, in return for which he would give them all the money he had in his trunk. "I am no coward," he kept repeating, "but I am so strong, so hard to die." He told Pernier not to be afraid, that he would not hurt him. About two hours later he died, "just as the sun rose above the trees."

James Neelly, in his letter to Jefferson, stated that he had Lewis "as decently buried as I could in that place — if there is anything wished by his friends to be done to his grave I will attend to their Instructions."

———⟫●⟨———

In most violent and unexplained events involving persons of historical importance, folklore usually enters the telling with passage of time. The mythology of Meriwether Lewis' death was undoubtedly already in oral tradition some 30 years later when an anonymous school teacher from the Cherokee Nation visited the Lewis grave. He found Priscilla Grinder, who was then in her late 60s, and listened to her story.

During her conversation with the school teacher, Priscilla Grinder added three men to the opening scene at Grinder's Stand. The trio arrived shortly after Lewis and his servants, whereupon Lewis drew a brace of pistols and ordered them to leave. Mrs. Grinder also added a third pistol shot. She omitted her previous statement that she had sent her children to the stables for the servants and instead said she was surprised to see them coming from the stables because she believed they had shared the cabin with Lewis. John Pernier, she added, was wearing Lewis' clothes — the same outfit Lewis had arrived in. When she asked Pernier about the clothes, he replied that Lewis had given them to him. The servants then searched for Lewis on the Trace and found him badly wounded and dressed in tattered clothing. Not long after they brought him back to the cabin, he died.

Whether these discrepancies were due to blurred memory on the part of Mrs. Grinder, or to other tales heard by the school teacher, no one can say. By the 1840s there was already an oral tradition of a coroner's jury assembled by Justice Samuel Whiteside immediately after the death to hold an inquest. The jury's decision supposedly was for suicide, but at least two of the five jurors were said to have decided for murder, yet were reluctant to name the killer. Failure to find any report of this inquest has led some historians to conclude that the county records were lost in a courthouse fire; others believed that the pages containing the report were torn from the record book.

According to Jill Garrett, who until recently was Maury County's official historian, there was no courthouse fire, the records still exist, and no pages are missing. Her further research into the matter indicated that local justices such as Samuel Whiteside did not begin forwarding reports to the county courthouse until the decade following Lewis' death. Findings of the coroner's jury, therefore, would be in Justice Whiteside's docket book, which apparently has been lost.

Supposedly, moccasin tracks and the print of an unusual rifle butt were found around the cabin on the morning after. The rifle butt's markings were recognized as belonging to Tom Runions, a part Indian who was suspected of being an occasional land pirate. Local residents believed that Runions would show no mercy to anyone who attempted to expose his alleged robberies and murders. The jurors may also have feared Robert Grinder because he sold "high wine" and whiskey illegally to the Indians. In 1904, the centennial of the Lewis and Clark expedition, a newspaperman went to the grave site to photograph the lonely monument. After talking with a number of people in the neighborhood, he wrote: "By the settlers of that vicinity, only one opinion was ever entertained — that Grinder had murdered Lewis for his money."

Yellow journalism was in full flower by the turn of the century, and in addition to Robert Grinder and Tom Runions, other names were soon on the list of possible murderers — Priscilla Grinder, James Neelly, and John Pernier. One elaborate theory concerned General James Wilkinson, who might have hired a murderer to stop Lewis from revealing the general's guilt as a traitor.

As for Neelly, he continued for three more years as agent to the Chickasaws and then was abruptly discharged by the Secretary of War for incompetence. After that he seems to disappear from the pages of history.

Soon after Lewis' death, Robert and Priscilla Grinder moved to a farm near Centerville, where they lived out their lives and left descendants who, for the most part, were substantial and responsible people. Tom Runions married one of their nieces, Perthania Grinder, and remained in the area.

John Pernier, the trusted servant, traveled straight from Grinder's Stand to Virginia to visit his former employer, Thomas Jefferson. He told Jefferson that Lewis had committed suicide, and Jefferson accepted that judgment. He recalled that Lewis "had from early youth suffered from hypochondriac affections . . . inherited by him from his father." Pernier then visited Lewis' family, presumably to claim $240 that he said his deceased master owed him for back wages. The family members refused to accept Pernier's story of suicide and fixed their suspicions upon the servant as a murderer.

Seven months after the death of Lewis, John Pernier himself died suddenly in Washington. Folklore has it that his throat was cut from ear to ear, but the man with whom he was boarding wrote Thomas Jefferson to inform him that Pernier deliberately ended his life with an overdose of laudanum. Jefferson recorded the event in a letter to a friend: "You will probably know the fate of poor Pierny, Lewis' servant, who lately followed his master's example."

The verdict for suicide by Jefferson, and by most modern scholars, has never been accepted by the people of the area around the scene of Lewis' death. Today, even though they are deeply concerned by the rapid changes taking place in middle Tennessee (construction of General Motors' huge Saturn automobile plant at Spring Hill, for example) they will stop whatever they may be doing to express their opinion on what happened at Grinder's Stand. And it's not unusual for descendants of the "suspects" to state that their ancestors "*might* have done it.*"

Not too long ago, vandals invaded a graveyard near Centerville and broke the tombstones of Priscilla and Robert Grinder. A descendant retrieved them and carried them off to Nashville for restoration. It was noted at the time that the name on the stones was Griner, not Grinder, proving that historians do not always get their spellings right. As to what really happened at Grinder's Stand, only Priscilla Grinder ever told. Still, "everybody knows what happened," one native of the area recently declared. "Robert Grinder came home that night, found Meriwether Lewis in bed with his wife, and shot him. The rest of the story she just made up."

The log structure (left), constructed in the 1930s, represents the early 19th century cabin of Robert and Priscilla Knight Grinder at Grinder's Stand that provided food and shelter to travelers along the Old Natchez Trace, in Tennessee. The burial place of Meriwether Lewis is on the distant far right. It is marked by a broken column to symbolize his untimely death. The Meriwether Lewis National Monument, as originally established and erected atop his grave site in 1848 by the State of Tennessee, became part of the Natchez Trace Parkway in 1961. Photographer: Glenn W. Peart. Courtesy of National Park Service.

4

━━━━◦➤◦◦◦━━━━

The Trail of Tears

"The forced removal of thousands of proud and prosperous Cherokees from their 35,000 square miles in the Southern uplands to less desirable land beyond the Mississippi stands as one of the blackest episodes in American history."

In the spring of 1838, Brigadier General Winfield Scott with a regiment of artillery, a regiment of infantry, and six companies of dragoons marched unopposed into the Cherokee country of northern Georgia. On May 10 at New Echota, the capital of what had been one of the greatest Indian nations in eastern America, Scott issued a proclamation:

The President of the United States sent me with a powerful army to cause you, in obedience to the treaty of 1835, to join that part of your people who are already established in prosperity on the other side of the Mississippi.... The emigration must be completed in haste.... The full moon of May is already on the wane, and before another shall have passed away every Cherokee man, woman and child . . . must be in motion to join their brethren in the west.... My troops already occupy many positions . . . and thousands and thousands are approaching from every quarter to render resistance and escape alike hopeless .... Will you then by resistance compel us to resort to arms? Or will you by flight seek to hide yourselves in mountains and forests and thus oblige us to hunt you down? Remember that in pursuit it may be impossible to avoid conflicts. The blood of the white man or the

59

blood of the red man may be spilt, and if spilt, however accidentally, it may be impossible for the discreet and humane among you, or among us, to prevent a general war and carnage.

For more than a century the Cherokees had been ceding their land, thousands of acres by thousands of acres. They had lost all of Kentucky and much of Tennessee, but after the last treaty of 1819 they still had remaining about 35,000 square miles of forested mountains, clean, swift-running rivers, and fine meadows. In this country which lay across parts of Georgia, North Carolina, and Tennessee they cultivated fields, planted orchards, fenced pastures, and built roads, houses, and towns. Sequoya had invented a syllabary for the Cherokee language so that thousands of his tribesmen quickly learned to read and write. The Cherokees had adopted the white man's way — his clothing, his constitutional form of government, even his religion. But it had all been for nothing. Now these men who had come across the great ocean many years ago wanted all of the Cherokees' land. In exchange for their 35,000 square miles the tribe was to receive five million dollars and another tract of land somewhere in the wilderness beyond the Mississippi River.

This was a crushing blow to a proud people. "They are extremely proud, despising the lower class of Europeans," said Henry Timberlake, who visited them before the Revolutionary War. William Bartram, the botanist, said the Cherokees were not only a handsome people, tall graceful, and olive-skinned, but "their countenance and actions exhibit an air of magnanimity, superiority and independence."

<hr>

Ever since the signing of the treaties of 1819, Major General Andrew Jackson, a man they once believed to be their friend, had been urging Cherokees to move beyond the Mississippi. Indians and white settlers, Jackson told them, could never get along together. Even if the government wanted to protect the Cherokees from harassment, he added, it would be unable to do so. "If you cannot protect us in Georgia," a chief retorted, "how can you protect us from similar evils in the West?"

During that period of polite urging, a few hundred Cherokee families did move west, but the tribe remained united and refused to give up any more territory. In fact, the council leaders passed a law forbidding any chief to sell or trade a single acre of Cherokee land on penalty of death.

In 1828, when Andrew Jackson was running for President, he knew that in order to win he must sweep the frontier states. Free land for the land-hungry settlers became Jackson's major policy. He hammered away at this theme especially hard in Georgia, where waves of settlers from the coastal lowlands were pushing into the highly desirable Cherokee country. He promised the Georgians that if they would help elect him President, he would lend his support to opening up the Cherokee lands for settlement. The Cherokees, of course, were not citizens and could not vote in opposition. To the Cherokees and their friends who protested this promise, Jackson justified his position by saying that the Cherokees had fought on the side of the British during the Revolutionary War. He conveniently forgot that the Cherokees had been his allies during the desperate War of 1812, and had saved the day for him in his decisive victory over the British-backed Creeks at Horseshoe Bend. (One of the Cherokee chiefs who aided Jackson was Junaluska. Said he afterward: "If I had known that Jackson would drive us from our homes I would have killed him that day at the Horseshoe.")

⸻⟫●⟪⸻

Three weeks after Jackson was elected President, the Georgia legislature passed a law annexing all the Cherokee country within that state's borders. As most of the Cherokee land was in Georgia and three-fourths of the tribe lived there, this meant an end to their independence as a nation. The Georgia legislature also abolished all Cherokee laws and customs and sent surveyors to map out land lots of 160 acres each. The 160-acre lots were to be distributed to white citizens of Georgia through public lotteries.

To add to the pressures on the Cherokees, gold was discovered near Dahlonega in the heart of their country. For many years the

Cherokees had concealed the gold deposits, but now the secret was out and a rabble of gold-hungry prospectors descended upon them.

John Ross, the Cherokees' leader, hurried to Washington to protest the Georgia legislature's actions and to plead for justice. In that year Ross was 38 years old; he was well-educated and had been active in Cherokee government matters since he was 19. He was adjutant of the Cherokee regiment that served with Jackson at Horseshoe Bend. His father had been one of a group of Scottish emigrants who settled near the Cherokees and married into the tribe.

In Washington, Ross found sympathizers in Congress, but most of them were anti-Jackson men and the Cherokee case was thus drawn into the whirlpool of politics. When Ross called upon Andrew Jackson to request this aid, the President bluntly told him that "no protection could be afforded the Cherokees" unless they were willing to move west of the Mississippi.

While Ross was vainly seeking help in Washington, alarming messages reached him from Georgia. White citizens of that state were claiming the homes of Cherokees through the land lottery, seizing some of them by force. Joseph Vann, a hard-working half-breed, had carved out an 800-acre plantation at Spring Place and built a fine brick house for his residence. Two men arrived to claim it, dueled for it, and the winner drove Vann and his family into the hills. When John Ross rushed home he found that the same thing had happened to his family. A lottery claimant was living in his beautiful home on the Coosa River, and Ross had to turn north toward Tennessee to find his fleeing wife and children.

<hr />

During all this turmoil, President Jackson and the governor of Georgia pressed the Cherokee leaders hard in attempts to persuade them to cede all their territory and move to the West. But the chiefs stood firm. Somehow they managed to hold the tribe together, and helped dispossessed families find new homes back in the wilderness areas. John Ross and his family lived in a one-room log cabin across the Tennessee line.

In 1834, the chiefs appealed to Congress with a memorial in which they stated that they would never voluntarily abandon their homeland, but proposed a compromise in which they agreed to cede the state of Georgia a part of their territory provided that they would be protected from invasion in the remainder. Furthermore, at the end of a definite period of years to be fixed by the United States they would be willing to become citizens of the various states in which they resided.

"Cupidity has fastened its eye upon our lands and our homes," they said, "and is seeking by force and by every variety of oppression and wrong to expel us from our lands and our homes and to tear from us all that has become endeared to us. In our distress we have appealed to the judiciary of the United States, where our rights have been solemnly established. We have appealed to the Executive of the United States to protect those rights according to the obligation of treaties and the injunctions of the laws. But this appeal to the Executive has been made in vain."

This new petition to Congress was no more effectual than their appeals to President Jackson. Again they were told that their difficulties could be remedied only by their removal to the west of the Mississippi.

For the first time now, a serious split occurred among the Cherokees. A small group of subchiefs decided that further resistance to the demands of the Georgia and United States governments was futile. It would be better they believed, to exchange their land and go west rather than risk bloodshed and the possible loss of everything. Leaders of this group were Major Ridge and Elias Boudinot. Ridge had adopted his first name after Andrew Jackson gave him that rank during the War of 1812. Boudinot was Ridge's nephew. Originally known as Buck Watie, he had taken the name of a New England philanthropist who sent him through a mission school in Connecticut. Stand Watie, who later became a Confederate general, was his brother. Upon Boudinot's return from school to Georgia he founded the first tribal newspaper, the Cherokee Phoenix, in 1827, but during the turbulence following the Georgia land lotteries he was forced to suspend publication.

And so in February 1835 when John Ross journeyed to Washington to resume his campaign to save the Cherokee nation, a rival delegation headed by Ridge and Boudinot arrived there to seek terms for removal to the West. The pro-removal forces in the government leaped at this opportunity to bypass Ross's authority, and within a few days drafted a preliminary treaty for the Ridge delegation. It was then announced that a council would be held later in the year at New Echota, Georgia, for the purpose of negotiating and agreeing upon final terms.

During the months that followed, bitterness increased between the two Cherokee factions. Ridge's group was a very small minority, but they had the full weight of the United States Government behind them, and threats and inducements were used to force a full attendance at the council which was set for December 22, 1835. Handbills were printed in Cherokee and distributed throughout the nation, informing the Indians that those who did not attend would be counted as assenting to any treaty that might be made.

During the seven days which followed the opening of the treaty council, fewer than five hundred Cherokees, or about 2 percent of the tribe, came to New Echota to participate in the discussions. Most of the other Cherokees were busy endorsing a petition to be sent to Congress stating their opposition to the treaty. But on December 29, Ridge, Boudinot and their followers signed away all the lands of the great Cherokee nation. Ironically, thirty years earlier Major Ridge had personally executed a Cherokee chief named Doublehead for committing one of the few capital crimes of the tribe. That crime was the signing of a treaty which gave away Cherokee lands.

Charges of bribery by the Ross forces were denied by government officials, but some years afterward it was discovered that the Secretary of War had sent secret agents into the Cherokee country with authority to expend money to bribe chiefs to support the treaty of

cession and removal. And certainly the treaty signers were hand-
somely rewarded. In an era when a dollar would buy many times its
worth today, Major Ridge was paid $30,000 and his followers
received several thousand dollars each. Ostensibly they were being
paid for their improved farmlands, but the amounts were far in excess
of contemporary land values.

John Ross meanwhile completed gathering signatures of Cherokees who were opposed to the treaty. Early in the following spring,
1836, he took the petition to Washington. More than three-fourths
of the tribe, 15,964, had signed in protest against the treaty.

When the governor of Georgia was informed of the overwhelm-
ing vote against the treaty, he replied: "Nineteen-twentieths of the
Cherokees are too ignorant and depraved to entitle their opinions to
any weight or consideration in such matters."

The Cherokees, however, did have friends in Congress. Representative Davy Crockett of Tennessee denounced the treatment of
the Cherokees as unjust, dishonest, and cruel. He admitted that he
represented a body of frontier constituents who would like to have
the Cherokee lands opened for settlement, and he doubted if a single
one of them would second what he was saying. Even though his
support of the Cherokees might remove him from public life, he
added, he could not do otherwise except at the expense of his honor
and conscience. Daniel Webster, Henry Clay, Edward Everett, and
other great orators of the Congress also spoke for the Cherokees.

When the treaty came to a final decision in the Senate, it passed
by only one vote. On May 23, 1836, President Jackson signed the
document. According to its terms, the Cherokees were allowed two
years from that day in which to leave their homeland forever.

The few Cherokees who had favored the treaty now began their final
preparations for departure. About three hundred left during that year
and then early in 1837 Major Ridge and 465 followers departed by
boats for the new land in the West. About 17,000 others, ignoring
the treaty, remained steadfast in their homeland with John Ross.

For a while it seemed that Ross might win his long fight, that perhaps the treaty might be declared void. After the Secretary of War, acting under instructions from President Jackson, sent Major William M. Davis to the Cherokee country to expedite removal to the West, Davis submitted a frank report: "That paper called a treaty is no treaty at all," he wrote, "because it is not sanctioned by the great body of the Cherokees and was made without their participation or assent. . . . The Cherokees are a peaceable, harmless people, but you may drive them to desperation, and this treaty cannot be carried into effect except by the strong arm of force."

In September 1836, Brigadier General Dunlap, who had been sent with a brigade of Tennessee volunteers to force the removal, indignantly disbanded his troops after making a strong speech in favor of the Indians: "I would never dishonor the Tennessee arms in a servile service by aiding to carry into execution at the point of the bayonet a treaty made by a lean minority against the will and authority of the Cherokee people."

Even Inspector General John W. Wool, commanding United States troops in the area, was impressed by the united Cherokee resistance, and warned the Secretary of War not to send any civilians who had any part in the making of the treaty back into the Cherokee country. During the summer of 1837, the Secretary of War sent a confidential agent, John Mason, Jr., to observe and report. "Opposition to the treaty is unanimous and irreconcilable," Mason wrote. "They say it cannot bind them because they did not make it; that it was made by a few unauthorized individuals; that the nation is not party to it."

The inexorable machinery of government was already in motion, however, and when the expiration date of the waiting period, May 23, 1838, came near, Winfield Scott was ordered in with his army to force compliance. As already stated, Scott issued his proclamation on May 10. His soldiers were already building thirteen stockaded forts — six in North Carolina, five in Georgia, one in Tennessee, and one in Alabama. At these points the Cherokees would be concentrated to await transportation to the West. Scott then ordered the roundup started, instructing his officers not to fire on the Cherokees except in case of resistance. "If we get possession of the women and children first," he said, "or first capture the men, the other members of the same family will readily come in."

—————◦◦◦◦—————

James Mooney, an ethnologist who afterwards talked with Cherokees who endured this ordeal, said that squads of troops moved into the forested mountains to search out every small cabin and make prisoners of all the occupants however or wherever they might be found. "Families at dinner were startled by the sudden gleam of bayonets in the doorway and rose up to be driven with blows and oaths along the weary miles of trail that led to the stockades. Men were seized in their fields or going along the road, women were taken from their spinning wheels and children from their play. In many cases, on turning for one last look as they crossed a ridge, they saw their homes in flames, fired by the lawless rabble that followed on the heels of the soldiers to loot and pillage. So keen were these outlaws on the scent that in some instances they were driving off the cattle and other stock of the Indians almost before the soldiers had fairly started their owners in the other direction."

Long afterward one of the Georgia militiamen who participated in the roundup said: "I fought through the Civil War and have seen men shot to pieces and slaughtered by thousands, but the Cherokee removal was the cruelest work I ever knew."

Knowing that resistance was futile, most of the Cherokees surrendered quietly. Within a month, thousands were enclosed in the stockades. On June 6 at Ross's Landing near the site of present-day Chattanooga, the first of many departures began. Eight hundred Cherokees were forcibly crowded onto a flotilla of six flatboats lashed to the side of a steamboat. After surviving a passage over rough rapids which smashed the sides of the flatboats, they landed at Decatur, Alabama, boarded a railroad train (which was a new and terrifying experience for most of them), and after reaching Tuscumbia were crowded upon a Tennessee River steamboat again.

Throughout June and July similar shipments of several hundred Cherokees were transported by this long water route — north on the

Tennessee River to the Ohio and then down the Mississippi and up the Arkansas to their new homeland. A few managed to escape and make their way back to the Cherokee country, but most of them were eventually recaptured. Along the route of travel of this forced migration, the summer was hot and dry. Drinking water and food were often contaminated. First the young children would die, then the older people, and sometimes as many as half the adults were stricken with dysentery and other ailments. On each boat deaths ran as high as five per day. On one of the first boats to reach Little Rock, Arkansas, at least a hundred had died. A compassionate lieutenant who was with the military escort recorded in his diary for August 1: "My blood chills as I write at the remembrance of the scenes I have gone through."

When John Ross and other Cherokee leaders back in the concentration camps learned of the high mortality among those who had gone ahead, they petitioned General Scott to postpone further departures until autumn. Although only three thousand Cherokees had been removed, Scott agreed to wait until the summer drought was broken, or no later than October. The Cherokees in turn agreed to organize and manage the migration themselves. After a lengthy council, they asked and received permission to travel overland in wagons, hoping that by camping along the way they would not suffer as many deaths as occurred among those who had gone on the river boats.

During this waiting period, Scott's soldiers continued their searches for more than a thousand Cherokees known to be still hiding out in the deep wildernesses of the Great Smoky Mountains. These Cherokees had organized themselves under the leadership of a chief named Utsala, and had developed warning systems to prevent captures by the bands of soldiers. Occasionally, however, some of the fugitives were caught and herded back to the nearest stockade.

One of the fugitive families was that of Tsali, an aging Cherokee. With his wife, his brother, three sons and their families, Tsali had built a hideout somewhere on the border between North Carolina and Tennessee. Soldiers surrounded their shelters one day, and the Cherokees surrendered without resistance. As they were being taken back toward Fort Cass (Calhoun, Tennessee) a soldier prodded Tsali's wife sharply with a bayonet, ordering her to walk faster. Angered by the brutality, Tsali grappled with the soldier, tore away his rifle, and bayoneted him to the ground. At the same time, Tsali's brother leaped upon another soldier and bayoneted him. Before the remainder of the military detachment could act, the Cherokees fled, vanishing back into the Smokies where they sought refuge with Chief Utsala. Both bayoneted soldiers died.

Upon learning of the incident, Scott immediately ordered that Tsali must be brought in and punished. Because some of his regiments were being transferred elsewhere for other duties, however, the general realized that his reduced force might be occupied for months in hunting down and capturing the escaped Cherokee. He would have to use guile to accomplish the capture of Tsali.

Scott therefore dispatched a messenger — a white man who had been adopted as a child by the Cherokees — to find Chief Utsala. The messenger was instructed to inform Utsala that if he would surrender Tsali to General Scott, the Army would withdraw from the Smokies and leave the remaining fugitives alone.

When Chief Utsala received the message, he was suspicious of Scott's sincerity, but he considered the general's offer as an opportunity to gain time. Perhaps with the passage of time, the few Cherokees remaining in the Smokies might be forgotten and left alone forever. Utsala put the proposition to Tsali: If he went in and surrendered, he would probably be put to death, but his death might insure the freedom of a thousand fugitive Cherokees.

Tsali did not hesitate. He announced that he would go and surrender to General Scott. To make certain that he was treated well, several members of Tsali's band went with him.

When the Cherokees reached Scott's headquarters, the general ordered Tsali, his brother, and three sons arrested, and then condemned them all to be shot to death. To impress upon the tribe their

Under heavy guard, Cherokee families, on foot, in wagons, and on horseback, are relocated to their new homeland in the West. From the painting "Trail of Tears" by Robert Lindneux. Courtesy of Woolaroc Museum, Bartlesville, Oklahoma.

utter helplessness before the might of the government, Scott selected the firing squad from Cherokee prisoners in one of the stockades. At the last moment, the general spared Tsali's youngest son because he was only a child.

(By this sacrifice, however, Tsali and his family gave the Smoky Mountain Cherokees a chance at survival in their homeland. Time was on their side, as Chief Utsala had hoped, and that is why today there is a small Cherokee reservation on the North Carolina slope of the Great Smoky Mountains.)

With the ending of the drought of 1838, John Ross and the 13,000 stockaded Cherokees began preparing for their long overland journey to the West. They assembled several hundred wagons, filled them with blankets, cooking pots, their old people and small children, and moved out in separate contingents along a trail that followed the Hiwassee River. The first party of 1,103 started on October 1.

"At noon all was in readiness for moving," said an observer of the departure. "The teams were stretched out in a line along the road through a heavy forest, groups of persons formed about each wagon. The day was bright and beautiful, but a gloomy thoughtfulness was depicted in the lineaments of every face. In all the bustle of preparation there was a silence and stillness of the voice that betrayed the sadness of the heart. At length the word was given to move on. Going Snake, an aged and respected chief whose head eighty summers had whitened, mounted on his favorite pony and led the way in silence, followed by a number of younger men on horseback. At this very moment a low sound of distant thunder fell upon my ear . . . a voice of divine indignation for the wrong of my poor and unhappy countrymen, driven by brutal power from all they loved and cherished in the land of their fathers to gratify the cravings of avarice. The sun was unclouded — no rain fell — the thunder rolled away and seemed hushed in the distance."

Throughout October, eleven wagon trains departed and then on November 4, the last Cherokee exiles moved out for the West. The overland route for these endless lines of wagons, horsemen, and people on foot ran from the mouth of the Hiwassee in Tennessee across the Cumberland plateau to McMinnville and then north to Nashville where they crossed the Cumberland River. From there they followed an old trail to Hopkinsville, Kentucky, and continued northwestward to the Ohio River, crossing into southern Illinois near the mouth of the Cumberland. Moving straight westward they passed through Jonesboro and crossed the Mississippi at Cape Girardeau, Missouri. Some of the first parties turned southward through Arkansas; the later ones continued westward through Springfield, Missouri, and on to Indian Territory.

A New Englander traveling eastward across Kentucky in November and December met several contingents, each a day apart from the others. "Many of the aged Indians were suffering extremely from the fatigue of the journey," he said, "and several were quite ill. Even aged females, apparently nearly ready to drop into the grave, were traveling with heavy burdens attached to their backs — on the sometimes frozen ground, and sometimes muddy streets, with no covering for the feet except what nature had given them . . . We learned from the inhabitants on the road where the Indians passed, that they buried fourteen or fifteen at every stopping place, and they make a journey of ten miles per day only on an average. They will not travel on the Sabbath . . . they must stop, and not merely stop — they must worship the Great Spirit, too; for they had divine service on the Sabbath — a camp meeting in truth."

Autumn rains softened the roads, and the hundreds of wagons and horses cut them into morasses, slowing movement to a crawl. To add to their difficulties, tollgate operators overcharged them for passage. Their horses were stolen or seized on pretext of unpaid debts, and they had no recourse to the law. With the coming of cold damp weather, measles and whooping cough became epidemic. Supplies had to be dumped to make room for the sick in the jolting wagons.

By the time the last detachments reached the Mississippi at Cape Girardeau it was January, with the river running full of ice so that several thousand had to wait on the east bank almost a month before the channel cleared. James Mooney, who later heard the story from survivors, said that "the lapse of over half a century had not sufficed to wipe out the memory of the miseries of that halt beside the frozen river, with hundreds of sick and dying penned up in wagons or stretched upon the ground with only a blanket overhead to keep out the January blast."

Meanwhile the parties that left early in October were beginning to reach Indian Territory. (The first arrived on January 4, 1839.) Each group had lost from thirty to forty members by death. The later detachments suffered much heavier losses, especially toward the end of their journey. Among the victims was the wife of John Ross.

Not until March 1839 did the last of the Cherokees reach their new home in the West. Counts were made of the survivors and balanced against the counts made at the beginning of the removal. As well as could be estimated, the Cherokees had lost about four thousand by deaths — or one out of every four members of the tribe — most of the deaths brought about as the direct result of the enforced removal. From that day to this the Cherokees remember it as "the trail where they cried," or the Trail of Tears.

PART II

Spoils and Scandal

A caravan of Conestoga wagon parties and traders heads southwest from Independence,
Missouri to Santa Fe and the end of the trail. From the painting, "On the Santa Fe Trail,"
by Frank Tenney Johnson. Courtesy of Wollaroc Museum, Bartlesville, Oklahoma.

5

Along the Santa Fe Trail

"The Cimarron Cutoff and Raton Pass opened the way for curious adventurers to the mystery and prosperity of old Santa Fe."

*F*orbidden cities, with their secrecy and unapproachableness acting as magnets, have always appealed to adventurous imaginations. From the time of its founding by the Spaniards in 1610, Santa Fe was taboo to the British, French, and other Europeans. During the first century of its existence, geography formed a protective shield around Santa Fe, but during the early 18th century explorers and traders from the East were drawn to its mystery. Like pilgrims approaching a forbidden monastery in Tibet, these early adventurers either were turned back or put under arrest and sentenced to long periods of imprisonment. The slowly fading Spanish empire was jealous of its Mexican colony, and Santa Fe was one of its farthest outposts. Trade with the outside world was strictly prohibited.

Legends began to spread telling of great wealth in Santa Fe. It was said that the men of that forbidden city wore buttons of silver on their trousers, and the women wore slippers of gold. So common were these precious metals that even the tires of carriages were made of silver and gold. Lured by these tales, brothers Pierre and Paul Mallet traveled from Canada in 1739 with a supply of knives, axes, and other trade goods. After reaching the Arkansas River, they followed what would later become the western end of the Santa Fe Trail, arriving

77

at their destination late in the summer. Naturally they were disappointed to find only a few hundred families in a small town "built of wood and without any fortifications, the garrison composed of but eighty soldiers . . . poorly armed." None of the gold and silver they had heard about was in evidence.

Despite the ban on foreign trade, the Spanish authorities allowed the Mallet brothers to sell their goods, but then refused to permit them to leave because they had "spied out the land." Only after months of negotiations with the Viceroy of Mexico did the Frenchmen obtain their release. Twice more the Mallets returned to Santa Fe with mule trains of goods, but each time their property was confiscated and they were escorted out of New Mexico. Throughout the remainder of the 18th century, occasional adventurers attempted to overcome the trade ban of the Spaniards, but with little success.

———————

In 1806 when Zebulon Pike was exploring the lower part of the nation's recently acquired Louisiana Territory, he and his small detachment of soldiers were captured by a Spanish patrol on the upper Rio Grande and taken into Santa Fe. Pike seems to have deliberately sought this enforced detention in order to obtain information about the area. After giving Pike and his men a guarded tour to Chihuahua, the Spanish military escorted them all the way to the United States boundary near Natchitoches, Louisiana, and released them.

During the years after Pike's expedition several more explorers and traders ventured toward Santa Fe, but few reached the city, and most of those who did were arrested and imprisoned in dungeons, where some remained until Mexico won its freedom from Spain in 1821. It was in June of that year that William Becknell, a young frontiersman, advertised in a St. Louis newspaper for "a company of men destined to the Westward for the purpose of trading for Horses and Mules, and catching wild animals of every description." By August, Becknell had seventeen men signed to his trading company, and they left Missouri on September 1, heading west. After crossing the Osage River they followed the Arkansas into Colorado and then turned south through

Raton Pass toward Santa Fe. They soon encountered a patrol of Mexican soldiers, but instead of being arrested or driven away, Becknell and his men were greeted in a friendly manner and invited to bring their trade goods into Santa Fe. The recent overthrow of Spanish rule had brought a liberalization of trading policies to Mexico.

Hurrying back to Missouri with a canvas bag full of silver coins that he had obtained for his merchandise, Becknell began organizing the first wagon train trading expedition to Santa Fe. To shorten the westward journey, he left the Arkansas River just west of present-day Dodge City and followed the Cimarron into New Mexico. He thus blazed the Cimarron Cutoff, a shorter route, but one that was more hazardous because of the scarcity of water and an increased danger of Indian attacks. Thenceforth there would be a bifurcated Santa Fe Trail — the Cimarron route and the Raton Pass route.

News of William Becknell's profitable ventures to Santa Fe quickly attracted other traders. For a few years the town of Franklin in central Missouri was the favored staging place, but after Independence was founded in 1827 it became the departure point for most caravans bound for Santa Fe.

—◄●►—

In 1831 the man who wrote the most enduring history of this "commerce of the prairies" became a Santa Fe trader almost by accident. He was Josiah Gregg, who at 25 abandoned the practice of law in Independence because a physician told him that he had only a few months to live. Determined to see Santa Fe before he died, Gregg joined a wagon train. Too weak to mount a horse, he started out in a carriage, but after a few days in the open air he acquired an insatiable appetite for the coarse food of the wagoners, and was soon able to ride horseback and stand his turn at guard watch.

Along the way, Gregg's party overtook a buffalo hunter who told them the "most melancholy news" of the death of a man traveling with the wagon train just ahead. "From his description we presumed it to be Capt. Smith . . . he was pierced by the arrows of a gang of Comanches who were lying in wait for him." The dead man was that celebrated explorer and fur trader, Jedediah Smith, the most literate of the Mountain Men. Smith and his wagon train had been traveling over the arid Cimarron Cutoff for three days without water. When he and a companion left the trail to search for water, Smith went on ahead, crossed a small rise, and vanished. Some weeks afterward, Mexican traders obtained Smith's silver-mounted pistols from a band of Comanches and learned how he died fighting to the end.

Josiah Gregg's journey to Santa Fe not only restored his health, it convinced him that in spite of physical discomforts and constant dangers, a man could grow rich much faster in the Santa Fe trade than by practicing law. Each year for the next eight years he took a wagon train of merchandise over the trail to Santa Fe. In 1843, at 36, he retired to Van Buren, Arkansas, and wrote a book about his experiences. *The Commerce of the Prairies* became a classic of American historical literature, and upon its content rests much of what we know about the first years of the Santa Fe Trail, the appearance of the unsettled country through which the trail passed, the routines of wagon trains, the economics of trading, what goods were in demand, and the attitudes and behavior of Indian tribes and Mexicans.

According to Gregg, for the first week after traders left Independence they usually traveled in detached parties. About forty miles out they would pass the junction of the two great western trails, one crude signboard pointing to Santa Fe, the other indicating "Road to Oregon." The former was a trail of commerce, the latter a trail of settlement. In romantic story and film the Oregon Trail has the edge, but in actuality the Santa Fe Trail's record is more varied and picturesque.

———❊———

About 150 miles west of Independence the separate wagon parties reached a timbered strip along Council Grove Creek, and there they always halted to make repairs, to organize into sizable and well-armed caravans, and to choose captains and lieutenants for the dangerous 575 miles to San Miguel, the only town of any consequence between Independence and Santa Fe.

Gregg described the departure of a wagon train from Council

Grove: " 'All's set!' is finally heard from some teamster — 'All's set' is directly responded from every quarter. 'Stretch out!' immediately vociferates the captain. Then the 'Heps!' of drivers — the cracking of whips — the trampling of feet — the occasional creak of wheels — the rumbling of wagons — form a new scene of exquisite confusion, which I shall not attempt further to describe. 'Fall in!' is heard from headquarters, and the wagons are forthwith strung out upon the long, inclined plain, which stretches to the heights beyond Council Grove."

Another 150 miles farther west on the high plains was Pawnee Rock, where travelers stopped to register their passage on the red sandstone landmark. "I cut my name among the many hundreds inscribed on the rock," Susan Shelby Magoffin noted in her diary on July 4, 1846. "It was not done well, for fear of Indians made me tremble all over."

The wagons most used on the Santa Fe Trail were modified Conestogas, huge vehicles capable of hauling at least two tons of merchandise that varied from candles, soap, tobacco, cloth, ribbons, washboards, and shoes to molasses, cider, flour, sugar, whiskey, coffee, and cured meats. Many traders used oxen for draft animals, four to six yoke to each wagon. Others preferred mules because oxen traveled slowly, made poor use of grass along the way, and their hooves sometimes wore out on the sand and rocks of the Southwest.

Although the caravans usually took the Cimarron Cutoff to San Miguel, the completion of Bent's Fort on the upper Arkansas in 1833 attracted a considerable number of traders, who then used the Raton Pass into Santa Fe. Charles and William Bent built an impregnable fort with thick adobe walls where travelers could enjoy security and hospitality. Here traders exchanged goods with Indians for marketable articles such as buffalo hides that could be obtained cheaply at Bent's Fort and sold for high prices in Santa Fe.

When war with Mexico was beginning in 1846, General Stephen W. Kearny marched his Army of the West from Fort Leavenworth over the Santa Fe Trail to Bent's Fort so he could use the fort as an assembly and supply base for the invasion of New Mexico. "Here a great many of the government wagons were unloaded and sent back to Fort Leavenworth for additional supplies," one of Kearny's officers noted. "Here also the caravans of traders waited the arrival of the army, thenceforward to move under the wing of its protection."

One of the best descriptions of life on the Santa Fe Trail during that momentous year of decision for the United States was recorded by 18-year old Susan Magoffin, who arrived at Bent's Fort just ahead of the Army of the West. Susan was traveling with her husband Samuel, who, with his brother James Magoffin, was engaged in a secret mission for the U.S. Government. Both men were veteran Santa Fe traders, well acquainted with Mexican officials, and according to legend they were carrying a sack of gold coins to be used "to secure New Mexico without the firing of a gun or the spilling of a drop of blood."

If Susan knew of this she did not reveal it in her diary. Perhaps she was too busy enjoying the journey along the Santa Fe Trail to be bothered with such matters. "Oh, this is a life I would not exchange for a good deal! . . . It is the life of a wandering princess, mine."

Susan was in early pregnancy, and to keep her comfortable Samuel had outfitted the most luxurious carriage yet seen in the West. It was cushioned with numerous pillows, and in easy reach were baskets, bags, boxes, wines, medicines, and books. Among the books, of course, was Josiah Gregg's *The Commerce of the Prairies*, which she consulted daily and sometimes quoted in her diary. The accompanying tent for use at night was carpeted and fitted with a dressing table and folding chairs. She and Samuel slept between silken sheets, and during the daily "noonings" when the wagon train stopped to rest and water the animals, they would recline on a buffalo skin in the shade of a wagon, sipping wine or "a little toddy with water."

Unfortunately for Susan, her luxurious carriage was suddenly overturned one day while the train was crossing a dry creek, and the rough jolting brought on severe pains. Soon after that, a thunderstorm wrecked the Magoffins' tent and she was rain soaked. By the time they reached Bent's Fort she was so ill that she had to spend her 19th birthday in bed. The next day she lost her child in a miscarriage.

None of this daunted the spirits of Susan Magoffin. While she was recovering, her brother-in-law James went on to New Mexico with his legendary bag of gold coins, and late in the summer of 1846 the Army of the West took possession of Santa Fe without firing a shot. When Susan arrived she joined in the celebration, delighting General Kearny by engaging him in a running flirtation. Some time later, after she became pregnant again, she noted in her diary: "I do think a pregnant woman has a hard time of it, some sickness all the time, heartburn, headache, cramp, etc. after all this thing of marrying is not what it is cracked up to be." Susan Magoffin had lost her romanticism and learned to face reality on the trail to Santa Fe.

⸺⸺⸻⸺⸺

Another young girl who made that journey in considerably less luxurious fashion during 1852 was Marian Russell, who with her mother and brother accompanied François Xavier Aubry's wagons and an Army supply train from Leavenworth. Marian's mother paid for their $500 transportation costs by cooking meals for three army officers enroute. Of this two-months' journey Marian later wrote: "Minute impressions flash before me, the sun-bonneted women and the woolen-trousered men that made up the cavalcade . . . the seven-year-old child in brand new coat with a silken fringed collar, sitting primly by mother's side, her eyes eager and her braids of long brown hair, bouncing . . . the wagons, five hundred of them, rolling and swaying along the old trail. . . . At night our wagons were spread out in a great circle. Ropes were stretched between them. Inside the enclosure thus formed the mules were turned loose to graze. Soon tents were pitched and cooking fires were blazing."

Young Marian Russell formed a warm friendship with the dashing François Aubry, and told of how he helped drive the Russells' tent stakes for night camp. "When Captain Aubry finished his task he came and took me on his lap. Sitting there in the shelter of his arms, I felt the great windy night closing down upon us, was conscious of the night wind and the vast turbulent prairie stretching away into infinity. The world seemed to me so big and black and terrible. I shivered in the Captain's arms, thinking that only here where the fire-light flickered on mother's face was warmth and comfort and home."

In 1852 Aubry was 28 years old, already a wealthy trader, and famous for his speedy horseback rides from Santa Fe to Independence. Born in Quebec, he emigrated to St. Louis at 19 and was soon hauling merchandise to Santa Fe. The secret of success, Aubry believed, was to make two or three trips to Santa Fe in each season. To accomplish this he began his famed endurance rides on fast horses back to Independence, which earned him the sobriquets of "Electric Traveler," "Skimmer of the Plains," and "The Telegraph."

In the spring of 1848 Aubry was the first trader of the season to bring wagons into Santa Fe. As soon as he sold his goods he announced that he would attempt to return to Independence in ten days. Accompanied by six hopeful companions, he rode out of Santa Fe on May 19. After the first three hundred miles all his fellow riders had fallen behind, and before he reached Fort Mann (near present-day Dodge City) he had worn out three horses and two mules. At the fort he bought fresh mounts, and eight days and ten hours after leaving Santa Fe he rode into Independence.

By mid-July the energetic Aubry had filled thirty wagons with newly purchased merchandise and was rolling on the trail to Santa Fe. With his usual audacity he rode far ahead of his train and sold his entire stock to Santa Fe merchants before the wagons arrived. In order to bring out a third train of goods before winter, he left Santa Fe early in September, riding alone this time and determined to break his previous speed record. In his saddlebag was a copy of a Santa Fe newspaper to document the time of his departure and convince skeptics in Independence.

Somewhere along the trail Alexander Majors, a trader bound for Santa Fe with twenty-five wagons, recognized his friend Aubry approaching at a gallop. Majors tried to wave him to a stop, but Aubry dashed past "merely nodding his head as the dust flew in our faces." Five days and sixteen hours after starting the 780-mile ride, Aubry arrived in Independence, setting a record that stands to this day.

"Indian Alarm on the Cimarron River," one of several illustrations by Josiah Gregg in his book, Commerce of the Prairies, *which depicted scenes travelers could expect to see along the Santa Fe Trail.*

In Aubry's swift rides, Alexander Majors may have seen the possibilities of the Pony Express, which twelve years later was started by the transportation company in which Majors held a partnership. Although the Pony Express did not use the Santa Fe Trail, the first mails to New Mexico were carried there irregularly on horseback. Then on July 1, 1850, subsidized by a government contract, the first mail wagons to follow the trail began a monthly service between Independence and Santa Fe.

To reduce travel time, relay stations were installed along the route, but the mail wagons never were able to make the run in less than seventeen days. During the early 1850s, after Indians became troublesome along the Cimarron, soldiers rode concealed beneath the canvas of the mail wagons, sometimes surprising bold warriors who rode in too close in their efforts to capture mules and horses.

Stagecoach service for passengers soon followed the wagon routes, and in a few years mails and passengers could make the trip from Independence to Santa Fe in eleven days. And even before the outbreak of the Civil War, which severely disrupted travel in the West, railroad enthusiasts were planning tracks of steel rails for Iron Horses to run along the old trail to Santa Fe.

Atchison, Kansas, on the Missouri River above Independence, was chosen as the eastern terminus of the Atchison, Topeka & Santa Fe Railroad, which received a generous land grant from the Government in 1863. Following the Arkansas River westward the rails of the A.T. & S.F. reached Dodge City in 1872, and before that year ended the track was at the Colorado line. After some financial delays the railroad moved into Colorado, passed Bent's Fort, and reached Pueblo in time to celebrate the nation's centennial year of 1876. It was obvious now that the A.T. & S.F. meant to use historic Raton Pass for its pathway into New Mexico.

But so did another railroad, the Denver & Rio Grande. Another complicating factor was Uncle Dick Wootton, a hard-bitten old trader who had secured charters from the legislatures of Colorado and New Mexico authorizing him to open a toll road through the pass. For several years he had lived well by collecting tolls from travelers bound to and from Santa Fe. Legend has it that the Atchison, Topeka & Santa Fe offered Uncle Dick a sizable life pension in exchange for the right-of-way and a guarantee from him of protection for the railroad's grading crews, who arrived there one cold winter's night ahead of the Denver & Rio Grande workers. At any rate, Uncle Dick organized an armed force to guard the graders, and a gunfight very nearly followed when a band of Denver & Rio Grande engineers and roustabouts challenged their rivals.

Victorious by right of possession, the A.T. & S.F. pushed its tracks on through Raton Pass. The main lines only skirted Santa Fe, however, and the city which originally had been the railroad's destination was served by a spur line from the village of Lamy, while the main tracks continued toward Albuquerque. In January 1880 the first trains began rolling into Santa Fe, and the weekly *New Mexican* announced with pride and a trace of nostalgic regret: "Old Santa Fe Trail Passes Into Oblivion."

6

Brides by the Boatload

*F*rom the first Oregon settlements through the California gold rush and until long after the Civil War, the scarcest commodity in the Old West was women. According to the 1850 census, percentages of females ranged from absolute zero in some sections to a high of 8 percent in favored California.

During this period, female-starved westerners considered it a privilege just to see a member of the opposite sex. A typical story concerns a young miner who learned one evening that a woman had arrived at another mining camp some forty miles distant. The young man went to his uncle and asked: "Uncle, will you lend me your mule tomorrow?"

"What do you want with my mule?"

"I've heard there's a woman over at the next camp, and I want to go and look at her."

The uncle lent his nephew the mule, and he was off at daybreak and never stopped until he covered the forty miles and had a good look at the lady.

In the course of time, the West's dearth of females attracted the attention of a number of social theorists and ingenious entrepreneurs. One of the first to propose a solution to the shortage was Catherine Beecher, sister of the famed Harriet and Henry Ward Beecher.

Catherine published a book called *The Duty of American Women to Their Country*, advocating "Go West, young woman" long before Horace Greeley thought up the phrase for young men. Miss Beecher, however, ignored the practicalities of getting there.

Not long afterward a New York widow, Elizabeth Farnham, attempted to organize a company of prospective brides for lonely California miners. She secured the endorsements of Horace Greeley, William Cullen Bryant, and Henry Ward Beecher, and published an announcement which quickly brought replies from two hundred interested women. Unfortunately, Mrs. Farnham fell ill and was not able to work actively at organizing the expedition; in the end, only three women agreed to go to California with her. Her plan had been widely advertised in the West, and a miner's diary entry of June 10, 1849, suggests the disappointment that must have followed her failure: "Went to church 3 times today. A few ladies present, does my eyes good to see a woman once more. Hope Mrs. Farnham will bring 10,000."

———※———

The most successful project for importing brides was that of Asa Shinn Mercer, who began his western career in Seattle in 1861. Mercer founded the University of Washington, becoming its first president, but was disappointed in the size of the student body — only a dozen or so young men. Realizing that his institution was unlikely to grow very rapidly in a territory where men outnumbered women nine to one, he decided that what was most needed was an importation of women to breed future students.

Mercer was a tall red-haired man in his mid-twenties, with intense dark eyes and an affable, persuasive manner. He convinced the Washington territorial legislature that hundreds of prospective brides could be obtained in New England, where there was an estimated surplus of 30,000 females, many of them left fatherless as a result of the raging Civil War. The territorial authorities gave Mercer's project their blessing, but no money. To finance the venture, he had to raise private contributions from hopeful bachelors.

In the early spring of 1864 Asa Mercer arrived in New England, ready to address all his powers of persuasion to that area's thousands of young single women. His most successful appearance was in Lowell, Massachusetts, where he pictured in glowing terms the advantages awaiting all young ladies who would leave their New England homes and migrate to Washington Territory to engage in school teaching. When some critics wondered publicly just whom the girls would teach if there were only childless bachelors in the West, Mercer ignored them and stressed an appeal to his listeners' desire for financial improvement.

His brief tour won him eleven converts, ranging in ages from fifteen to twenty-five. Each paid $225 passage money, and in March 1864 the little party with Mercer in charge, sailed from New York. After crossing the Panama Isthmus, they reached Seattle on May 16. As Mercer had hoped, most of his "school teachers" were soon married; only one, a Miss Ann Murphy, became homesick and returned to Lowell.

<hr/>

Hailed as a hero, Mercer was soon afterward elected to the territorial legislature. By the next year he was ready to go back east, make a longer and wider canvass, and return to Seattle with an entire shipload of girls. His plans included enlisting the aid of President Lincoln, but only a few days before he reached New York, April 19, 1865, Lincoln was assassinated.

Shocked but undaunted, Mercer went on to Washington, D.C., waited until the furor surrounding the President's assassination had died down, and then sought an audience with President Andrew Johnson. Although Johnson did not oppose the female emigration scheme, he would offer no financial assistance from the government. In desperation, Mercer turned to General Ulysses Grant, a man who had soldiered in the West and knew how urgently women were needed there. Grant cheerfully wrote out an order authorizing Mercer's use of a troopship for transporting his school teachers to Washington Territory.

Elated by this good fortune, Mercer immediately headed for New

England to round up his cargo. He was now in a position to offer bargain rates, only twenty-five dollars per passenger, and those who could not afford that sum could pay later. In his speeches, he asked for female volunteers below the age of twenty-five, guaranteeing employment as soon as they arrived in Washington Territory.

Both in New England and New York, Mercer ran into opposition from the press. One editor accused him of "seeking to carry off young girls for the benefit of miserable old bachelors," and a number of papers attempted to undermine his efforts by publicly ridiculing those who joined the expedition. But in spite of opposition, Mercer signed up about four hundred girls, issuing contracts guaranteeing the holders passage to Washington Territory.

⟞⟩❂❨⟝

On the first day of August, Mercer arrived in New York to prepare for his departure. His first step was to seek possession of the promised military transport ship. Armed with the written order from General Grant, he called on Quartermaster-General Montgomery Meigs, who was a stickler for military regulations. Declaring that Grant had acted without authority, Meigs refused to permit use of a government vessel for transporting females anywhere. The dismayed Mercer protested that he must have a ship; four hundred young women were ready and eager to sail; they had his written promises guaranteeing transportation to Washington Territory. Meigs replied that he would sell him a ship at a bargain, $80,000.

Time was pressing, but Mercer tried to raise the money. When that failed, he attempted to contract passage with a shipping line. The best price he could get was $120,000, fare for four hundred passengers. He hurriedly postponed the sailing date, and began sending frantic messages for help to his friends in the West.

On September 30, when the New York Times interviewed him about his plans, Mercer confidently announced that his list of applicants had grown to 650, and that they would be sailing within a few weeks. He made careful replies to questions concerning the matrimonial chances for the girls. "Although this is not a matrimonial venture," the newspaper commented, "it being expressly stipulated that the wages of the girls shall be adequate for their support without recourse to marriage, there is not the most distant probability that any young woman who desires to marry will be prevented."

❦

It was Ben Holladay, king of the stagecoach and overland mail lines, who saved the day for Asa Mercer. Holladay also owned the California, Oregon & Mexican Steamship Company, and he volunteered to buy one of General Meigs' military ships and transport the girls at low rates.

At last, on January 15, 1866, the steamship Continental was ready to clear the port of New York with the Mercer Belles aboard. All the delay and bad publicity, however, had cut Mercer's proud cargo to only about one hundred single women, a dozen married couples, and fourteen single men.

When the passengers boarded the Continental , they found everything in confusion. No repairs had been made to the vessel's interior fittings since it was last used for transporting soldiers, and the galley was in such condition that no meals could be served the first day. Off Staten Island, the Continental anchored to await a pilot boat; as the boat approached, a man standing in the bow began shouting: "Where is Mercer? I want to see Mercer!" Mercer quickly hid in a coal bin, suspecting the caller might be a creditor armed with a legal summons which would further delay the voyage. Actually the man was a Maine farmer who had sold his farm at Mercer's suggestion and wanted to take his family west with the expedition.

As the ship headed south through calm waters, the passengers settled down to the usual routines of ocean voyaging. The food was monotonous; for seventeen days they were served nothing but fried salt beef, parboiled beans, and tea steeped in salt water. The girls were on the point of rebellion because Mercer was dining at the captain's table, where the diet was more varied, but when Mercer heard of their dissatisfaction he deserted the captain and began sharing the poor fare of his charges.

Aboard the Continental was a special newspaper correspondent who, after the fashion of the day, signed his dispatches with a cognomen, "Rod." His real name was Roger Conant, a bachelor in his early thirties. According to Flora Pearson — who later recorded her experiences — he flirted with "first one and then another of the fair sex, evidently with serious intentions each time, but the ardent wooer failed to make a permanent impression; his charmers suffered his devotions for a brief season and then gave him the cold shoulder."

There were other shipboard flirtations, involving four of the vessel's engineers and a grizzled California miner who had booked passage at the last minute. "Around him [the miner] revolved as regularly as the planets in their orbits, five unmarried females, who were known as 'the Constellation.' How the much-sought man escaped entanglement in the matrimonial mesh will never be known — possibly he made haste upon landing to lose himself in the foothills of California."

Asa Mercer himself fell victim to the mood of romantic enchantment that seemed to hover over the Continental. In the words of Flora Pearson, "he succumbed to the fascination of one of the most accomplished of our maidens, but she would have none of him." However, when he formed a second attachment, to a Miss Annie Stephens of Baltimore, his "passion was reciprocated."

Among the personalities aboard, as described by Miss Pearson, was a dyspeptic young lady nicknamed "Spepsy," an exclusive maid whose mouth always had a "prunes and prisms expression," and who showed deep disdain for all her surroundings until she "grew chummy with the captain's daughter and ate at the table with the royal household." Another interesting member of the party was "the plain spoken Miss S. who was locked in her room at the command of the ship's master." Annoyed by the flirtatious actions of his engineers, the captain ordered them to remain in their quarters and not mingle with the female passengers. Miss S. disliked this order, and to show her contempt for the captain she drew a chalk mark across the deck by the saloon door and lettered a huge sign along it: *Officers Not Allowed Aft*. The captain retaliated by confining Miss S. to her quarters also.

When the Continental reached Rio de Janeiro, the passengers all went happily ashore, and Rod of the New York Times was able to send dispatches back by mail boat to his paper. For some reason, he had little to say in print about "the marriageable young ladies on board," devoting most of his florid prose to descriptions of Rio. In his private diary, however, which remained unpublished for many years, the greater part of Roger Conant's entries was concerned with the female passengers whom he usually referred to as "virgins." He described numerous flirtations, including his own, and hinted that it was not unusual for some of the virgins to occasionally get into the wrong berths.

——————

Conant took a violent dislike to Mercer, ridiculing him for his watchfulness over his charges, and complaining that he forbade card playing and dancing and would allow no one to use the fine library donated to the expedition by philanthropist Peter Cooper. Mercer also ordered the girls to bed every night at 10 p.m., but they took revenge by making faces at him while he read sermons to them at evening services.

One of the liveliest of the girls was Almira Huntoon, nicknamed "Pontoon," who was among a group who visited a wholesale liquor store in Rio. According to Conant, when Miss Huntoon was invited to choose a wine from six samples set before her, instead of merely sipping she drank a full glass of each kind. "She seemed to feel very happy," Conant noted in his diary. "Raising her dress a little she danced a jig around the room and attempted to sing a song . . . She then started up 'We Won't Go Home Till Morning' and another which she called 'We'll Get as Tight as a Brick.'"

After leaving Rio, the Continental sailed on around the Horn to the Chilean port of Lota, anchoring there for several days to take on coal and supplies. Rod went ashore with some of the girls to buy souvenirs, and later sent a dispatch to the Times : "Ever since our arrival at this port, the Continental has been completely overrun, night and

day, with Chilean officers. So intense has been their admiration for
the ladies that every inducement has been held out to persuade them
to remain in Chile. Offers of marriage; offers of schools at fabulous
prices, and offers of positions as housekeepers flowed in abundance."

In his more vivid diary account of this affair, which almost turned to
disaster for the expedition, Conant said that when several of the in-
fatuated girls were preparing to leave the ship permanently with a
group of Chilean officers, Mercer leaped to the gangway, pistol in
hand. "No one," he shouted, "takes one of these girls from the ship
except they pass over my dead body." The ship's captain avoided an
immediate showdown by ordering the ladder drawn up and promising the girls they might go ashore next day. That night while all on
board were asleep he lifted anchor and set sail.

On April 25, the girls landed in San Francisco, where they were
hailed by crowds of enthusiastic male Californians. Mercer permitted
eleven members of his valuable cargo to remain there, and as this was
the end of the journey for the Continental, he arranged further passage on the brig Tanner. They continued north for Seattle, and on
May 29, 1866, more than four months after leaving New York,
Mercer's Belles reached their destination.

"All the men in Seattle that could get new suits did so," reported
a member of the reception committee, "and others got new overalls
and were on the dock when the Tanner arrived. Mr. Mercer thought
they seemed to think they would get a wife immediately, so he made
a speech to them before they landed, telling them that the women
were all of the best and if the men wanted them for wives they must
do it in the good old way. All were well treated when they came
ashore, and were taken into homes until they married or got employment as milliners, dressmakers, school teachers, etc."

In less than a month, at least thirteen of the girls had achieved the
matrimonial objectives of their long voyage west. Asa Mercer himself

married Annie Stephens six weeks after their arrival, and he made no more journeys east in search of prospective brides. Perhaps he had found what he had been searching for. In the course of time, all of his girls except one found husbands. The exception was Elizabeth Ordway, who had signed on to be a school teacher, and a school teacher she was for many years. "Nothing could induce me," she said in later life, "to relinquish the advantages of single blessedness."

As for Mercer, his later life is worthy of a brief footnote. Whether it was the strain and excitement of his two expeditions, or something else, Mercer was never again able to settle down and fulfill the bright promise of his youthful twenties. He became a drifter, moving first to Oregon to found a periodical, engage in the grain trade, and work as an employee of the state government.

In 1876 he moved on to Texas, operating four newspapers, none too successfully. In 1883 he drifted north to Wyoming, founded a live-stock journal, and there met his downfall. During the Johnson County War between the settlers and the big cattlemen, he sided with the settlers and published an exposé of the Johnson County invasion, *The Banditti of the Plains*, in which he named names in bold print. Copies of his book were searched out and burned, the plates were destroyed, and he was thrown into jail. For the remainder of his life, Mercer lived on the verge of poverty, accomplishing nothing of importance, and finally died in 1917 at the age of seventy-eight.

Holding her newborn baby, Amanda Tomlinson Bower Belknap, wife of Secretary of War William Worth Belknap, pleads for help on her husband's behalf to Rep. Joseph Blackburn, whose wife, Therese, was a close friend. Rep. Blackburn (D-Kentucky) was a member of the House Committee on Expenditures in the War Department that was hearing the charges made against the Secretary of War.

7

The Belknap Scandal

*"Public disgrace, an impeachment trial and a ruined career were
all part of this strange story of the Grant Administration."*

One of the clichés of American history is that the administration of President Ulysses Grant was riddled with corruption. Actually it was far less corrupt than the lusty era it encompassed — the Gilded Age of the robber barons which included such well-known names as the Vanderbilts, Goulds, Fisks, Carnegies, and Rockefellers. The two major scandals which gave the Grant administration its stigma occurred early in the election year of 1876. The President's confidential secretary, Orville Babcock, was involved in the first affair — alleged bribery by the Whiskey Ring. Grant's Secretary of the Treasury, Benjamin Bristow, accused Babcock of conspiring with a group of distillers to evade the whiskey tax. Although Babcock was exonerated by a jury, Grant soon afterward dismissed him from his post in the White House.

Only a week later the second scandal, involving Secretary of War William W. Belknap, exploded in the nation's Capital. As events unfolded, the Belknap story resembled a dime novel of the period, with its scheming ladies of society, orphaned infants, domestic intrigues, journeys to Europe, secret exchanges of money, rumored suicides, hints of illicit sex, flights to Canada, and sisters wedded to the same husband.

Washington dispatches of March 1, 1876, reported that Secretary of War Belknap would probably offer his resignation within twenty-four hours as the result of discoveries made by an investigating committee which were of such a nature as to make his remaining in the cabinet impossible.

Early in the morning of that day, Secretary Belknap received a message from his old friend, Hiester Clymer, Democratic congressman from Pennsylvania and chairman of the House Committee on Expenditures in the War Department. The message requested his presence at a meeting at 10:30 a.m. concerning testimony given on the previous day by Caleb P. Marsh, who held a War Department post-tradership at Fort Sill, Indian Territory. No one can say what the Secretary's emotions were as he read this message because no one can be certain of how much he knew about Marsh at that time.

During the ensuing hour or so he spent with the committee, Belknap must have learned a great deal about Marsh that he had not known before. If he was completely unaware of past relationships between the post trader and the two Mrs. Belknaps, one deceased, the Secretary of War must have listened with shocked surprise to the recorded words of Caleb Marsh. In brief, Marsh testified that for the past six years he had been sending regular sums of money — a total of about $25,000 — to the Belknaps as payment for his government appointment.

After hearing the testimony, Belknap sat as if stunned. He was a handsome man, tall, robust, with curly blond hair and a full silky beard. He faced a committee of five men, four of whom he counted as friends — the two Republicans, Lyman Bass and Lorenzo Danford, and two of the Democrats, Joseph Blackburn and Hiester Clymer (the fifth was W. M. Robbins). Blackburn had soldiered for the Confederacy, but his wife and Belknap's wife had been friends since their girlhood days in Kentucky. As for Clymer, he had been Belknap's roommate at Princeton University, and their friendship had survived political differences.

The law which Belknap's friends accused him of violating was explicit: *Every member of Congress, or any officer or agent of the government, who, directly or indirectly, takes, receives, or agrees to receive, any money, property or other valuable consideration, whatever, from any person, for procuring or aiding to procure, any contract, office or place from the government or any department thereof . . . shall be imprisoned not more than two years, and fined not more than $10,000.* In Belknap's case the disgrace would be greater than the penalty of law.

Belknap's first reaction was to ask for a delay so that he might employ legal counsel. The committee agreed to adjourn until 3 p.m. Belknap secured the services of Montgomery Blair, a leading Washington lawyer, and the two men appeared before Clymer's committee that afternoon for a second reading of Marsh's testimony.

Belknap now made his first statement. "I have heard the charges read," he said. "Some things are true, some things are not true, and some things I know nothing about. But make your charge and put anything in it you may please, it makes no difference what, as to my guilt, which I will acknowledge without reserve. Only grant my wish that this investigation shall be pursued no further as affecting any member of my family."

The committee objected to this. The two wives of the Secretary were involved in Marsh's testimony; their names could not be removed. Hiester Clymer, however, suggested that Belknap had one other alternative — he could resign his office. After some discussion, the committee agreed to adjourn until the next morning, at which time Belknap would be expected to make a new statement.

Although these proceedings were closed to the press, intimations of what was occurring leaked to alert correspondents. New York newspapers of March 2 carried the first hints of the charges against Belknap, but President Grant apparently had not received or read copies before mid-morning of that day.

Around nine o'clock, after a late breakfast, the President was going through his mail in the White House drawing room when he was informed that Secretary Bristow wanted to see him. "I wondered why he came so early," Grant said afterward, "but I invited him into the room and we talked for a time over some matters referred to in my mail." Bristow appeared to be worried, and after some hesitation declared: "There are some very sad stories in circulation about one of your Cabinet." Grant replied that he had heard nothing. "They are dreadful stories," Bristow continued, "almost too bad to be believed." The President demanded an explanation, and just as Bristow began telling what he had heard about the Secretary of War, Belknap himself appeared, accompanied by Secretary of the Interior, Zachariah Chandler.

"Chandler looked very sober," Grant later related, "and Belknap was changed so you would hardly have known him. He looked as if he had not slept for a week. I got up and shook hands with him and asked him what was the matter. He went on to tell me in an incoherent way about the Congressional investigation; that it was going to damage him very much, and he said he had written his resignation and brought it with him. He took out the letter and I read it.

"I said to him that I would regret very much his leaving the Cabinet, for I had confidence in him. At that he burst into tears and took hold of my hand. . . . I understood that he was expecting an investigation that he could avoid by resigning; that the facts if exposed would not damage him so much as his wife. He spoke of his dead wife, too. I told him he had a great many friends and they would help him out, but he said it was impossible; that he had shouldered all the blame and would be ruined. He insisted it would save me and the government a great deal of trouble if his resignation was accepted. I tried again to induce him to wait a while, but he said he must go before the commission that morning, and wanted to tell them he was no longer an officer of the government. So I wrote him a letter accepting the resignation, and after thanking me for that and for what he called my kindness to him in the past he went away with Chandler."

<hr />

In spite of Belknap's efforts to shield the reputations of his wives, the full story of their dealings with Marsh was revealed that afternoon in the House of Representatives. With no preliminary warning, Belk-nap's former friend, Chairman Clymer, arose on the floor of the House and asked unanimous consent to submit a report "of so grave a nature that I am quite certain, when it is heard, the House will agree that I am justified in asking that permission at this time." Clymer went on to explain that his committee had received a letter of the President of the United States accepting Belknap's resignation, and therefore must demand that the "late Secretary of War be dealt with according to the laws of the land." He then proceeded to read the full text of Marsh's testimony which named both of Belknap's wives.

Once the secret was out, Washington became a city of wild rumors. Newspapers published extra editions, at least one reporting that Belknap had killed himself. Before the Belknaps had any opportunity to answer the charges, editorial writers were judging them: "The result of inordinate extravagances and the general demoralization of the day." "An entire loss of the principles of honesty and integrity." "What is the matter with the President?"

As he must have foreseen, President Grant was held responsible for the entire affair. When Hiester Clymer informed his colleagues in the House that the President had accepted Belknap's resignation, murmurs of amazement arose from the floor and galleries. It was immediately assumed by almost everyone that this was a sly move on the President's part to protect his Secretary of War from impeach-ment. Actually, as has been noted, Clymer himself had recommended resignation to Belknap as a way out of his predicament. After an hour's debate, the House voted unanimously to impeach Belknap, although he was no longer in office.

—————

When William Belknap graduated from Princeton in 1848, he went west to Keokuk, Iowa, where he opened a law office. At the be-ginning of the Civil War he joined an Iowa regiment, and by 1864 had become a provost marshal general attached to Sherman's army in Georgia.

It was at this time that he became acquainted with two brothers named Tomlinson and their sisters, Carita and Amanda, from the Kentucky Bluegrass. As was not uncommon in Kentucky, the Tomlinsons were divided in their loyalties, the brothers joining the Confederate forces, the sisters remaining pro-Union. Early in the war, Amanda made a Union flag with her own hands, presenting it with an appropriate speech to a Kentucky Union regiment.

In the summer of 1864 the Tomlinson sisters learned that their brothers had been captured. With an impetuosity that was typical of this pair of adventuresses, they set out for Georgia to seek paroles for their erring brothers. They were also in character when they scorned the lower echelons and went straight to the top man, General William Belknap.

If Belknap could have foreseen his future he would have dispatched the Bluegrass belles straight back to Kentucky, but he was charmed by Carita (Carrie) and Amanda (Puss), and both girls were entranced by the handsome, silken-bearded Iowan. Parole regulations at that time forbade his releasing the Tomlinson brothers, but he promised to look after their best interests. (Six years later Belknap gave a post-tradership to James Tomlinson, the only ex-Confederate to receive one of these lucrative assignments.)

Shortly after the war ended, Belknap married Carita and settled down in Keokuk as a collector of internal revenue. When Secretary of War John Rawlins died in 1869, Grant summoned Belknap to Washington to fill the vacated office.

Carrie Belknap at last had reached her natural element, the social whirl of Washington. According to the Washington Star, during the winter of 1869-70 she was "the most brilliant of the Cabinet family, generous, sympathetic in disposition, handsome in person, courteous in manner, and ready in conversation." But her reign was to be brief.

Meanwhile, Carita's sister Amanda had married H. L. Bower, a Cincinnati merchant who died soon afterward, leaving her several thousand dollars. One of Amanda Tomlinson Bower's closest friends in Cincinnati was Mrs. Caleb Marsh, wife of the man who was later to testify against her and Belknap. Amanda entrusted a considerable part of her small fortune to Marsh to invest for her, and in the spring of 1870 she arrived in Washington in the role of an independent young widow, to visit her sister Carrie.

Early that summer the two sisters left the humid climate of the Capital to go to Long Branch on the New Jersey shore. Everybody who was anybody always summered at Long Branch — the Grants, members of the Cabinet, influential congressmen and well-to-do families from New York. Later in the season Caleb Marsh and his wife appeared at Long Branch, and Amanda introduced them to Carrie. Marsh was a furniture dealer and tea importer, a slender, balding oval-faced man with a gray moustache. He was the opposite in manner and temperament of his vivacious, flirtatious wife, but he was apparently charmed to have the company of three such women at Long Branch. The Marshes invited Carrie and Amanda to visit in their New York home.

While in New York, Carrie Belknap fell ill (she was in advanced pregnancy) and for three or four weeks Mrs. Marsh was her constant attendant. As soon as Carrie was convalescent she felt impelled to repay the Marshes for their kindness. Whether it was Carrie or Amanda who first conceived the idea of offering Caleb Marsh a post-tradership, no one can be certain, but according to Marsh's later testimony Carrie broached the subject to him.

"If I can prevail upon the Secretary of War to award you a post," he quoted her as saying, "you must be careful to say nothing to him about presents, for a man once offered him $10,000 for a tradership of this kind, and he told him that if he did not leave the office he would kick him downstairs."

After the sisters returned to Washington, Marsh visited the Capital and learned from Carrie Belknap that the post-tradership at Fort Sill was expiring. On August 16, 1870, Marsh went to see Belknap, filled out an application form, and soon afterward received the appointment. The reasons why Belknap gave the post to Marsh are obscure.

Undoubtedly, the friendship of their wives had much to do with it, but Marsh was a businessman of good reputation, and perhaps Belknap felt he was as well qualified as the preceding post trader, John S. Evans.

Soon after receiving his appointment, Marsh learned that his prede-cessor at Fort Sill was extremely disappointed to have lost the tradership. The two men met in Washington, and Evans agreed to pay Marsh $12,000 a year for the privilege of continuing the business. This was all very surprising to Marsh, but when he notified the Secretary of War of his arrangement with Evans, he received no objections.

In fairness to Belknap it should be said that regulations govern-ing post-traderships were not of his making. They were a part of the spoils system which he had inherited, and he followed the system. Before the war the traders were known as sutlers, selected by local boards of Army officers who kept close watch on their operations. After the war, with the rapid increase in reservation Indians and the concentration of large numbers of soldiers on Western posts, the traders became big businessmen dealing in thousands of dollars' worth of goods every year. Profits were enormous, and it was inevitable that appointments would be handled from Washington under the spoils system which demanded percentage contributions "for the good of the party" in power.

John Evans' profits at Fort Sill must have been considerable or he would never have offered Marsh $12,000 for the privilege of retain-ing the post. In November 1870 he sent Marsh the first quarterly payment of $3,000, and Marsh promptly forwarded $1,500 to Carita Belknap. Perhaps he considered himself so fortunate to be receiving $12,000 a year for doing nothing that he felt honor bound to divide the bonanza with his benefactor. Carita's child had just been born and she was quite ill, but the money was deposited in a bank to her order.

Late in December, Carita died. The Marshes came to Washington for the funeral, and afterwards went to the Belknap house. They learned that Amanda (Puss) Bower had agreed to stay with Belknap and take care of her dead sister's child. She may have already made up her mind to marry Belknap; he had just turned forty, was still handsome and vigorous. During this brief visit, Amanda invited Marsh to go up to the nursery and see the baby. Marsh was a kindly, sentimental man, and when he looked down at Carita's baby, he said: "This child will have money coming to it before a great while." Amanda replied: "Yes, the mother gave the child to me and told me that the money coming from you I must take and keep for it."

On the witness stand six years later, Marsh could not remember exactly what he next told Amanda. "It seems to me I said that perhaps the father ought to be consulted . . . yet I can give no reason for it, for as far as I know the father knew nothing of any money transactions between the mother and myself."

Amanda Bower, however, took care of that contingency. She let Belknap know that she had entrusted part of her estate to Caleb Marsh for investment, and that there would be income from him in regular installments.

⟝⟞

Amanda (Puss) Tomlinson Bower was the prettier of the sisters — a tall, stately brunette with fine features, head, and carriage, a splendid complexion, black glossy hair and dark flashing eyes. During her stay in William Belknap's house as foster mother to his young child she observed a brief period of mourning, and then quickly moved into Washington social circles.

In June 1871 the first episode of her Washington career ended tragically with the death of the Belknap infant. As there was now no excuse for Amanda Bower to remain in Washington (she had reached no understanding of marriage with Belknap at this time) she returned to Cincinnati. Meanwhile the payments from Marsh continued to come regularly, in Belknap's name, and the Secretary forwarded the amounts to Mrs. Bower. Assuming that Belknap was innocent of the reasons for the payments, he could have done this without becoming suspicious. It was common practice for women, who had practically no legal rights in that day, to entrust their estates to responsible male relatives, and Belknap may have thought he was standing as a sort of guarantor between Marsh and Mrs. Bower. The fact that he endorsed the drafts instead of insisting that they be made out directly to her is an indication that he suspected no fraud.

Over the next three years Amanda thoroughly enjoyed the income from her estate and the $6,000 yearly payments from Caleb Marsh, traveling about the country and making at least two excursions to Europe. Apparently she reached a romantic understanding with William Belknap sometime in 1873, but she postponed the wedding for another journey to Europe where she bought an expensive collection of furniture, numerous Parisian dresses, and forty pairs of shoes. In December 1874 they were married at Harrodsburg, Kentucky, Amanda wearing a wedding trousseau designed by Worth of Paris.

Amanda Tomlinson Bower Belknap now descended upon Washington, determined to become the queen of official society. She persuaded her husband that they must move into a more fashionable house in the West End, a three-story, bow-windowed brick at 2022 G Street. She purchased a fine carriage and ordered additional costumes from Paris. She installed an English maid and a French chef, and her receptions and dinners were soon the talk of the Capital.

———⟫●⟪———

In 1875 Amanda retired briefly from society to give birth to a daughter, but by the end of the year she was on the move again. She convinced her husband that he must aim higher in politics than a mere Cabinet post. As a step on the road to greater fame, he decided to run for senator from Iowa. In December, while he was visiting his home state to announce his candidacy, Amanda went to New York to do her Christmas shopping. While there she talked Caleb Marsh out of a $750 advance payment, the only money she ever received directly from him.

Two months later, with Marsh's unexpected testimony before the Clymer committee, her glittering world abruptly collapsed. For several months the Democrats had been digging into the post-tradership spoils system, and John Evans, who was weary of paying Marsh $12,000 a year, was a willing informant. When the Clymer committee summoned Marsh to Washington he was frightened into telling all he knew.

Marsh was so panic-stricken that on March 3 he fled to Canada in fear of becoming involved in a criminal trial. He later changed his mind and returned to Washington for more questioning. Mrs. Belknap also was reported to have panicked, taking her baby in her arms one night to make a plea for help to Representative Blackburn, the committee member whose wife was one of her oldest friends. The illustrated weekly, Day's Doings, spread across its front page a lurid drawing of this dramatic scene. Amanda later denied the whole story.

For the next several weeks, Amanda Belknap was the most publicized woman in the nation, newspapers devoting almost as much space to her as to the Secretary of War. The Washington Delilah, some called her, although there was considerable disagreement among editors as to whether it was Carita or Amanda who had delivered "Samson" Belknap over to the Philistines.

In general, the Washington press was kind to Amanda, applauding her for attempting to take the blame from her husband's shoulders. "She has been not only admired but loved during her residence here," said the Star. "It is the one pleasant feature in this deplorable business that her own sex with one accord commiserate Mrs. Belknap. While possessed of every charm of mind and person which would seem calculated to excite the envy and jealousy of other women, Mrs. Belknap has so conducted herself toward them as to win from them admiration and esteem."

Every newspaper correspondent in Washington attempted to interview Amanda Belknap, but only a few female members of the press succeeded in reaching her. One quoted her as saying she did not consider herself a criminal or that she had done anything wrong in using her influence to obtain government posts for her friends. "If I have sinned, others have doubly sinned; if I am guilty of crimes others are guilty of double crimes." Another described an interview with her in the Belknap parlor. "She was plainly dressed in heavy black silk; a simple knot of cherry ribbon fastened the ruche at her throat; the soft dark hair was simply parted, and a dainty little cap of French muslin, with cherry ribbons, covered her head. Not a bit of jewelry was visible. We talked in low tones as one would talk in the presence of death." During the interview Mrs. Belknap declared that her husband had no money. "Every penny we have belongs to me, and when this is done we shall have precious little."

Saturday evening March 4, as the result of rumors in Washington that Belknap was planning to escape and join Caleb Marsh in Canada, a Secret Service detail was posted around the Secretary's residence on G Street. Sunday morning Mrs. Belknap noticed a man standing below her windows and went down to ask him what he was doing there. He admitted that he was shadowing the house, and asked if the Secretary was at home. Belknap came downstairs, and when he was told that his house was under surveillance he began shedding tears. But he offered no objections when the officers in charge requested permission to station two men inside the house.

That evening local Washington police replaced the Secret Service. All this activity around the G Street residence started new rumors that Belknap had escaped and was making his way down the Potomac in a tugboat. On Monday morning these reports were demolished after an Army officer visited Belknap's house on unfinished War Department business. When the officer came outside, he told waiting reporters he had just talked with Belknap. "Words fail to express how this man has suffered and aged during the last few days," he said. "His flowing silky beard was knotted and tangled, his hair was unkempt, great black rings were under his eyes, and his sunken cheeks made up a picture of woe and despair that would have touched a heart of stone. I was so moved that I sprang forward with a word of comfort. . . . Belknap caught me by the hand and burst into tears. He was completely unmanned. He choked and sobbed: 'I am going to prove it to the people of this country that I am an honest man before this business.' "

—⟫●⟪—

Congress meanwhile was moving toward an impeachment of Belknap. Under the Constitution only the House can impeach, and only the Senate can try impeachments. On April 3 the House submitted to the Senate five articles of impeachment, demanding that Belknap "be put to answer the high crimes and misdemeanors of his office herein charged against him."

Three days later the sergeant at arms of the Senate served a summons on Belknap. His lawyers argued that he could not be impeached because he had already resigned. A few anti-Administration Republicans joined with Democratic senators to vote down the argument 37 to 27, and the impeachment trial began. The proceedings dragged on into the summer, competing for public attention with the Centennial Exhibition in Philadelphia, the bitter Presidential campaign between Samuel Tilden and Rutherford Hayes, and the Custer Massacre.

A considerable amount of time was spent in legal maneuvering, and then a procession of witnesses presented conflicting testimony concerning telegrams, bank drafts, and the operation of post-traderships in the West. Caleb Marsh's testimony was ambiguous at times; he did not entirely share Belknap's determination to shield Amanda. Little was revealed, however, that had not been known before the tedious proceedings began. Late in July the trial ended, almost anti-climactically, with an acquittal.

—⟫●⟪—

A free man with a blackened reputation, Belknap remained in Washington to earn a living practicing law, but relations between him and his wife were almost at the breaking point. Soon after the impeachment trial ended, she went off to Europe with her young daughter for a self-imposed exile of two years. When she returned to Washington she was restless, constantly journeying to New York or to fashionable resorts. In 1889 she made her last grand appearance at the inaugural ball for President Benjamin Harrison; then when the weather turned warm she went to Coney Island, which had replaced Long Branch as a fashionable shore resort. The press made much of her appearance in a sleeveless red-and-white French bathing suit with a brief skirt and sheer silk stockings.

Belknap was now suffering from rheumatic gout, and as usual was having difficulty meeting family expenses. One day he remarked glumly to a friend: "Some morning they'll find me dead in bed, and the War Department clerks will have a holiday." On October 12, 1890, his prediction came true. He was found in a grubby little room adjacent to his law office, dead of a heart attack. Amanda Belknap and her 16-year-old daughter were away on holiday in New York. President Harrison ordered the War Department closed for his funeral, and a surprising number of public figures who had remained silent for fourteen years openly expressed their opinions that Belknap had been a victim of circumstances in the post-tradership affair. One quoted the dead man: "The mistake of my life was in tendering my resignation with the chivalric intention of shielding my wife."

Engraving of William Worth Belknap. From A History of the American People *by Woodrow Wilson.*

PART III

Heroes, Heroines, and Outlaws

Jim Bridger is photographed clad in buckskins which he wore infrequently. Taken from the diary of the Washburn Expedition to the Yellowstone and Firehole Rivers *by Nathanial Langford, 1905. Courtesy of the Montana Historical Society, Helena.*

8

Jim Bridger

"Jim Bridger may have stretched the truth sometimes, but this illiterate, rough-and-tumble 'Mountain Man' was an important figure in the winning of the West."

Fort Bridger, Bridger Peak, Bridger Trail, Bridger Lake, Bridger's Pass, Bridger National Forest, several Bridger creeks and Bridger towns — these are names fixed on maps of the American West as memorials to a man who explored that wild land for half a century. His name can be found in almost any book about the West. He is an important figure in histories of the fur trade, the Oregon Trail, the Gold Rush, the Mormon migration, and the Indian wars. He never learned to read or write but he could draw maps as accurately as a trained topographer; he could speak French, Spanish, and a dozen Indian tongues; he invented much of the oral folklore of the mountain men, and he could quote Shakespeare line by line.

James Bridger was born in Richmond, Virginia in 1804, but while he was still a child his family went west to the St. Louis area. There in 1822 he learned about William Ashley's offer of employment to one hundred "enterprising young men to ascend the Missouri River to its source, there to be employed for one, two, or three years." Although Bridger was only 18, he had been working as a blacksmith; Ashley's partner, Andrew Henry, liked the looks of the tall, gray-eyed youngster and signed him on.

Ashley and Henry wanted to make fur trappers of Bridger and the other young men. Demand for furs, especially beaver skins, had reached the point where it could not be met by the old method of trading with Indians.

On the way up the Missouri by keelboat, Bridger became acquainted with Thomas Fitzpatrick, Jedediah Smith, Jim Clyman, and Bill Sublette — all destined as was he to become giants among the "mountain men." At the mouth of the Yellowstone in the heart of beaver country, they built Fort Henry, and Jim Bridger was soon lugging heavy iron traps up mountain streams. He learned that a successful beaver trapper had to wade for miles in icy waters so as to leave no scent, and that the best lure was a bundle of twigs smeared with a beaver's musk glands. He also learned about Blackfeet Indians, who claimed the beaver country as their own and did their best to kill all intruders. He discovered that other tribes might be friendly one day, hostile the next. After participating in his first Indian fight with Arickarees, he decided that no white man could survive in that hostile country unless he learned everything the Indians knew — and then a little more.

⸺⊰•⊱⸺

In his first two years with the Ashley-Henry trappers, Jim Bridger studied the ways of the Indians as other men study books. He learned to read the meaning of every turned leaf, broken twig, or sudden flight of birds. He concentrated upon the land, its valleys and peaks, its streams and forests. Explorers who traveled with Jim Bridger in later years described him as a walking atlas of the Rocky Mountains. "The whole West was mapped out in his mind," said General Grenville Dodge, "and such was his instinctive sense of locality and direction . . . he could smell his way when he could not see it."

During the winter of 1824-25, Bridger and several of his companions were holed up in a canyon on Bear River. Arguments arose as to whether this turbulent, rapids-filled stream ran north, south, east, or west. Such questions of geography fascinated Bridger; he volunteered to explore Bear River. He was the youngest member of the party, not yet 21 and at first the other trappers thought he was merely boasting. But he set to work building a bull-boat, an almost unsinkable vessel of willow trunks and buffalo skin sealed with tallow. He had a rough ride down the boiling canyon but eventually came to quieter waters, with a large lake in the distance. He had proved that Bear River flowed south, but also made a more important discovery — Great Salt Lake.

With other mountain men, Bridger helped establish the seasonal rituals of the developing fur industry. During the autumns they organized themselves into brigades, each party making thorough sweeps of the hostile Indians' favorite hunting grounds. When winter came they gathered at pre-designated sites to build fortified camps. Springtime brought another brief trapping period, and then came the summer rendezvous. The rendezvous originally served as a delivery point for pelts taken during the year; from there they were shipped to St. Louis. But Indians by the hundreds were soon coming in to trade, and during the 1830's the annual rendezvous became a brawling revel, a "foo-faraw" as the trappers called it. They held shooting matches, raced horses, gambled, and chased Indian girls.

In 1830, Bridger and four of his associates pooled their savings, bought out their employers, and formed the Rocky Mountain Fur Company. They hoped to become as wealthy as Ashley and Henry, but trouble lay ahead. John Jacob Astor's American Fur Company, which had been operating farther north, began expanding into the central Rockies. Astor's company was rich and powerful, and for the next few years ruthlessly harassed its ambitious rival.

Bridger was especially irate because the American Fur Company set the Crow Indians against him. He had always got along well with the Crows, but in 1831 on Powder River they stampeded his company's 300 horses. Bridger and his men had to track them on foot for several days, eventually re-capturing the animals after a sharp fight. That same year Bridger tangled with the Blackfeet again, taking two arrows in his back. One barbed head remained imbedded against his spine for three years until his friend, Dr. Marcus Whitman, efficiently removed it.

Such misadventures Jim Bridger was willing to accept as part of the natural environment. Responsibility for operating a big fur enterprise was not to his taste, however, and he had no regrets when the Rocky Mountain Fur Company disbanded in 1834. Tom Fitzpatrick, Milt Sublette, and he worked out an arrangement with the American Fur Company whereby they would confine their activities to the east side of the Rockies.

With harassment ended and dreams of great wealth out of his mind, Bridger found time to enjoy life again. He married the daughter of a Flathead Indian chief; he made a visit to St. Louis to see civilization again; and he met an eccentric Scottish nobleman named William Drummond Stewart. Stewart was fascinated by the lean, self-assured mountain man, and Bridger delighted in Stewart, finding him a willing believer of his tall tales and a splendid victim for practical jokes.

When Stewart made a return visit in 1837, he brought along artist Alfred Jacob Miller to paint Western scenes. He also brought Jim Bridger a present — a full suit of armor. Bridger and the other trappers enjoyed wearing the armor and posing for Miller. Miller sketched Bridger on horseback in the suit of mail, and placed him in the foreground of his well-known painting, "Rendezvous."

By the late 1830's it was obvious to Bridger and his partners that fur trapping was no longer big business. Beaver were scarce, Indians more hostile, and the demand for furs was declining. In 1839 on Green River they held their last big summer rendezvous. It was like a final military review for the survivors of a long war; many of Bridger's original companions had been killed by Indians. Like old soldiers on the eve of mustering out, they faced the future with apprehension. "Only with reluctance does a trapper abandon his dangerous craft," observed Adolphe Wislezenus, who was present at that final rendezvous. "A sort of serious homesickness seizes on him when he retires from his mountain life to civilization."

Jim Bridger had no intention of returning to civilization. He had noted a rapid increase in the number of emigrants whose wagon

trains were rolling westward to Oregon, and he had come to the
shrewd conclusion that a man could make a good living by building
a wayside oasis at some strategic point along the trail — a place
where travelers could rest, obtain fresh supplies, shoe their animals,
and repair harness and wagons. He was ready to begin part two of his
long career in the West.

As a site for his emigrant haven, Bridger chose a grassy valley along
a fork of his beloved Green River. He built log cabins and corrals,
installed a blacksmith shop, and ordered supplies from St. Louis.
This was Fort Bridger, the only way station on the rugged 620-mile
stretch between Fort Laramie and Fort Hall. From 1843 until his
troubles with the Mormons in 1853, Bridger's fort was a busy and
exciting halfway point for thousands of westering travelers.

These were also Bridger's most prosperous years. He became
wealthy, not only from travelers in the summer season but from a year-
round fur trade. He made Fort Bridger into a sort of permanent
rendezvous for his old trapper comrades and Indian friends.

Bridger was in his forties now, settling down to become a family
man with three children. He sent his oldest daughter, Mary Anne,
up to Marcus Whitman's mission school in the Oregon country; he
wanted all his children to learn the mysteries of reading and writing.
Not long afterward his Indian wife died, interrupting the even flow
of his life. He grew restless and made long trips into the mountains,
hunting, trapping, and exploring remote areas of the Rockies.

One day in June 1847 he was heading east for Fort Laramie when
he met Brigham Young and a pioneer party of Mormons en route west
to find a promised land where their followers could prosper and live
free of religious persecution. The Mormon leaders had heard of
Bridger; in fact, they had hoped to find him at his fort. They had been
told that he knew more about the Salt Lake Basin than any living
man. At Young's request Bridger agreed to stop for a conference, and
although it was midday the Mormons immediately corraled their
wagons and went into camp.

The meeting would prove to be a fateful one for Bridger. With his usual frankness he answered the questions put to him. Perhaps he was too outspoken. He had seen an army of tenderfeet heading west, and undoubtedly considered these zealous Easterners greener than most. When one of his questioners claimed that the Mormons were being divinely guided, Bridger cautioned against settling the Utah country on faith alone. Apparently this was taken as a reflection upon their religion and some were offended. One of his remarks on the prospects of growing corn in the basin eventually developed into a derogatory Bridger myth. Supposedly he told Brigham Young that he would give a thousand dollars a bushel for all the corn that could be raised in Salt Lake valley. Afterwards Bridger denied that he ever said it (the only written record of the conference makes no mention of it) but the remark was used against him for years.

Although the Bridger-Young meeting was outwardly cordial, each man seemed to distrust the other. What Bridger thought of Young and his associates is not on record. Some of the Mormons were impressed with Bridger's knowledge of the West; others disliked his appearance and manner of conversation. From that day a coolness between Bridger and the Mormons would deepen into outright antagonism.

In 1849 when Bridger assisted Captain Howard Stansbury of the Army Engineers in opening a more direct trail into Utah, he found the Mormons unfriendly to the project. When Stansbury recommended to the Army that Fort Bridger be made into a military post, the Mormons not only opposed the move but claimed that Fort Bridger and the Green River valley were a part of their territory.

During these years, Bridger was also plagued with personal tragedies. His daughter Mary Anne was slain by Cayuse Indians in a massacre at Marcus Whitman's mission school. His second wife, a Ute Indian, died in childbirth.

As always when events closed in upon him, he went back to the primitive wilderness, living for a time with Chief Washakie's Shoshones, leaving his fort in the care of others. He had a rough-and-tumble romance with Washakie's daughter, Little Fawn, during which he had to engage in a slashing, gouging fight with a Shoshone rival. The romance ended happily with a genuine Christian wedding ceremony performed by an old friend, Father Pierre De Smet.

For two or three years Bridger enjoyed the pleasant routine of spending his summers at his fort and then wintering with his wife's people. Meanwhile the Mormons were moving into the Green River country, establishing ferries and rival trading posts along the trails. When the Indians became troublesome, the Mormons accused Bridger of selling arms and ammunition to them and inciting them to war.

In the summer of 1853 a 150-man posse of Brigham Young's "avenging angels" rode northward with orders to arrest Jim Bridger as an outlaw. He escaped just in time and with his wife and children hid in the mountains until the "angels" departed. When the Bridgers came back to the fort they found the buildings gutted, thousands of dollars in merchandise gone, the premises stripped, all the livestock taken away. Little Fawn wanted to summon the Shoshones for a war of extermination against the Mormons, but Bridger was more realistic. He employed a government road surveyor to survey the fort and 3,900 acres of land around it, and then dispatched the papers to the General Land Office in Washington for recording.

For the time being he would wait out the Mormons, let them simmer down. He took his wife and children east to Missouri, invested most of his remaining funds in a farm near Westport for the security of his family, and then returned to Fort Laramie to seek some new way of earning a living. At the age of fifty he was about to embark on part three of his Western career — Jim Bridger as guide and scout.

In the autumn of 1854, Sir George Gore, an Irish nobleman with $200,000 a year to spend as he pleased, arrived at Fort Laramie. Sir George brought along forty servants and a train of wagons filled with liquors, foodstuffs, a complete hunting arsenal, and a library of literary classics. When Sir George met Bridger he was entranced, for here in the flesh was the frontiersman he had read about in the works of James Fenimore Cooper — a bronzed, sinewy, resourceful man of the wilderness. He immediately offered to put him on his payroll as guide, and Bridger accepted.

The two men constantly amazed each other, but they got along so well that they roamed the Yellowstone and Powder River country for almost two years — hunting and fishing, drinking Sir George's fine brandies, and trying to out-yarn each other. It was Sir George who introduced Shakespeare to Bridger, and Jim liked some of the plays so much that he memorized long passages, delighting his employer by reciting them back to him in mountain-man dialect. But Bridger was not impressed by another of Sir George's favorites. Baron Munchausen, he declared, was nothing but a damned liar.

At Fort Benton in the spring of 1856 the long odyssey ended. Bridger drew his two years' wages and took a boat down the Missouri to see his family. After a happy reunion at Westport he began thinking about the Green River country and his dispossessed fort. He decided that the best way to get it back was to pay a visit to the government in Washington, D.C. Like most of Bridger's moves, this one was shrewdly timed.

A wave of anti-Mormon feeling was sweeping the country, much of it fanned by the nativistic Know-Nothing party. Wild tales of plural marriages, plots for territorial expansion, and mistreatment of non-Mormons were being published in the press. The Mormons reacted by becoming suspicious of every move made by the Federal Government. Brigham Young was constantly quarreling with officials sent out from Washington, and some of the more vehement zealots did begin to mistreat travelers crossing the Territory, the most cold-blooded affair being the Mountain Meadows Massacre. When Jim Bridger arrived in Washington to plead his case he found willing listeners, among them President James Buchanan, and was promised the assistance of the Government in recovering his fort and lands.

A few months later the U.S. Government declared that the Territory of Utah was in insurrection, and ordered an infantry regiment at Fort Laramie to march for the Green River country. The regiment's civilian guide was Jim Bridger.

The so-called Utah War consisted of more words than bullets, although the Mormons proved to be adept at guerrilla raiding. During the winter of 1857-58, the worst enemy of the U.S. soldiers was the snowy weather, and had Bridger not been present to guide them out of blizzards they might have met with disaster. He showed the men how to survive in skin tepees as the Indians did, and at the same time he advanced his own interests by leasing Fort Bridger to the Army for a supply base. Colonel Albert Sidney Johnston, in command, regarded Bridger's advice so highly that he attached him to his personal staff with the rank of major.

In the spring of 1858 the imbroglio ended with a peace settlement and Jim Bridger guided the army to Salt Lake City for a parade through its deserted streets. His score with the Mormons was even, but there was no exultation in his heart. Back home at Westport, the one real romance of his life had ended with the death of Little Fawn.

Returning to the farm, he arranged for a tenant family to take care of his children, and then went back to earning a living the best way he knew. In 1859 he guided Colonel William F. Raynolds on an exploration of the Yellowstone, revisiting mountain areas he had not seen for fifteen years. He considered the expedition a paid vacation. In 1861 he helped Captain E. L. Berthoud route a stagecoach road directly from Denver to Salt Lake City (it is still in use as a highway). In 1862-63 he operated an ingenious ferry run by cables and pulleys across the Platte River — that is, when the Army was not using him as a scout against the increasingly hostile Indians.

"We had Major Bridger with us as a guide," Lieutenant Caspar Collins noted after one of these expeditions. "He knows more of the Rocky Mountains than any living man." Young Collins was amused by Bridger's dining habits. "He would take a whole jackrabbit and a trout about 18 inches long and put them on two sticks and set them up before a fire, and eat them both without a particle of salt, and drink about a quart of stong coffee."

When the Civil War ended back East and soldiers in the West began returning home, Bridger decided to go home, too — back to Westport. He was past sixty now, and cold and dampness made his bones ache. But he had scarcely unpacked his saddlebags when he received an urgent summons from General Grenville Dodge to report to Fort Riley. The whole plains country was exploding into an Indian war, and Jim Bridger was needed.

His first major assignment was to serve as cavalry scout for General Patrick Connor's Powder River Expedition in the summer of 1865. Westerners would remember 1865 as "the bloody year on the Plains." Cheyenne, Sioux, and Arapaho were raiding everywhere, hitting stagecoaches, wagon trains, ranches, small settlements, and understrength military patrols.

To stop the raiding, General Connor decided to attack hostile base camps in Powder River country. Three thousand soldiers (including a number of former Confederates known as Galvanized Yankees) moved out in a three-pronged invasion, with Jim Bridger scouting for Connor's column.

After establishing a supply camp on the Powder, Connor pushed on toward Tongue River. On August 26, the general was riding with Bridger. They halted on a ridge, Connor surveying the northern hills with his field glass, Bridger merely shading his eyes with his hand. "Column of smoke over yonder," Bridger said.

"Where?" Connor asked.

"Over by that saddle-shaped range."

Connor scanned the horizon closely. "No column of smoke to be seen," he declared positively.

Bridger did not bother to reply. He mounted his horse and rode on, muttering to one of his comrades about "these damned paper-collar soldiers" telling him there were no columns of smoke.

Later in the day Connor reconsidered and ordered Captain Frank North to take his Pawnee Scouts and reconnoiter the saddle-shaped range. An Indian village was there, of course — hostile Arapahoes

— and three days later Jim Bridger was in the thick of the Battle of Tongue River. It was the last and one of the most arduous Indian fights of his career, a running battle for ten miles. He came out without a scratch, but forever resented the fact that Connor never apologized for doubting he had seen the smoke.

When the Powder River Expedition returned to Fort Laramie, Bridger boarded a stagecoach eastbound for Missouri, but the Army stopped him at Fort Kearny. A regiment was forming there under command of Colonel Henry B. Carrington. Its mission was to establish three forts along the Bozeman Trail and keep the route to Montana open for emigrants and supply trains. One of Carrington's lieutenants described Bridger at that time: "A plain farmer-like man dressed in the customary store clothes garments, low-crowned felt hat, never affecting long hair or showy fringed buckskin suits, though he may on occasion have donned them for convenience."

The expedition reached Fort Laramie in June 1866, and Bridger was present at the confrontation between Carrington and Red Cloud when the latter made his dramatic speech: "Great Father sends us presents and wants new road. But White Chief goes with soldiers to steal road before Indian says yes or no!" Red Cloud then strode angrily out of the council, and Bridger knew the Army was going to have trouble along the Bozeman Trail.

In those post-Civil War years military funds were tight, and before Carrington marched north he received an order to save money by discharging his civilian scout, Jim Bridger. The colonel was indignant. He scrawled an endorsement, "Impossible of Execution" across the order and sent it back to headquarters. His regard for Bridger's services was corroborated by his wife, Margaret, who wrote: "Our sterling friend Bridger had a head full of maps and trails and ideas, all of the utmost value to the objects of the expedition."

—————◦◦◦◦————

The Indian trouble that Bridger had foreseen at Laramie came on gradually through the late summer and autumn of 1866. Carrington built his three forts, establishing headquarters at Fort Phil Kearny. Hostile Indians harassed his trains and wood cutters; his soldiers who were trained to fight Confederates disregarded Bridger's advice and ran into ambushes. "Your men who fought down South are crazy," Bridger told Carrington. "They don't know anything about fighting Indians."

On December 21, 1866, in spite of Bridger's warnings and Carrington's direct orders, Captain William J. Fetterman and eighty men allowed themselves to be decoyed into an ambush. Not one soldier survived the Fetterman Massacre, and the weakened fort itself might have fallen if a blizzard had not come raging out of the north almost immediately afterward.

During the long days of waiting for a relief column to reinforce Fort Phil Kearny, Bridger volunteered to maintain an outer guard. His legs were stiff from arthritis, but he beat his way out through the snow to scout the hills. He then posted two men on every high point, each pair in sight of two other guard positions so as to form a continuous signal link to the fort.

With the arriving reinforcements on January 16 came orders relieving Carrington of command. Bridger, however, would remain; the Army could not spare him even though his eyesight was failing and rheumatism was crippling his legs. Not until the autumn of 1867 did he receive his final discharge. He took a brief look at the Union Pacific Railroad pushing westward from Cheyenne and knew that the West of his day was gone forever.

Major James Bridger went home to Westport where he became Grandpa Bridger. He ran a little grocery store, cultivated his apple trees, listened to fiddle music, told tall tales to children, and sold off pieces of his land to eke out his existence. After he became crippled and almost blind he would sit on his porch staring toward the West that he remembered. He died on July 17, 1881, having outlived his time.

POSTSCRIPT

Jim Bridger lives on in place names on the land he explored, in the folklore of the mountain men. As Davy Crockett personifies the Eastern frontiersman, Bridger represents his Western counterpart. Bridger has never become a ring-tailed, roaring superman like Crockett; he is more often a spectator than the central figure of his tall tales.

Captain W. F. Raynolds was one of the first to record some of Bridger's yarns. In 1859-60, while Bridger was guide for Raynolds' engineering survey of the Yellowstone country, they spent several weeks in winter camp. The old mountain man entertained the young captain with stories which the latter described as "Munchausen tales too good to be lost." One of them told of a large tract of sage perfectly petrified, with all the leaves and branches in perfect condition, the rabbits, sage hens, and other animals also petrified and as natural as when they were living; and even more wonderful — petrified bushes bearing diamonds, rubies, sapphires, and emeralds as large as walnuts. "I tell you, sir, it is true," declared Bridger, "for I gathered a quart myself."

General Nelson Miles later recorded another of Bridger's petrified stories:

"Jim, were you ever down to Zuni?"

"No, thar ain't any beaver down there."

"But Jim, there are some things in this world besides beaver. I was down there last winter and saw great trees with limbs and bark and all turned into stone."

"Oh," replied Jim, "that's peetrifaction. Come with me to the Yellowstone next summer, and I'll show you peetrified trees a-growing with peetrified birds on 'em a-singing peetrified songs."

Many of his stories centered around the Yellowstone's famed Obsidian Cliff which he sometimes transformed into a mythological Crystal Mountain. "It's a mountain of crystal rock, an' so clear that the most powerful field glasses can't see it, much less the naked eye. You'll wonder, per'aps, how a thing that can't be seen nohow was ever discovered. It came about in this way. You see, a lot of bones and the carcasses of animals an' birds wus found scattered all around the base. You see, they ran or flew against this invisible rock and jest killed themselves dead. You kin feel the rock an' that's all. You can't see it. It's a good many miles high, for everlastin' quantities of birds' bones are jest piled up all around the base of it."

———>•<———

One of his favorite camping grounds, he said, was opposite a bald, flat-faced mountain so far distant that any sound in camp would not echo for a period of six hours. Before retiring for the night he would shout "Time to get up!" and the call would then roll back at the pre-cise hour he wished to awaken.

———>•<———

He also liked to tell about a seventy-foot snow that fell in the Great Salt Lake valley, trapping vast herds of buffalo and preserving their carcasses. "When spring came, all I had to do was to tumble 'em into Salt Lake and I had pickled buffalo enough for myself and the whole Ute nation for years. But there ain't been no buffalo in that region since."

———>•<———

He had many exaggerated tales of Indian fights, and from the Indians he learned to tell long, involved, almost pointless recitations resembling our modern shaggy-dog stories. One of these concerned a pack of bears which followed him around everywhere; at the end of the story he had 250 bears surrounding him in camp as he was frying bacon.

"What did you do?" someone would ask Bridger.

"Oh, didn't do nothing."

"Well, what did the bears do!"

"Oh, they did nothing, only they just sot around."

⎯⎯⎯⎯⎯⎯⎯

Bridger became so well known for his tall tales that when he would come back from explorations of the Yellowstone and tell about geysers and boiling springs, no one would believe him. A newspaper man who met Bridger prepared an article from his accounts of the wonders of Yellowstone, but after consulting with one of Bridger's trapper friends he decided not to send it to his paper. "Them stories are just a pack of old Jim's lies," said the trapper, "and anybody who prints 'em for truth would be laughed out of the nation."

Jim Bridger has been the prototype for many a hero in stories of the West, some of them classics, but like his tall tales none of the fictionalized characters can match the real man, nor are the imagined adventures any more dramatic or romantic than the true life and times of the Old Man of the Mountains.

An engraving depicts Virginia Reed in later years. Her diary, written at age 12, provided considerable insight into the ordeal of the Donner Party during their 1846–47 winter in the Sierra Nevada Mountains.

9

---◦◦◦---

A Girl with the
Donner Pass Party

*"'Thank God we have all got thro, and we did not eat
human flesh.' The letters of a 12-year-old girl with the
Donner party tell a moving story of an ill-fated trip to
California in the 1840's."*

lmost all the records of overland journeys by covered
wagon to the Far West have come from the pens of adults
who, whether they were male or female, viewed events
from a different perspective than that of their children.
Children's accounts of overland journeys are rare indeed. Few kept
diaries, and those who wrote later of their experiences had already
lost much of the wonderment of childhood.

Virginia Elizabeth Reed, 12 years old, managed to find time en
route to write to a cousin back home letters filled with misspelled
words and observations of events which most adults would have
omitted. By some miracle these records of a young girl's overland
journey have survived, and they provide not only the fresh and
spirited viewpoint of a child experiencing a great American adventure but also describe one of the most harrowing of all western
journeys. Virginia Reed's family traveled with the Donner party
which was trapped in the snows of the Sierras during the winter of
1846-47, a predicament from which some members survived only by
resorting to cannibalism.

The adventure began on a sun-filled April morning in 1846, when a crowd began gathering in the small town of Springfield, Illinois, to bid farewell to thirty-one friends and neighbors who were that day starting to California. The organizer of the party was James Frazier Reed, and drawn up beside his house was an extraordinary covered wagon.

Reed's daughter, Virginia, had already christened it the "pioneer palace car," and it was as palatial as an overland wagon could be made in that day. Heavy 12-inch boards extended over the wheels on each side, running the full length of the wagon to form a foundation for a roomy second story in which beds had been placed. The entrance was at the side, like a stagecoach; when one entered, it was like stepping into a cozy living room. At right and left were spring seats with comfortable high backs where the passengers could sit and ride with as much ease as on the seats of a Concord coach. For cold nights and mornings, a small sheet-iron stove had been braced in the center, the vent pipe running out the top through a circle of tin which prevented fire being set to the canvas roof.

Under the spring seats were compartments for storing work baskets, a medicine chest, and spare clothing packed in canvas bags. A small mirror hung directly opposite the entrance. "Knowing that books were always scarce in the new country," Virginia afterwards recalled, "we also took a good library of standard works."

Besides Virginia and three younger children, occupants of this wagon were James Reed's young wife, Margaret, and his mother-in-law, known to all Springfield and her family as Grandma Keyes. Grandma Keyes was 75, an invalid, and she had to be carried out of the house and placed on a large feather bed, propped up by pillows in the second floor of the pioneer palace car. Her two sons, remaining behind, begged her to stay with them, but Grandma Keyes was determined to go to California.

James Reed was not leaving Springfield because he needed to better his fortunes. He owned a thriving furniture factory, was well off financially, and was a close friend of two rising young politicians, Abraham Lincoln and Stephen A. Douglas. Reed burned with the "western fever"; his ambition was to become Indian agent for all the territory west of the Rocky Mountains, and his political friends had promised their aid in this undertaking. Reed had hoped that Lincoln, with whom he had soldiered in the Black Hawk War, would be in Springfield that morning to see him off, but the future President was away on circuit court duties. Mary Todd Lincoln and her small son Robert were present to represent the family.

As Virginia later remembered that leave-taking, "we were all surrounded by loved ones, and there stood all my little schoolmates who had come to kiss me goodbye. My father with tears in his eyes tried to smile as one friend after another grasped his hand in a last farewell. Mama was overcome with grief. At last we were all in the wagons, the drivers cracked their whips, the oxen moved slowly forward and the long journey had begun."

The eight oxen drawing Reed's two-story wagon were large Durham steers, the preferred draft animals for plains crossings. They were not bridled, but were yoked to the tongue of the wagon. Instead of riding, the drivers walked alongside with a stock or whip, controlling the oxen with a simple "whoa," or "haw, or "gee."

Across Missouri and into Kansas the wagons rolled, the first weeks uneventful. "Our little home was so comfortable that mama could sit reading and chatting with the little ones and almost forget that she was really crossing the plains."

Death, which was to follow this wagon train all the way across the West, struck first near the Big Blue River in Kansas. On a day late in May, Grandma Keyes died quietly. James Reed hewed a coffin for her out of a cottonwood tree, and they buried her under the shade of an oak, planting wild flowers in the sod. John Denton, an English gunsmith who had joined fortunes with the Reeds at Springfield, carved an inscription on a stone: "Sarah Keyes, Born In Virginia."

At Independence Rock, July 12, Virginia wrote her first letter about this to a cousin in Illinois, sending it back east by an obliging traveler on horseback. "Gramma died, she became speechless the day before she died. We buried her verry decent We made a nete coffin and buried her under a tree we had a head stone and had her name cut on it and the date and yere verry nice and at the head of the grave was a tree we cut some letters on it the young men soded it all ofer and put Flores on it We miss her verry much every time we come into the Wagon we look at the bed for her."

Long afterward in 1891, Virginia learned that the grave had not been disturbed. "The wilderness," she said, "blossomed into the city of Manhattan, Kansas, and we have been told that the city cemetery surrounds the grave of Sarah Keyes."

⟶⟫●⟨⟵

By the time the Reeds reached the valley of the Platte, the original Springfield train had increased to forty wagons. They were in Indian country now, and at nights when they drove into camp they formed the wagons into a circle. "We have come thro several tribes of Indians, the Caw Indians, the Soux, the Shawnies," Virginia noted. "At the Caw villiage, paw counted 250 Indians . . . the Caw Indians are going to war with the Crows. We have to pass thro ther Fiting grond. The Soux Indians are the pretiest drest Indians thare is. Paw goes bufalo hunting most every day and kils 2 or 3 bufalo every day. Paw shot an elk. Some of our compian saw a grisly bear. We have the thermometer 102° — average for the last 6 days."

Early on the afternoon of July 4 the wagons rumbled into Fort Laramie, and Virginia wrote of the grand dinner and celebration: "Severel of the gentlemen in Springfield gave paw a botel of licker and said it shoulden be opend till the 4th day of July and paw was to look to the east and drink it and they was to look to the West and drink it at 12 o'clock paw treted the company and we all had some lemminade."

After leaving Fort Laramie, the Springfield train again increased considerably in length, many other wagons joining it for the hard passage through the Rockies. During a stopover at Fort Bridger, the leaders debated whether they should take the long trail by way of Fort Hall or a shorter route known as the "Hastings Cut-off," said to be 200 miles shorter. Disagreement followed, and the train divided into two sections, one group heading for Fort Hall, the other taking the shorter route. James Reed decided to go with the "Hastings Cut-off" party. Before leaving Fort Bridger, this group elected a new captain. His name was George Donner. The Reeds were riding with death for certain now, the ill-fated Donner party.

As they drove toward Great Salt Lake, they found the cut-off was no road at all, not even a trail. Heavy underbrush blocked the way, so thick it had to be cut down and used for a roadbed. A month was spent in reaching the lake, and the oxen were unfit for the long desert crossing that lay ahead. "It was a dreary, desolate alkali waste," Virginia wrote afterwards. "not a living thing could be seen; it seemed as though the hand of death had been laid upon the country."

<hr />

They were now into September and time was running out for the crossing of the high, snowy Sierras. The oxen began dying for lack of water. Hoping to save his Durhams, Reed unhitched them from the palace car and sent them ahead with two of his drivers in search of a water hole. Somehow, along the way the oxen panicked, escaping from the drivers in the night. A week was wasted in search of them, but they could not be found. "The Indians had taken them," Virginia wrote in one of her letters, "so some of the companie took thare oxons and went out and brout in one wagon and cashed [cached] the other two and a grate many things." The fine palace car had to be abandoned, and they moved into a smaller vehicle.

October 5 "the hand of death" showed itself again. During a quarrel with a man named John Snyder, James Reed was forced to defend himself; he killed Snyder with a knife. As soon as the deed was done, Reed's anger turned upon himself; he ran and hurled his knife into the Humboldt River.

That night the wagon company's members held council, voting to banish Reed from the train even though the killing was in self-defense. They agreed to care for his wife and children, provided he did not show himself again. He was given a horse and some food, but no rifle, and was told he could pay for his crime by going ahead to Fort Sutter and seeking help for the company in crossing the mountains.

As Reed was saying farewell to his wife, Virginia slipped a rifle and ammunition from their wagon and waited outside the camp in the darkness until her father rode out. He took the weapon and ammunition, gave her a silent hug, and rode westward alone into the desert.

For a day or so, Reed left messages along the way in the form of scattered feathers of birds he had killed for food. Then for two weeks there was no further trace of him. The oxen drawing the Reed wagon died; Mrs. Reed had to ride muleback, one child on her lap. Virginia and her younger sister and brother shared another mount. "We went on that way a while and we come to a nother long drive of 40 miles between Marys River & Truckeys Rivers . . . We had to walk all the time we ware traveling up the Truckey River."

At last on October 19, Virginia and her mother learned that James Reed was still alive. "We met a Mr. T. C. Stanton and 2 Indians that we had sent on for provisins to Captn Sutters Fort before papa started. Thay had met pa, not fur from Sutters Fort. He looked very bad. He had not ate but 3 times in 7 days and the three last days without any thing. Thay gave him a horse and he went on."

By the time they reached the Sierra approaches, autumn snows were falling. On the slopes the snow reached to their waists. "The farther we went up, the deeper the snow got so the wagons could not go . . . the mules kept fallin down in the snow head formost . . . well the

Weman were all so tired of carrying there children that they could not go over that night so we made a fire and got somthing to eat & ma spred down a bufalo robe & we all laid down on it & spred somthing over us & ma sit up by the fire & It snowed one foot on top of the bed & we got up in the morning & the snow was so deep we could not go over & so we had to go back to the cabin built by emigrants 3 years ago."

The party broke into small sections but soon they could go no farther. The Donner families camped near a lake; Mrs. Reed and her children joined a group that found an old cabin farther up the slope. They built more log shelters, killed all the surviving oxen, packed the meat in snow for preservation, and used the hides for roofing.

The snow continued falling, the days passed, the carefully rationed ox meat was all consumed. Virginia's mother recooked bones that she had thrown out; she cut strips of rawhide from her roof and boiled them into a sort of gluey paste. "We had nothing to eat then but ox hides. O, Mary I would cry and wish I had what you all wasted."

When the ox hides were gone, the Reeds moved into a cabin with the Patrick Breens, an Iowa family who had joined the train at Independence, Missouri. "The Breens were the only Catholic family in the Donner party," Virginia recalled long afterward, "and prayers were said aloud regularly in that cabin night and morning. Our only light was from little pine sticks split up like kindling wood and kept constantly on the hearth. I was very fond of holding these little torches so that he [Mr. Breen] might see to read."

On Christmas Day, Mrs. Reed was able to give her children a special treat. She had hidden away a few dried apples, some beans, a bit of tripe, and a small piece of bacon. She said as they all sat down to Christmas dinner: "Children, eat slowly, for this one day you can have all you wish."

But after Christmas nothing was left. She trapped field mice on the snow, she slit her dog's throat and fed him to her children. "We had to kill little Cash the dog & eat him. We eat his entrails, also feet, hide and everything about him. O, my Dear Cousin, you dont know what trubel is yet . . . We lived on little Cash a week and after Mr. Breen would cook his meat and boil the bones two or three times we would take the bones and boil them 3 or 4 days at a time."

———⟫●⟨———

Despairing of rescue, Mrs. Reed decided to start out with Virginia and cross the mountains to obtain food for the younger children. But neither she nor her daughter could climb through the high passes in the bitter cold. "We went on a while and could not find the road so we had to turn back," Virginia wrote. "I could go on verry well while I thout we wer gitting along but as soon as we had to turn back I could hardly git along but we got to the cabins that night & I froze one of my feet verry bad. That same night thare was the worst storme we had that winter & if we had not come back that night we would never got back." They lived out another seven weeks on boiled ox hides.

Down in the lake camp, more grisly events were occurring; some of the survivors were eating their frozen comrades. At last, after many died and hope was all but gone, on February 19, 1847, a relief party from Sutter's Fort arrived with food. James Reed had made his way across the Sierras and found help. "I can not describe the death-like look they all had," he wrote in his diary. "Bread Bread Bread was the begging of every child and grown person except my wife." His daughter Virginia recorded: "O, Mary, you do not know how glad we was to see him." Thirty-six of the original party of eighty-seven had perished in the Sierra snows. One of them was the Reed family's good friend John Denton, the English gunsmith who had carved the headstone for Grandma Keyes's grave.

———⟫●⟨———

From California a month later Virginia made one of her few references to the cannibalism always associated with the tragic Donner party. "There was 3 died and the rest eat them, they was 10 days without anything to eat but the Dead . . . O Mary I have not wrote you half of the trubel we have had but I hav wrote you anuf to let you know that you dont know what trubel is but thank God we have all got thro, and we did not eat human flesh." Because she wanted her cousins to come and live in California, she asked them not to let her letters dishearten them, but added a warning: "Never take cutofs and hury along as fast as you can."

She wrote that the Reeds were all very well pleased with California, particularly with the climate. "It is a beautiful Country, it is mostly in vallies. It aut to be a beautiful Country to pay us for our trubel getting there." She especially liked the "Spanyards"; she thought they were the best riders she had ever seen. "They have a spanish sadel and wodon sturups and great big spurs 5 inches in diamter . . . Tell Henrietta if she wants to get married to come to California. She can get a Spanyard anytime."

Virginia Reed lived a long and happy life in California. "She was a handsome young lady," one of her admirers said of her, "and was noted for her superior equestrianship, having obtained several first premiums at county fairs for graceful riding." Instead of marrying a "Spanyard," she chose an Army officer, John M. Murphy, who became one of the first real-estate operators in the state. When Murphy lost his eyesight, Virginia led him each day to and from his office in San Jose. After he died she continued the business, becoming a pioneer as a real-estate saleswoman as she had been a pioneer in crossing the Plains and the Rockies. She outlived almost all the survivors of the Donner party, dying at the age of 87 in 1921.

Ely S. Parker, a former general and Civil War veteran, was appointed on April 13, 1869 by President Ulysses S. Grant to be the first Indian Commissioner of Indian Affairs. Photographer: C. D. Fredericks & Co. Courtesy of Chicago Historical Society ICHi-26500.

10

Ely S. Parker:
"One Real American"

"Lee's sincere compliment was more than earned by this Seneca Indian who served both the white and the red man with equal talent and integrity."

In various paintings of Lee's surrender to Grant at Appomattox can be seen a dark-complexioned lieutenant colonel with a thick, black, down-curved mustache. Usually he is in the background, sometimes standing against a wall, sometimes seated at a writing desk. The writing desk is significant, for it was this swarthy lieutenant colonel who, because of his excellent penmanship, was ordered by Grant to transcribe the final surrender terms. He was a Seneca Indian born on the Tonawanda reservation in New York as Hasanoanda, but who early in life anglicized his name to Ely Samuel Parker.

Some of the other officers present at the surrender said afterward that when General Lee was introduced to Colonel Parker, he looked at the Indian searchingly and with evident surprise. "After he had stared at me for a moment," Parker later told friends, "he extended his hand and said, 'I am glad to see one real American here.' I shook his hand and said, 'We are all Americans.'"

Ely Parker's travels from his humble birthplace on an Indian reservation to an appointment on General Grant's staff and then later as the first Indian Commissioner of Indian Affairs was a continual struggle against racial prejudice. Although obstacle after obstacle was thrown across his path, from the days of his youth Ely

Parker was determined to persevere until he had proved himself the equal of any man.

Parker was born in 1825, a descendant of Tonawanda Senecas who fought the British during the Revolutionary War. During that war an English officer named Parker was captured by the Senecas and adopted into the tribe. The Englishman lived for a time with Ely Parker's ancestors, and after he departed the younger boys of the family, including Ely's father, assumed Parker's name for use in their associations with white men.

———◦◦◦———

During the early 1830's Ely's parents sent him to a mission school. "Learn all you can," his father told him, but the boy was just becoming accustomed to school life when the Seneca reservation was thrown into turmoil. By bribery and chicanery the Senecas were defrauded of much of their land in New York and assigned a tract in Kansas. Seneca leaders were determined to defend their treaty rights, but the younger men were so disillusioned by the government's actions that many fled to Canada to start a new life. Ten-year-old Ely joined the exodus, quickly discovered that he would have to earn a living, and went to work as a hostler's boy for Army officers at a Canadian military post. Soon the officers began teasing him because of his poor English. After a few days of this the proud young Seneca had had enough. He resolved to master the English language; he would learn to speak and write it so well that no white man would ever laugh at him again.

Returning to his people's reservation, Ely entered an academy and concentrated on the study of English speech, reading, and penmanship. By the time he was 15, his proficiency in the language was so superior that the Seneca leaders took him to Washington to help defend the Tonawanda land claims before Congress. He met and impressed Webster, Clay, and Calhoun, and was invited to dine at the White House with President James K. Polk.

Convinced by this experience that he could best help the cause of the Indians by studying law, young Parker persuaded a law firm in

Ellicottville, New York, to permit him to begin his career as a student in their office. After three years of reading law, preparing briefs, drawing up forms, and attending court proceedings, he was pronounced competent to practice. Then came a crushing blow. When he applied for admission to the bar, he was told that only white male citizens could be admitted to practice. No Indians need apply.

Disheartened by this injustice, Parker drifted about for a few weeks, but instead of becoming embittered he made careful inquiries into which of the white man's professions or trades an Indian could be admitted. He finally decided upon engineering. Entering Rensselaer Polytechnic Institute, he mastered all the courses in rapid succession and soon found employment as a civil engineer on the Erie Canal. Parker's capabilities brought rapid promotions, and before he was 30 the U.S. government sought him out to supervise construction of levees and government buildings. In 1860 his duties took him to Galena, Illinois. Although he was a giant of an Indian now — with huge muscular arms and legs and an enormous chest — he was a quiet, soft-spoken man. In Galena he met another quiet man of about his age, a clerk in a harness store, and they became good friends. The clerk was a former Army captain named Ulysses Simpson Grant.

A few months later the Civil War began and Grant began talking of raising an Illinois regiment. As it was the custom in that war for volunteers to enter the Army through their state military organizations, Parker decided to return to New York and recruit a regiment of Iroquois Indians. He went first to Albany, saw the governor, and asked for a commission to raise an Indian regiment. The governor told him bluntly that he had no place for Indians in the New York Volunteers, and suggested that he return to work as a civilian.

Accustomed by now to the prejudices of white men, Ely Parker shrugged off the rebuff and took a train to Washington to offer his services to the War Department as an engineer. Confident that his wide experience would secure him an immediate appointment in the Union Army, which was in acute need of trained engineers, Parker called upon Secretary of State Seward whom he had known as senator from New York.

Parker later told of the interview: "Mr. Seward in a short time said to me that the struggle in which I wished to assist was an affair between white men and one in which the Indian was not called to act. 'The fight must be settled by the white men alone,' he said. 'Go home, cultivate your farm, and we will settle our troubles without any Indian aid.'"

Parker returned to the Tonawanda reservation as Seward advised him, but he also let his friend Ulysses Grant know that he was having difficulties getting into the Army. A few months later a special mounted messenger in a Union Army uniform delivered a sealed letter to Ely Parker. It contained an officer's commission and orders to report to General John E. Smith as an engineer in one of Grant's divisions facing Vicksburg.

—————⊃•⊂—————

From the spring of 1863 until the end of the war, Ely Parker was with Grant at Vicksburg, Lookout Mountain, Missionary Ridge, The Wilderness, Cold Harbor, and Petersburg. After Grant took command in Virginia, he assigned Parker to his staff with the rank of lieutenant colonel, and much of the general's official correspondence of that time was transcribed in the neat penmanship of the Seneca Indian. Parker also continued his engineering duties, especially in the operations around Richmond. While laying out entrenchments he would ride casually about on his black horse, apparently unmindful of enemy fire. "I don't believe I am to be killed by a bullet," he remarked, and seemed surprised one day when his hat and coat were perforated by bullets. "The Indian," as almost everyone called him, soon became a familiar figure.

He especially valued two friendships formed during this period. One was with Mathew Brady, the photographer who frequently visited Grant's headquarters to make photographs (Parker appears in several of them). The other was with President Lincoln who expressed a deep interest in the American Indian. Lincoln told Parker that he hoped the nation would find a way to requite past injustices done to his people.

In April 1865 when General Lee agreed to meet for a discussion of surrender terms, Parker accompanied General Grant to the McLean farm house. "Grant sat at a small oval table," Parker said afterward, "and Lee took his seat at a square-topped stand. The rest of us sat or stood where it was most convenient. . . . Lee began talking about the Mexican War and other reminiscences. He seemed composed but was quite stiff in his dignity. Grant seemed relaxed but as he smoked he was thinking hard." While the two generals discussed the terms of surrender, Grant used a pencil to scribble them upon the sheet of a manifold order book. He called Colonel Parker to his side and read the sentences over with him. Then he presented the statement to Lee who read it and requested that a clause be inserted allowing horses and mules to be retained by his men. Grant replied that he would issue a special order so that Lee's men could keep their animals for farming; the surrender terms would be put into ink as he had written them.

"When I made the copy in ink," Parker said, "I put the original in my pocket." He later framed it and kept it as a prized memento of the occasion.

—————⟫●⟨—————

Instead of returning to civilian life as an engineer, Parker accepted Grant's offer to remain with him as his personal secretary. When the general made his grand tour of the nation after the assassination of President Lincoln, Parker accompanied him, his burly figure always alert in case an attempt should also be made upon Grant's life.

In 1866, after being awarded a brevet as brigadier general, he accepted the first of a series of government assignments to act as mediator in conflicts with Indian tribes. The fact that an Indian — although dressed as a white man — was present as a representative of the United States made considerable impression upon the Choctaws and Seminoles. After the Fetterman Massacre at Fort Phil Kearny, he journeyed to the Far West as a member of a special commission to negotiate with the hostile Plains Indians. As General Parker traveled up the Missouri River, various bands of Teton Sioux were surprised and pleased when they discovered that the Great

Father in Washington had sent out an Indian to parley with them. They told Parker that they had agreed to cede their lands and live in peace on reservations in exchange for promises of livestock, seed, and implements to till the soil, but none of the promises had been kept. Parker returned to Washington with many ideas for reformation of the nation's Indian policy, but he had to wait a year until his old friend Ulysses Grant was elected President.

Confident that Parker could deal with Indians more intelligently than any white man, President Grant named him Commissioner of Indian Affairs. When Parker took office, he found the Indian Bureau even more graft-ridden than he had expected. Instead of serving the Indians as they were supposed to be doing, corrupt officials and agents were actually forcing some tribes to acts of hostility.

Parker was convinced that a clean sweep should be made of the long-entrenched bureaucrats, and with Grant's support he established a system of appointing agents recommended by various religious bodies of the nation. Because so many Quakers volunteered to serve as Indian agents, the new plan became known as Grant's "Quaker policy," or "peace policy" for the Indians. In addition a Board of Indian Commissioners made up of public-spirited citizens was formed to act as a watchdog over the operations of the Bureau of Indian Affairs.

Within a year Ely Parker completely revitalized the Bureau of Indian Affairs. Because of his military background, he was able to eliminate much of the long-standing distrust between the civilian-oriented bureau and the War Department. And because he was an Indian he won the confidence of the suspicious Plains tribes who had been waging intermittent warfare for five years. Except for an inexcusable attack by U.S. Army troops upon a band of Piegan Blackfeet, there was at least a cessation of organized warfare on the northwestern frontier during Ely Parker's tenure of office. The Kiowas and Comanches continued to raid in Texas but considered themselves to be at peace with the United States.

As a result of the "Piegan massacre," tribes on the upper Plains began mild demonstrations of hostility. Indian agents were held prisoners at several agencies along the Missouri, and rumors spread that the Sioux were planning a general war. The most belligerent war leader among the Indians at this time was Red Cloud, who had united the northern Plains tribes and forced the United States to abandon its forts above the North Platte and pull its troops out of territory claimed by the Indians north of that river. Whether Red Cloud would remain peaceful or continue to wage war was one of the questions facing Commissioner Parker when he took office. To win Red Cloud over, Parker arranged for him and twenty-two other Sioux leaders to make a state visit to Washington.

"I have come to see you," Red Cloud greeted Parker when the delegation arrived on June 1, 1870. "When I heard the Great Father would permit me to come to see him I was glad and came right off. Telegraph to my people, and say that I am safe."

Parker took his Sioux visitors on a tour of the Capital, showed them through the Navy Yard and Arsenal, and had a 15-inch Rodman gun fired off for them. Red Cloud was visibly impressed; he carefully measured the diameter of the gun and examined the powder grains used in the charge.

For the journey from Fort Laramie, the Sioux had been outfitted with white man's clothing, and it was obvious that most of them were ill at ease in their tight-fitting black coats and button shoes. When Commissioner Parker told them that Mathew Brady had invited them to visit his studio to have their photographs taken, Red Cloud said it did not suit him to do so. "I am not a white man, but a Sioux," he explained. "I am not dressed for such an occasion."

Parker understood immediately, and let his visitors know that if it so pleased them they could dress in buckskins, feathers, and moccasins for dinner at the White House with President Grant.

During his visit, Red Cloud made it plain that his people would not tolerate being robbed by dishonest traders and agents, that they had no intention of surrendering any more territory, and that they expected to be well paid for land which they had already surrendered.

"The government stole Denver from us," he said. "You never gave us anything for it." Yet it was apparent that he trusted Ely Parker. When he left Washington, he told the commissioner that he would spend the remainder of his life working for peace, and he never went back on his word. The Seneca Iroquois had won over the Teton Sioux, thus stopping "the spread of the threatened hostilities among the Sioux at the north, and their southern allies, the Cheyennes, Arapahoes, and Comanches of the southern plains who were awaiting the outbreak of hostilities among the Sioux to join in its bloody work."

———————

Like most crusaders, General Parker also began creating enemies, especially among political bosses who had long been using the Indian Bureau as a lucrative branch of the spoils system. He discovered that as soon as he replaced a dishonest agent with an honest agent, the spoilsmen would devise new ways of siphoning off funds from the Indians — through beef contractors, freighters, steamboat operators, and traders. Often a frontier politician would pose as a friend of an Indian tribe and offer to act as the tribe's agent in Washington to push special appropriations through Congress. The agent or lobbyist usually secured power of attorney from the chiefs to claim as much as one-third of any appropriation money for his services. Although funds appropriated for Indians were distributed through the Indian Bureau, the agents were bold enough to appear on the reservations on allotment days to collect their 33⅓ percent from individual Indians as they left the pay table.

To halt such practices, General Parker instructed his paymasters to inform each Indian that all the money given him was his, and that he owed nothing to any agent or attorney claiming to have obtained the money for him from Washington. Reaction to this from the spoilsmen was smoldering anger. They did not dare to denounce Parker publicly for shutting off thousands of dollars of the Indians' money from their pockets. But a growing number of shady dealers, contractors, and politicians began keeping a close watch on "that

Indian Ely Parker," laying traps for him, and awaiting a chance to ac-
cuse him of anything that might bring about his removal from office.

⊂●○⊃

In 1870 a small band of his enemies in Congress managed to delay
passage of funds for purchase of supplies for reservation Indians.
Thousands of formerly hostile warriors had been pacified and located
on reservations through promises of regular allotments of food and
supplies, but because Congress would not give him funds, Parker
could not purchase foodstuffs. By early summer it became evident to
several reservation agents that their hungry charges were preparing
to break away in search of wild game. If they did this they would surely
come in conflict with settlers and soldiers again. Warning telegrams
began arriving daily upon the commissioner's desk.

Parker responded immediately to the warnings by cutting through
government red tape. He obtained food and supplies on credit and
arranged for hasty transportation by wagon trains and steamboats. The
Indians received their meat and flour in time to avoid starvation, and
another useless series of Indian wars was avoided. Parker, however,
had broken a few minor regulations, and this gave his enemies the
chance they had been waiting for.

The first attack came unexpectedly from a man Parker had once
believed to be his friend — William Welsh, a missionary to the
Indians. Welsh had been one of the first members of the watchdog
Board of Indian Commissioners, but resigned soon after accepting the
appointment. His motive was not made clear until December 1870
when he wrote a letter for publication in several Washington newspapers. Welsh charged General Parker with "fraud and improvidence
in the conduct of Indian affairs," and blamed General Grant for
putting into office a man "who is but a remove from barbarism." As
events unfolded it became evident that Welsh believed the reason the
Indians went on the warpath was their heathenism and the only
solution to the Indian problem was to convert all of them to Christianity. When he discovered that Parker was tolerant of the Indians'
primitive religions, he took a violent dislike to the "heathen"

commissioner and resigned. Welsh was also suspicious of Parker because of his military background; he considered the Army an enemy
of missionary endeavors.

As soon as Welsh's letter appeared in print, Parker's political
enemies seized upon it as a perfect opportunity to remove him from
office. Within a week, the House of Representatives Committee
on Appropriations adopted a resolution to inquire into the charges
against the Commissioner of Indian Affairs, and summoned Parker
to a grilling that continued for several weeks. For the committee,
Welsh drew up a list of thirteen charges of misconduct. At the end
of the inquiry, Ely Parker was exonerated of all charges and was com-
plimented for convincing the Indian tribes "that the government is
in earnest, and that it may be trusted," thus saving the Treasury
millions of dollars by avoiding another war on the Plains.

Only General Parker's closest friends knew how agonizing the
entire affair had been to him. Welsh's attack he considered a betrayal,
especially the implication that as an Indian "but a remove from barbarism" he was not fit to serve as Commissioner of Indian Affairs.

For several months he debated what his next course of action
should be. Above all he wanted to help the advancement of his race,
but if he remained in office with political enemies constantly sniping
at him because he was an Indian himself, he feared that he might do
his people more harm than good. He also wondered if his continu-
ance in office might not be a political embarrassment to his old
friend President Grant.

General Parker still had one more major objective to accomplish,
however, and that was abolition of the Indian treaty system. For
years he had considered the making of treaties between the United
States and Indian tribes as a tragic farce, the principal cause of mis-
understandings, land frauds, and wars. "The Indian tribes of the
United States are not sovereign nations," he wrote in 1869, "capable of making treaties, as none of them have an organized government
of such inherent strength as would secure a faithful obedience of its

people in the observance of compacts of this character . . . great injury has been done by the government in deluding this people into the belief of their being independent sovereignties, while they were at the same time recognized only as its dependents and wards."

In 1871 a proviso forbidding the making of further treaties with Indian tribes was added to the regular Indian appropriation bill and was enacted into law. Satisfied with this accomplishment, Parker turned in his resignation late that summer. Privately he told friends he was leaving because he had become "a rock of offense." Publicly he said he wanted to go into business to better provide for his family. He had recently married Minnie Sackett, the daughter of a prominent New Yorker.

Turning his back on his past, General Parker moved to New York City and began a new career in the financial world. To his own astonishment and that of his friends he soon acquired a considerable fortune. He purchased a fine house in Fairfield, Connecticut and began devoting much of his time to Indian matters.

As Grand Sachem of the Iroquois his name was Donehogawa, or Keeper of the Western Door of the Long House. This highest honor of the Six Nations carried with it responsibility for guarding the rights and interests of his people. He was soon carrying on a wide correspondence with tribesmen and friends, signing his name as Donehogawa, and for the first time in years felt himself to be an Indian again.

Once more, however, fate interrupted the even flow of his new life. A trusted associate in his financial firm embezzled considerable sums of money from clients and could not replace the losses. As Parker was bondsman for the defaulter, he immediately consulted his lawyers. "You won't have to pay," they told him. "You are an Indian, and the law does not hold you to it. The bond is not worth the paper it is written on because you are an Indian."

Parker was indignant. "I am a man," he declared. "If the law does not compel me to pay, my honor does."

After he had paid off the embezzled funds, he was almost penniless, but he had made enough friends and learned enough about the business world to fight his way back to the top again. Some years later when a financial panic wiped Parker out for the second time, he decided he had had enough of the pressured world of money changing. He was preparing to retire to a quiet life in the Connecticut countryside when friends persuaded him to help in the reformation of the New York Police Department. Among his associates in this work were Theodore Roosevelt, a dynamic young reformer; Frederick Grant, son of President Grant; and Danish-born Jacob Riis, a crusading newspaper reporter.

In his book *The Making of an American*, Jacob Riis recorded his impressions of Ely Parker during the last years of the Seneca Indian's long and varied career: "I suppose it was the fact that he was an Indian that first attracted me to him. As the years passed we became good friends, and I loved nothing better in an idle hour than to smoke a pipe with the general in his poky little office at police headquarters. When, once in a while, it would happen that some of his people came down from the Reservation or from Canada, the powwow that ensued was my dear delight. He was a noble old fellow. His title was no trumpery show either. It was fairly earned on more than one bloody field with Grant's Army. . . . It was not General Parker, however, but Donehogawa, Chief of the Senecas and the remnant of the once powerful Six Nations . . . that appealed to me, who in my boyhood had lived with Leather-Stocking and with Uncas and Chingachgook. They had something to do with my coming here, and at last I had for a friend one of their kin. I think he felt the bond of sympathy between us and prized it, for he showed me in many silent ways that he was fond of me."

Not until he was stricken with paralysis at his desk in 1893 did General Parker finally retire from active life. Two years later, August 30, 1895, he died at his home in Fairfield, Connecticut.

11

The Ordeal of Surgeon Tappan

*"It was an army doctor's duty to save the lives of his men.
Benjamin Tappan did — by losing his own!"*

The role of the army doctor in the American West has been largely over-shadowed by more flamboyant characters — cowboys, gunfighters, dashing cavalry leaders. Most doctors in the Indian-fighting army bore the title "assistant surgeon." They were usually civilians under military contract, and were considered to have rank equal to that of a second lieutenant.

In the far-flung network of forts and trails across the West it was not unusual for command responsibility to fall upon an army doctor. An assistant surgeon was often assigned to small escort parties and scouting patrols traveling in dangerous country. If no trouble occurred, his duties were light, but if a sudden raid put the officer or officers in charge out of action, the surgeon assumed command.

During the spring of 1866 in the Apache country of Arizona, three army doctors became separately involved in a harrowing struggle for survival against Indians and the desert. Their story is representative of what doctors of medicine could expect to experience at that time and place in the service of the Army.

On March 25, Assistant Surgeon John E. Kunkler marched out of District of Arizona headquarters at Tucson with a small detachment of First Cavalry California Volunteers. Because of a shortage of regular officers, Dr. Kunkler was in command. He and his men had served throughout the Civil War in the Southwest and when the war ended had volunteered to remain another year to guard stagecoach routes against Apache raiders. Now at last they were on their way home to be mustered out.

Early in the afternoon Kunkler led his men into Picacho Station, finding there two men near exhaustion and starvation. One was Corporal John Berg, Company F, Fourteenth U.S. Infantry, the other a civilian teamster, Stevens Sumner. They were survivors of an Apache attack against a small escort troop which had occurred three days earlier. According to Kunkler, Corporal Berg "was in a bewildered and exhausted condition; the teamster had an arrow wound in his scalp, not serious."

Their story was pieced together by Kunkler. On March 7, Berg and five soldiers had been detailed to escort Captain James F. Millar and Assistant Surgeon Benjamin Tappan of the Fourteenth Infantry from Fort Yuma to Fort Grant, a journey of almost 300 miles across arid land inhabited almost exclusively by hostile Apaches. One wagon was provided to transport baggage and supplies, with Stevens Sumner, a civilian employee of the quartermaster, as teamster. For sixteen days the march was uneventful.

Then, about two o'clock in the afternoon of March 22, near Cottonwood Springs, they were attacked suddenly by a large party of Tonto and Pinaleno Apaches — perhaps seventy-five or a hundred Indians. The place selected for the ambush was typical — a canyon broken by boulders which narrowed the trail to thirty paces. The Apaches, armed with guns and arrows, concealed themselves in a brush-filled arroyo parallel with the trail and attacked without warning.

Captain Millar, the only officer, was killed almost instantly, a bullet through his heart. One soldier was also killed in the first moments of attack; two others attempting escape were pursued and slain. Dr. Tappan received two wounds through the body and one in the foot. Teamster Sumner was struck a glancing blow on the head by an arrow.

The five survivors — Corporal Berg and two privates who had escaped unhurt, the slightly wounded teamster, and the thrice-wounded

Dr. Tappan — fled south on foot. The Apaches, eager to seize the spoils from the army wagon, soon abandoned pursuit.

Tappan, as an acting second lieutenant, was in command. And his men were without food and had very little water. Their only weapons were an army six-shooter and a derringer which Tappan had on his person at the time of attack. The country through which they were escaping was a dry plain covered with cactus and broken by dry ravines. The officer decided their best hope of survival was to find a waterhole, then work their way southwest to the stage route.

Tappan, however, was weak from loss of blood, and his foot wound was so painful that after marching a few miles he was forced to discard his boot. Before nightfall they found a waterhole, but it was dry.

All of the following day the surgeon held his men together while searching desperately for water. On the morning of the twenty-fourth, he attempted to resume the march, but by nine o'clock his strength failed him. He suggested that the party split up. If the Apaches found them, five exhausted men could offer little resistance.

Perhaps, if each of them went in a different direction, some would survive. The men refused to leave the doctor alone; they knew he could not travel another mile on his swollen foot. It was finally decided that Corporal Berg and Stevens Sumner would go in search of water and assistance. The two privates and Dr. Tappan would make camp and wait for the pair to return.

Tappan agreed reluctantly. He gave his derringer to Berg, and the corporal and the teamster started out. They searched all day without finding any water or trails of any kind. Before nightfall they tried to rejoin Tappan, but without natural landmarks to guide them, they became lost.

At dawn the next day, Sumner made a careful study of the horizon and finally decided that sunlight reflecting from a peak far to the southwest marked the Picacho stage station. It was approximately thirty-five miles away, and this was their third day without water, but he persuaded Corporal Berg to make a try for it. Much of the way Sumner had to help the faltering soldier, but they staggered into Picacho early in the afternoon. The station was deserted. The waterhole, the horse trough, the barrels were all dry. They dropped in the shade of the stage stop and waited. Two hours later Surgeon Kunkler and his California Volunteers found them and gave them food and water.

As soon as Kunkler learned of the desperate plight of Dr. Tappan, he selected one of his best horsemen to ride back to Tucson with a message for help. Within a few hours a search party had departed and a fast messenger was en route to Fort Grant to start another party from there. Among these men was Dr. Charles Meyers, a colleague of Dr. Tappan and the third surgeon to become involved.

After unsuccessful searches across the lonely desert country, the two parties rendezvoused at Cottonwood Springs late on the 27th. The following morning they discovered the bodies of Captain Millar and the three enlisted men.

The Apaches, Dr. Meyers said, had stripped Millar's body, "cut off the genital organs and the upper part of the ears, then turned the body over on its face and shot nine arrows into the back, which were sticking in it when I saw the body."

One of the enlisted men had been killed as he rode in the wagon and had been "thrown out by the Indians and had a gaping lance wound inflicted in the left loin after death." The second enlisted man evidently had attempted to escape with Dr. Tappan's party, but had been overtaken by the Apaches and tortured to death.

"His left arm was broken close to the shoulder and twisted until it assumed the appearance of a twisted rope; his whole scalp was skinned off from the eyebrows upward down to the back of his neck; whereas in scalping a victim after death the Indians merely cut the central portion of the scalp, and from the above indications, therefore, it is almost certain that this man was tortured before he died. After stripping the body the Indians fired seven arrows into the back, which were in it when seen by me."

The third enlisted man had managed to flee 250 yards west of the wagon but had been overtaken, slain, and stripped. "By the man's side was found paper of the cartridges he had torn, and also the marks of the butt of the musket, while loading." He had died fighting while his surviving comrades escaped to the south.

After burying the bodies, the search party picked up the trail of Dr. Tappan and the four men with him. Their footprints were six days old, but accompanying the search party was a first-rate civilian guide accustomed to trailing in difficult country. Near sundown the expedition was camped at the same dry waterhole which Tappan's party had reached on their first day's march.

Captain J. B. Hager, in command of the combined detachment of fifty-eight men, now began to find himself in a predicament similar to that of the party for which he was searching. His men had exhausted their water supplies.

"March 29," he reported later, "I pursued the trail over the mountains to the desert south of them. The trail was difficult to follow on that portion of the desert and the progress was exceedingly slow, but it was finally followed to a point about five miles from the water hole in the mountains.

"At this point the men (Tappan's) were all together, but here they divided, each taking a different direction. By this time the command was out of water, and the day very warm. It being impossible for want of water to follow up either of these trails I determined to cross the desert to Picacho, about thirty miles, hoping to find some trace of them and also to find water there.

"I intended, if water was obtained there, to prosecute the search from that point. I found no trail during our transit through the desert, and was so unfortunate as to find no water at Picacho. The men were suffering dreadfully. Some fell fainting by the wayside, and another showed some symptoms of insanity. We reached Picacho at 7 o'clock in the evening.

"I dispatched a man to point of mountain with all the canteens of the detachment with orders to return as soon as possible and meet the command, which would leave Picacho at twelve o'clock at night for that well. This man was met returning not until long after sunrise, and not until many of the men had arrived within a few miles of the well. I have no doubt this supply of water saved the lives of several men."

Meanwhile, one of the two soldiers left behind with Dr. Tappan had been found by travelers on the stage road north of Tucson. "He was completely bewildered, but on getting some water soon revived and was able to point out the direction and something near the spot where he left the doctor and the other man." He told his rescuers that the day after Corporal Berg and Stevens Sumner had left to go in search of water, Dr. Tappan had ordered him and the other soldier to try to save themselves as best they could.

In obedience to the surgeon's order, the two soldiers had set out in different directions. (This accounted for Captain Hager's finding four trails leading in different directions from Tappan's last camp.)

Tucson headquarters soon afterward dispatched two other expeditions, one "a party of Mexicans mounted, men who are accustomed to the country." On March 31, the Mexicans found the second of the soldiers who had left Dr. Tappan on the 25th. This man had kept himself alive by living on moisture from cactus plants until he found a spring in the mountains. Dr. Tappan, he reported, had told him "to look out for himself as he did not expect to live."

The search would go on for another ten days, but there was now no hope for Assistant Surgeon Benjamin Tappan. As a temporary commanding officer he had managed the survival of all his men. But he himself had escaped the Apaches only to be claimed by the implacable desert. In official records his death date is recorded as March 22, the day of the attack. The exact date, the exact place, no man will ever know.

12

How Standing Bear
Became a Person

*I*n the spring of 1877 a representative of the Office of Indian Affairs arrived on the Ponca Reservation and informed Standing Bear and other chiefs that the Poncas must move to Indian Territory. Although the Poncas had lived for more than a century at the confluence of the Niobrara and Missouri Rivers, and had never engaged in war against the United States, the removal was in accordance with a new Governmental policy to concentrate all Indians in large regional reservations or within Indian Territory.

Only 170 Poncas, or about one fourth of the tribe, agreed to go voluntarily. In April a company of soldiers and a civilian agent, E. A. Howard, arrived to enforce the removal order. Standing Bear and White Eagle protested strongly that the Government had no right to remove the Poncas from their land, but Howard said that if they refused to go peaceably, he must order the soldiers to move them by force.

"The soldiers forced us across the Niobrara to the other side, just as one would drive a herd of ponies," White Eagle said afterward, "and the soldiers pushed us on until we came to the Platte River." For fifty days the Poncas marched southward across Nebraska and Kansas, enduring drenching rains, burning suns, roaring tornadoes, biting flies, severe illnesses, and several deaths. Standing Bear's daughter was one of the victims, and Agent Howard prevailed upon the citizens of Milford, Nebraska to permit her to be buried in the local cemetery.

At last, on July 9, they reached the Quapaw Reservation which was to be their temporary home. Living wretchedly in army tents, they had little to do except scrounge for food to supplement their meager rations, and fight off mosquitoes. As summer wore on, a disease unknown to these northern Indians swept through their camps. Malaria, against which they had no resistance, destroyed one of every four Poncas before the year's end.

⟨⟩

Early in 1878 the Poncas were informed that the Government had assigned them a permanent reservation on the west bank of the Arkansas River. No funds were available, however, for food, medicine, or shelter. After walking 150 miles to their new homes, the Poncas

Chief Standing Bear of the Poncas spoke convincingly for his people in the court of law. Courtesy of Nebraska State Historical Society.

were again struck by chills and fevers. "We were as grass that is trodden down," said Standing Bear. "How many died we did not know. At last I had only one son left; then he sickened. When he was dying he asked me to promise him one thing. He begged me to take him when he was dead, back to our old burying ground by the Swift Running Water, the Niobrara. I promised. When he died, I and those with me put his body into a box and then in a wagon and we started north."

Sixty-six Poncas made up the procession, all of Standing Bear's band, that followed the old wagon drawn by two gaunt horses. In the bitter weather of January 1879, this funeral cortege crossed the plains to the Niobrara. After their solemn task was done, they decided to stay in the north with their old friends, the Omaha Indians who still had a reservation not far from the frontier town of Omaha, Nebraska.

For some weeks, however, Indian Office agents had been in search of Standing Bear's Poncas. When they were located, Secretary of the Interior Carl Schurz asked the War Department to arrest the runaways without delay. The order went to General George Crook, whose headquarters were at Omaha, and he sent a company of soldiers to the reservation. Standing Bear and his people made no resistance; they were arrested and brought back to Fort Omaha to await arrangements for transportation to Indian Territory.

For much of his life George Crook had been fighting Indians, meeting them in councils, making them promises he could not keep. From a grudging admiration for their courage, his attitude had changed through the years to a feeling of respect and sympathy for his former enemies. When he saw the Poncas in the guardhouse at Fort Omaha, he was appalled by their pitiable condition. He was impressed by Standing Bear's simple statements explaining why he had left Indian Territory to come back north, and by the chief's stoical acceptance of events over which he had lost control. "I thought God intended us to live," Standing Bear said to Crook, "but I was mistaken. God intends to give the country to the white people, and we are to die."

Crook expressed his sympathy. Instead of merely promising to do something to prevent Standing Bear from being returned to Indian

Territory, he went to see an Omaha newspaperman, Thomas Henry Tibbles, and enlisted the power of the press. While Crook held up orders for transfer of the Poncas, Tibbles spread their story across the Nation. A young Omaha lawyer, John L. Webster, then volunteered his services to take the Indians' case into court, and he was soon supported by the chief attorney for the Union Pacific Railroad, Andrew Poppleton.

Both lawyers bent all their energies toward preparation of a case before General Crook received orders from Washington compelling him to start the Indians southward. The judge chosen to hear the case was Elmer S. Dundy, a rugged frontiersman with four main interests in life: good literature, horses, hunting, and the administration of justice. Before the trial could begin, a messenger had to be sent up the Missouri River to summon the judge back from a bear hunt.

With Crook's tacit agreement, Judge Dundy issued a writ of habeas corpus upon the general, requiring him to bring the Poncas into court and show by what authority he held them prisoners. Crook obeyed the writ by presenting his military orders from Washington, and the United States district attorney appeared before the judge to deny the Poncas' right to the writ on the ground that Indians were "not persons within the meaning of the law."

Thus began on April 18, 1879, the now almost forgotten civil rights case of Standing Bear v. Crook . Standing Bear's lawyers argued that an Indian was as much a "person" as any white man and could avail himself of the rights of freedom guaranteed by the Constitution. When the U.S. attorney claimed that Standing Bear and his people were subject to rules and regulations established by the Government for tribal Indians, Webster and Poppleton replied that Standing Bear and all Indians had the right to separate themselves from their tribes and live under the protection of United States laws like anyone else.

The climax of the trial came when Standing Bear was given permission to speak for his people. "I want to go back to my old place north," he said. "I want to save myself and my tribe. If a white man had land, and some one should swindle him, that man would try to get it back, and you would not blame him. Look on me. Take pity on me, and help me save the lives of the women and children. My brothers, a power which I cannot resist crowds me down to the ground. I need help. I have done."

Judge Dundy ruled that an Indian was a "person" within the meaning of the habeas corpus act, that the right of expatriation was a natural, inherent, and inalienable right of the Indian as well as the white race, and that in time of peace no authority, civil or military, existed for transporting Indians from one section of the country to another without the consent of the Indians, nor to confine them to any particular reservation against their will.

"The Poncas are amongst the most peaceable and friendly of all the Indian tribes," Judge Dundy said. "If they could be removed to the Indian Territory by force, and kept there in the same way, I can see no good reason why they might not be taken and kept by force in the penitentiary at Lincoln, or Leavenworth, or any other place which the commander of the forces might, in his judgment, see proper to designate. I cannot think that any such arbitrary authority exists in this country."

———

When Judge Dundy concluded the proceedings by ordering Standing Bear and the Poncas released from custody, the audience in the courtroom stood up and, according to a newspaper reporter, "gave out such a shout as was never heard in a courtroom." General Crook was the first to reach Standing Bear to congratulate him.

After studying Judge Dundy's written opinion (a brilliant essay upon human rights) the U.S. attorney decided to make no appeal to a higher court. Standing Bear was now officially a "person." The Government assigned him and his band a few hundred acres of unclaimed land near the mouth of the Niobrara. He was back home again, but more important than that he had also taken one step forward down the long, hard road toward justice for all American Indians.

Enjoying their profits from the holdup of the First National Bank, in Winnemucca, Nevada, Butch Cassidy and his gang sport stylish and expensive garb as they pose for a photograph at the Schwartz Gallery, in Fort Worth, Texas. Afterward, they daringly sent a copy of the group portrait, along with a thank you note, to Winnemucca bank officials. Seated (from left) are: Harry Longabaugh (Sundance Kid), Ben Kilpatrick and Robert Parker (Butch Cassidy); standing are Bill Carver (left) and Harvey Logan. Courtesy of Pinkerton, Inc.

13

Butch Cassidy and the Sundance Kid

*L*ike the gods on Mt. Olympus, outlaws of our Old West hold various ranks in the hierarchy of American mythology. Because Butch Cassidy and the Sundance Kid lived so close to our own time — their outlawry flourishing into the 20th century — they were hardly more than demigods before 1969. That year a motion picture appeared linking their names in the title, and its popular appeal opened a flood of inquiry into the "real" Butch and Sundance and their Wild Bunch that quickly lifted them to the top ranks in the pantheon of outlaw gods.

Butch and Sundance did not meet until they were in their thirties, the former growing up in Utah, the latter in Wyoming. Until they were adults they used the names given them at birth. Butch was Robert LeRoy Parker, born April 13, 1866, near Beaver, Utah. The Sundance Kid was Harry Longabaugh, and his origins are less clearly documented. Some sources give his birthplace as Plainfield, New Jersey; others Lancaster County, Pennsylvania. His birthdate varies from 1866 to 1870. The file on Longabaugh kept by Pinkerton's National Detective Agency stated that he was arrested for stealing a horse and served eighteen months in jail at Sundance, Wyoming while still a teenager. He was released on February 4, 1889. During one short period of employment on a Wyoming Ranch, he is said to have thrashed three cowboys, threatened to kill the cook, and committed armed robbery in the town of Lusk.

Any impartial observer of the two future partners certainly would have chosen the young drifter, Harry Longabaugh, as most likely to lead a life of crime. As for Robert LeRoy Parker, he appears to have been a tow-headed innocent, nurtured within a hard-working Mormon family in the sparsely settled Sevier River country of central Utah. His forebears were "handcart pioneers," Mormons who walked and pulled carts across the Great Plains in 1856. He was almost a sure bet to become a respectable cowboy or perhaps owner of one of the small ranches in the Circle Valley area.

Some say that "bad company" must be blamed for turning young Parker down the road to crime; others credit the attitudes of his social peers at that time and place in America. This was the age of the robber barons, of unfettered financial combines that were ruthlessly gobbling up the wealth of the country without regard for the general public. In the West, small ranchers and farmers looked upon the giant stock-raising ventures financed from the Eastern states or from Europe as mortal enemies who were grabbing every acre of good land, monopolizing water sources, and operating hand-in-glove with the gouging railroads.

⸻⸱⸱⸱⸺

When Robert LeRoy Parker was still in his early teens he fell under the influence of a cowhand named Mike Cassidy, who not only taught him how to ride, rope, brand, and shoot, but also how to rustle cattle and horses. Mike Cassidy became young Parker's idol, and after the older man fled the country to avoid arrest, the boy and two of his friends were suspected of rustling on their own.

About eighteen at the time, Parker left home for Telluride, Colorado, a mining town where many restless young men from Utah found employment. While there he formed a friendship with two more "bad companions," Tom McCarty and Matt Warner, whose opulent style of living won the admiration of the greenhorn from Circle Valley. They were the nucleus of the so-called "McCarty Gang," and their prosperity came from the proceeds of bank robberies.

On June 24, 1889, Robert LeRoy Parker joined the pair in a

robbery of the San Miguel Valley Bank at Telluride. In this endeavor they used the classic three-man heist that Butch Cassidy was to perfect over the next few years — one man to hold the horses, one man to hold the gun, one man to grab the money.

With a few thousand dollars apiece the three scattered in different directions, Parker riding north to Brown's Park, a rugged, sparsely inhabited area where Green River flows along the Utah-Colorado-Wyoming borders. He had heard that outlaws hid out there, and for the first time in his life he knew he had crossed the line from prankish pilfering to genuine outlawry. How he spent his stolen money during the months he was at Brown's Park is not known. Some of it undoubtedly went for expensive clothing, saddles, and other horse gear, and he stayed for a while at the Bassett Ranch, where there were two daughters he favored. Anyway, he must have been short of funds by the time he moved on to Rock Springs, Wyoming, where he took a job in William Gottsche's butcher shop. By this time he had adopted a pseudonym, calling himself Ed and borrowing the last name of the "bad companion" of his youth, Mike Cassidy. Ed Cassidy of the butcher shop was soon known around Rock Springs as Butch Cassidy, the name that Robert LeRoy Parker lived with until the legendary gunfight in faraway Bolivia brought it to an end.

During his days in Rock Springs and Brown's Park, Butch apparently met a number of the men who under his leadership would develop into the Wild Bunch. They included Harvey (Kid Curry) Logan, Bill Carver, Ben (Tall Texan) Kilpatrick, Deaf Charley Hanks, Harry Tracy, Bob Meeks, and Elzy Lay, who may have been a closer friend to Butch than was Sundance. (Butch's sister, Lula Parker Betenson, claimed that many of the incidents attributed to Sundance in the 1969 motion picture were based on the exploits of Elzy Lay.)

At the time of the Johnson County War between cattle barons and homesteaders in 1892, Butch and his friends operated on the fringes of the conflict, their sympathies entirely with those who rustled cattle from the big livestock corporations. Sometimes the Wild Bunch hid out with the local outlaws in a valley which could be entered only through an easily defended opening in a high red sandstone ridge, a passageway so narrow that horsemen had to enter single file. This was Wyoming's Hole-in-the-Wall, 250 miles northeast of Brown's Park. In that area the Wild Bunch soon became known as the Hole-in-the-Wall Gang.

The name Butch Cassidy probably first appeared in Wyoming court records in 1892 when he was arrested for stealing a five-dollar horse from a ranch in Fremont County. Butch claimed that he had bought the horse from a rustler, and court hearings and delays continued until July 10, 1894, when he was finally sentenced to two years at hard labor.

Although he was paroled before completing the sentence (January 1896), the thirty-year-old Cassidy was so embittered by what he considered unfair treatment by the law that he could hardly wait to rejoin his old cronies and engage in more profitable crimes than stealing five-dollar horses. On August 13, with Elzy Lay and Bob Meeks, he robbed the Bank of Montpelier in Idaho. For this exploit they stationed fresh horses at fifteen-mile intervals over an escape route of a hundred miles or more. Butch did not invent this system, but he developed it to a high art. After Sundance joined him, they extended their horse stations over longer and longer distances, using the most swift-footed mounts in the West.

Chroniclers of the Montpelier robbery disagree as to whether the outlaws fled to the Hole-in-the-Wall or to Robbers Roost, a remote and mountainous area of southeastern Utah marked by deep winding canyons and high buttes. Butch was almost certainly at Robbers Roost during the winter of 1896-97, living in a rather comfortable community of log cabins and tents with others of the Wild Bunch and their women. It was probably during this interlude that he formed the lasting friendship with Harry Longabaugh, the Sundance Kid. Elzy Lay was also there with his new wife, Maude, and Sundance probably had his mistress, Etta Place, with him.

Much mystery and many contradictions surround the beautiful green-eyed, chestnut-haired Etta Place, if indeed that was her real name. Was she the granddaughter of the Earl of Essex? Was she a young music teacher from Denver, or Telluride? Or was she Betty Price of Fanny Porter's sporting house in Hell's Half Acre of San Antonio? Her origins and her final destiny are both lost in the mists of outlaw mythology.

By the spring of 1897, Butch was evidently running short of cash again. On April 21, he and Elzy Lay rode into Castle Gate, Utah. They dismounted, waited for the payroll train for the Pleasant Valley Coal Company to roll in, and as soon as the clerks took possession of the payroll, the outlaws pulled their revolvers and seized the bags of money. What made the robbery so remarkable was the immediate presence of dozens of miners lined up waiting to be paid. While the miners stared in astonishment, Butch and Elzy leaped into their saddles and started a fast relay ride back to Robbers Roost.

Train robberies almost as daring as the payroll holdup soon followed, but the affluent railroads brought the relentless Pinkerton detectives into the chase. These professional manhunters began issuing identification flyers with full descriptions of suspected desperadoes. For the first time lawmen throughout the West received photographs or drawings of members of the Wild Bunch. In 1898 Pinkerton's described Butch Cassidy as being 5 feet 7 inches tall, weighing 165 pounds, with a light complexion, flaxen hair, deep set blue eyes, and a small red scar under the left eye. "Kid" Longabaugh, as Pinkerton's then listed Sundance, was described as about the same size as Butch, but with darker skin, black hair parted in the middle, and a carefully trimmed black mustache.

To conceal their identities from railway men and detectives, train robbers wore masks, which makes it as difficult for the historian as it was for the lawmen to determine which of the various train holdups of the period were executed by Butch and Sundance and their associates. As Geronimo was blamed for every Indian raid in the Southwest only a decade earlier, the Wild Bunch received credit for every train robbery, even though they might have been hundreds of miles from the scene.

The trademarks of a well-planned Wild Bunch train robbery were no loss of life of train crew or outlaws, no molestation of passengers, and the use of tremendous quantities of dynamite, which usually turned baggage cars into piles of debris. One such explosion scattered thousands of banknotes across the sage-dotted landscape. Train robberies near Wilcox, Wyoming, on June 2, 1899; Folsom, New Mexico, July 11, 1899; and Tipton, Wyoming, August 29, 1900, are generally attributed to the Wild Bunch, with Butch and Sundance planning and participating in the first and third. Butch's good friend Elzy Lay was badly wounded before being captured after the Folsom robbery and was sentenced to a long term in the New Mexico penitentiary. With the Pinkerton detectives ceaselessly in pursuit, several others of the Wild Bunch were now being arrested or gunned down.

———◦◦◦◦———

After the Tipton train robbery, Butch and Sundance decided to have one more go at a bank before departing their familiar Rocky Mountain country. They chose a far distant town, Winnemucca in western Nevada, and took Bill Carver with them for third man. At high noon of September 19, 1900, after studying the layout of the First National Bank, they rode boldly into town without their train robbery masks. Within five minutes they had more than $32,000 in their possession and were galloping out of Winnemucca. Others of the Wild Bunch probably helped with the swift escape, most likely Harvey Logan and Ben Kilpatrick. With fast horses stationed at close intervals, they rode a hundred miles north of Winnemucca while posses were still being formed to pursue them.

As soon as they were well into Idaho each of the robbers set off alone in a different direction. From their subsequent actions it appears that they were aware that this successful bank robbery marked the approaching end of the Wild Bunch. By varied routes they made their ways out of the mountain fastnesses of their youth and late in the year met by pre-arrangement more than a thousand miles away in Fort Worth, Texas.

There they went on a wild spree, bought expensive suits of clothes,

The train robbery at Tipton, Wyoming, on August 29, 1900, resulted in quick formation of a posse, including Deputy U.S. Marshall Joe LeFors (seated, third from left). The group secured their horses in a stock car and boarded an attached way car in Rawlins, Wyoming for the 65-mile train ride to the Tipton railroad yards and the nearby robbery site for pursuit on horseback. Courtesy of Pinkerton, Inc.

fancy shirts and shoes, and derby hats, which were then the height
of fashion. Butch also purchased a bicycle and learned to perform ac-
robatic feats on it.

One day in December, Carver, Logan, Kilpatrick, Butch, and
Sundance went around to the Schwartz photo gallery dressed in their
resplendent finery and sat for a photograph together. They ordered
a dozen prints, and Butch with his usual bravado mailed one to the
First National Bank in Winnemucca, thanking the bankers for
making it possible for the Wild Bunch to dress so elegantly. The
photograph, however, set the alert Pinkertons on their tail, and
perhaps suspecting this, the outlaws moved on to San Antonio.

It was while they were in San Antonio, probably at Fanny Porter's
place, that Butch, Sundance, and Harvey Logan discussed plans to
go to South America. Logan was not enthusiastic, but apparently it
was he who suggested they rob one more train to build up their
financial resources before leaving the country. On July 3, 1901, they
stopped a Great Northern express near Wagner, Montana, demolished
the baggage car, and made off with thousands of dollars in unsigned
banknotes. A few months later, while trying to exchange some of the
notes for regular greenbacks, Logan was caught and jailed.

Meanwhile Butch, Sundance, and Etta Place were enjoying the
sights of New York City before sailing for South America. With
plenty of funds in hand they bought the finest tailored clothes the
city offered. Dressed like a high society couple, Etta and Sundance
visited De Young's gallery on Broadway and had a full length photograph made. Etta wore a velvet gown and displayed a watch she had
bought at Tiffany's. Scarcely anyone viewing this pair would have
placed their origins anywhere west of the Hudson River.

———⟫●⟪———

Difficult as it is to document the movements of Butch and Sundance
within their own country, their trail across South America is a morass
of confused identities, slipshod official records, and deliberately contrived blind alleys — all overlaid with the imaginative prose of
various traveling journalists.

Part of a letter that Butch wrote to Elzy Lay's mother in Utah still exists. It was dated August 10, 1902, and he was writing from Cholila, Chubut Province, in southern Argentina. Evidently the fugitive trio had purchased a ranch near Cholila and may have used the names George Parker, Harry Longabaugh, and Senora Longabaugh. At times, however, during the South American period, Sundance called himself Harry E. Place or Lewis Nelson. Butch sometimes used Thompson, Ryan, Maxwell, or Gibbon as a last name.

For some reason, possibly because they had run out of money, the three left the Argentina ranch early in 1906. In March of that year, a bank at Mercedes was robbed. A woman was said to have held the horses for the two male banditos. From time to time other robberies followed at widely separated places, in Bolivia as well as in Argentina.

Legend has it that some time in 1906 or 1907, Etta Place fell ill and asked Sundance to take her back to the United States. Traveling as Mr. and Mrs. Harry E. Place, they stopped briefly in New York, then continued by train to Denver, where she entered a hospital. Some have speculated that she had appendicitis, others that she was pregnant. Anyway she paid her hospital bill and departed — to vanish physically as she entered the myths of outlaw women.

As for Sundance, he returned to South America where he joined Butch for numerous undocumented robberies of banks, railroad trains, and pack-mules carrying gold. One day in 1908 (or was it 1909 or 1911?), the audacious pair rode into the town of San Vicente in Bolivia. There they were surrounded by Bolivian cavalry. After many years of using revolvers harmlessly in robberies, Butch Cassidy finally had to kill his first man.

The end of the violent shootout is disputed; Butch and Sundance were killed, or Sundance was killed but Butch escaped, or Butch and Sundance both escaped.

Like all legendary bandits, Butch and Sundance refused to die. Until well into the 20th century rumors of their living presence constantly arose. Some serious researchers claimed that there never was a shootout at San Vicente, and that both men returned to the United States. Butch's sister stated in a university press book published in

1975 that he visited the family home in 1925. Sundance rejoined Etta Place in Mexico City; they lived for a time in New Mexico; he did not die until 1957 and is allegedly buried at Casper, Wyoming. Butch took the name William T. Phillips and lived in Spokane, Washington, until his death in a nursing home on July 20, 1937.

We may believe what we choose to believe, but in truth outlaw gods are immortal, stamped into the American consciousness as firmly as our most honorable heroes. Butch and Sundance will live forever, each generation of us adding to, or withdrawing something from, the enduring myth.

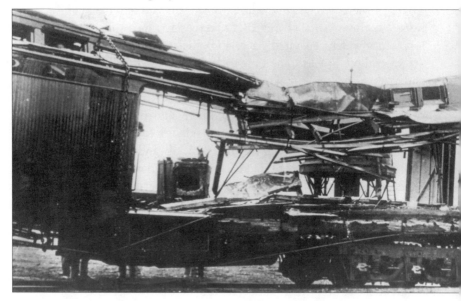

One trademark of a Butch Cassidy train robbery was the use of large amounts of dynamite to splinter the sides of an express car. Notice, the safe is visible in the center among debris of the car destroyed near Wilcox, Wyoming. Courtesy of Pinkerton, Inc.

PART IV

Seeds of Change

Sketches of Blackfoot Indians individually and in camp. By Frederic Remington.

14

Story of the Plains Indians

efore the Spaniards brought the horse to America, there were no Plains Indians as we know them in our history. Tribes lived on the Plains, of course, but their nomadic range was restricted. They hunted the buffalo, but most of them also depended upon some form of agriculture for food. Their only domesticated animal was the dog; when the tribes moved from one place to another they used their dogs as beasts of burden.

In 1541, one of Coronado's men noted that Indians on the Texas Plains used a sort of Moorish pack saddle with girths on their dogs, while at the same time the animals pulled travois poles loaded with baggage. "When the load gets disarranged," he said, "the dogs howl, calling some one to fix them right." Another of the Spaniards observed that the dogs had sores on their withers like pack animals. "These dogs carry the Indians' houses [tipis] and they have the sticks of their houses dragging along tied to the pack saddles, besides the loads which they carry on top, and the load may be, according to the dog, from 35 to 50 pounds." In Plains Indian sign language the sign for dog was made by separating the first and second fingers and drawing them in front of the chest like spread travois poles.

When the Southwestern Indians first saw Coronado's horses they were terrified, believing the mounted Spaniards to be monsters with the heads and trunks of men and the bodies of four-legged animals. Rumors spread across the Plains that these ferocious beings devoured people. This attitude changed quickly, however, and within a few years after the first horses came to the West, they were viewed as sacred animals which the gods had presented to the earth people. Some tribes welcomed horses to their villages by spreading cloths on the ground for them to walk upon. As none of the tribes had a name for the horse, they had to invent one. Understandably the word "dog" was often used — "the Great Dog of the White Men" being a common designation. The Sioux named it *sunka wakan*, or mysterious dog, and the Blackfeet called it elk dog.

At first they used horses as big dogs, fastening larger travois to the animals and loading them with heavier burdens, but long after the tribes obtained horses, they still continued to use dogs to haul light loads. When Francis Parkman was at Fort Laramie in 1846 he saw a large number of dogs carrying Oglalla Sioux children and small puppies in baskets attached to travois. As the dogs crossed a stream "the little black-eyed children, from one year of age upward, clung fast with both hands to the edges of their basket, and looked over in alarm at the water rising so near them, sputtering and making wry mouths as it splashed against their faces. Some of the dogs, encumbered by their load, were carried down the current, yelping piteously, and the old squaws would rush into the water, seize their favorites by the neck, and drag them out."

Before the coming of the horse, most of the tribes we know as Plains Indians lived on the fringes of the Great Plains or along rivers, dwelling in permanent villages, hunting whenever opportunity afforded, and engaging in the growing of corn, melons, squash, beans, tobacco, and other native crops. They also practiced the arts of pottery making, weaving, and skin dressing. Typical semi-agricultural Plains Indians were tribes belonging to the Caddo-speaking confederation which included the Wichitas and Pawnees and extended from the Arikaras of North Dakota to the Wacos far down in Texas.

When Coronado and his men marched northward across the flat dry Plains in what is now Kansas in search of the golden cities of Quivira, they found Quivira but the cities were only villages of grass houses glowing under the sun. The Quivirans were Wichita

Indians. "The houses were of straw," recorded one of the disillusioned Spaniards, "and most of them round, and the straw reached
down to the ground like a wall. They have something like a sentry
box outside, where the Indians sit or recline." The "sentry boxes" were
brush-arbors which many southern Plains Indians use to this day.

The Wichita grass house was a marvel of engineering with simple
materials. The supporting timbers were upright logs, forming the
sides of a square, with forks at the tops across which other timbers were
laid. Long, flexible poles were pulled over this frame to form a dome,
and then were bound firmly with elm bark. Smaller poles were next
fastened horizontally around the circumference of the structure.
When this was done, the builders were ready to attach the bundles
of long grass, laying them on shingle fashion, beginning at the bottom and fastening the bundles so that each round was overlapped by
the one above. All were tied on with elm bark so adroitly that only
the keenest eye could detect the fastenings. The inner diameter of a
house varied from thirty to fifty feet, with a fire-hole sunk in the center of the earthen floor. Opposite doorways facing east and west and
a smoke-hole near the top furnished sufficient ventilation.

Platforms around the inner wall served as seats and beds, and as
many as fifteen persons could live comfortably within a structure that
was cool in summer and warm in winter. In 1834, George Catlin
painted a Wichita grass house village, which must have been about
the same as the ones seen by Coronado three centuries earlier. Catlin
called the Wichitas by the name Pawnee-Picts, given them by French
traders — Panis Piques — because the Wichitas delighted in tattoo-
ing their bodies with colorful designs.

During their stay among the Wichitas in Kansas, the starving
Spaniards replenished themselves from the tribal fields of corn, beans,
melons, and pumpkins, and found plums of "excellent flavor" and
grapes of "fairly good flavor." Wichitas pulped and dried their wild
fruits for preservation into the winter months, mixing some with dried
buffalo meat to make pemmican. Their balanced diet probably
accounted for the fine physical condition of the Wichitas, noted ad-
miringly by the Spaniards, most of whom were a foot shorter than

their towering hosts. "The women are comely," Coronado said, "with faces more like Moorish than Indian women."

Available nearby for the Wichitas and all the other semi-agricultural tribes on the Plains were the great herds of buffalo. "We have proof," said one of the Spaniards, "that vast numbers of buffalo exist there, as many as anyone could imagine." No matter how plentiful the buffalo were, hunting them without horses was a time-consuming occupation, and may explain the origin of the sharp division of labor between the sexes in Indian tribes. The men were the hunters, and long walks on foot to find a herd, long waits before the animals could be maneuvered into position for a kill, long hauls of meat back to the villages, left little time for males to help with household and agricultural tasks.

Before the coming of the horse, several methods were used to hunt buffalo on foot. One of the oft-told tales is that of Indians chasing herds off high cliffs so that the animals fell to their deaths below and could then be butchered for skins and meat. This method was sometimes used by the Crow, Blackfoot, and other tribes along the fringes of the Rockies where precipices and herds were more easily brought together. On the vast stretches of the Great Plains, only luck and chance would bring a herd, a hunting party, and a cliff in proximity.

The most common method was for large numbers of hunters to encircle a segment of a herd and then rush in on foot and kill as many buffalo as possible before they escaped. Some tribes on the Northern Plains devised an entrapment in which piles of rocks and logs were placed in a V-shape, the wide end of the V being a good grazing ground while the narrow end led into a natural or man-made corral where the captured buffalo could be slain as they milled around.

According to Rudolph Kurz, a Swiss artist who traveled through the West in the 1840's, the Assiniboins trapped buffalo by building circular enclosures of logs and boughs, leaving a single narrow entrance. They then set up two rows of stakes diverging from either side of the entrance and forming a passageway wide enough for a herd to move through. "As soon as the hunters are aware of a nearby herd, one of them, disguised as a buffalo, goes out to meet it, and by imitating the cry of a calf, by bellowing, by shaking his buffalo robe, and resorting to all sorts of motions endeavors to attract the attention of the animal nearest him." The natural curiosity of buffalo usually excited them into following the decoy, who on hands and knees crawled slowly and deliberately back toward the enclosure. "If the decoy makes but one bungling movement," Kurz said, "he may betray himself, startle the animals, cause them to take flight, spoil the hunt, expose himself to ridicule, and lose his reputation as a skilled and practiced huntsman to whom only this most difficult undertaking might be entrusted."

From years of observation, the Plains hunters knew that the leader of a small herd was more likely to be a cow than a bull. Nicolas Point, a Jesuit missionary, called her the "queen," and said that if a hunter could approach close enough to bring her down "you will see the entire herd group itself around her, manifesting nothing but amazement. Recharge your rifle, or better, if you are not far distant, take another arrow, but don't hurry. Wait until the herd has calmed down. Then shoot again, and continue in this way until you have bagged a sufficient number."

Hunting in winter when snows were deep and lakes ice-covered was an advantage to tribes that had snowshoes. Buffalo were slowed by deep drifts, giving snowshoed hunters a chance to approach close enough to kill them with lances. Whole herds could sometimes be trapped on slippery ice. Even after the horse came to the Plains, much winter hunting was done on foot. Buffalo skins obtained in cold months supposedly made warmer bedding and garments than those taken in the summer hunting season.

━━━━◦○◦◦━━━

"The Comanches," said Captain Randolph Marcy in 1852, "are the most expert horsemen in the world." Many others who knew the Comanches of the 19th century corroborated Marcy's statement. "In racing horses and riding," George Catlin agreed, "they are not equaled by any other Indians on the continent." Perhaps the reason for this Comanche superiority was that they were among the earliest of the Plains Indians to obtain horses.

Not until at least a century after the soldiers of Coronado amazed the southern tribes with the mounts did horses begin to appear on the Texas Plains, the home of the Comanches. Most of these horses came from New Mexico, center of Spanish settlement, either escaping to roam wild or being captured in raids made principally by Comanches. Others came from northern Mexico where Spaniards were establishing ranches; they forbade the Indians of Mexico to ride mounts — although some did, even before the Comanches.

As early as the 18th century traders from Mexico — known as Comancheros —made long journeys into the Plains to trade horses to the Comanches for buffalo skins and other pelts. By the first half of the 19th century, the Comanches had so many horses they reversed the trading process and used their mounts as mediums of exchange for guns and other manufactured goods. In 1840 when the Comanches met with the Cheyennes on the Arkansas River near Bent's Fort to make peace between the tribes, there were long discussions about what gifts should be exchanged on this ceremonial occasion. "The Comanches have many horses," said one of their chiefs, "as many as we need. We do not wish to accept any horses, but we shall be glad to receive other gifts. We have made a road to give many horses to you."

For a century the Comanches had indeed been making a road to furnish horses to all the tribes who lived north of them. Even before they obtained horses, the Comanches were a far-ranging people, and because of their close blood-kinship with the Shoshone, the latter tribe was mounted earlier than many Indians who lived south of them. The Shoshones in turn traded some of the animals to neighboring tribes, and lost a considerable number to the Blackfeet who took them in raids.

At the height of their power as horse Indians, a single Comanche band roaming the Southern Plains often traveled with several thousand animals. In the 1850's, Captain Marcy noted that it was not unusual for a Comanche warrior to possess between fifty and one hundred mounts, and one chief was known to have more than a thousand. By comparison, a Sioux warrior was considered to be extremely wealthy if he owned as many as thirty horses, a Cheyenne twenty, a

Cree five or six. Usually, the farther north a tribe lived from Comanche country, the fewer were their horses.

The Comanches acquired their vast herds by trading, by raiding,
by capturing wild horses, and by breeding. Captain Marcy discovered
their fondness for their mounts when he tried to buy an especially
swift one from a chief. The Comanche leader could not be persuaded
to part with the horse for any amount of presents. He said if he were
to trade him, it would prove a calamity because it often required all
the speed of that particular animal to insure success in a buffalo
chase. The horse's loss therefore would be felt by all the tribe, and the
chief would be looked upon as a very foolish man if he let the animal go. "Besides," said the chief, patting the horse on the neck, "I love
him very much."

The first use the Plains tribes made of horses was to transfer to them
the burdens formerly carried by their dogs. This made it necessary to
develop complex travois accessories. Longer and heavier lodgepoles
and stronger rawhide ties were needed. After the Indians learned to
ride and began making wooden saddles, these were found to be excellent hitch supports for the travois poles.

As soon as they adopted the larger travois they were able to add
cages made of bent willows to the rawhide travois rests so that
children and old people would not fall off while traveling. Later
they covered the cage frameworks with hides or blankets to serve as
sunshades.

For journeys when lodgepoles were not used, they quickly learned
the technique of fastening packhorse luggage to their mounts. Double
saddlebags made of rectangular pieces of dressed animal skins could
be thrown over the saddle and secured at the cantle by a slit opening. Women riders often placed these bags over the center of the
saddle, covered them with a buffalo robe, and used the arrangement
as a comfortable seat. For some reason saddlebags came to be considered as woman's luggage, and men seldom carried them. Women
also were responsible for transporting the parfleche bags in which

Plains Indians stored their food and clothing. In the days of dog travois, most tribes had some sort of folding rawhide skin to protect valuable articles in transit. With the coming of the horse, these were considerably enlarged, developing into parfleches which were made of rawhide or tanned buffalo skin and shaped somewhat like a large envelope two or three feet long and about one and a half feet wide. When folded and fastened together in pairs, parfleches could be removed from the travois and attached to the horse's back or saddle.

Long before they obtained horses, the Plains tribes were using buffalo rawhide for ropes and straps, and they quickly applied these to their animals for bridles, hobbles, ties, halters, and lariats. Some tribes also wove buffalo hair into quite serviceable ropes for similar uses.

Saddles as we know them came much later. The first Indian saddles were little more than pads of soft animal skins, stuffed with dried grass or deer hair, and were girthed to horses with wide rawhide straps. Gradually the pad saddles became more complex, with stirrup straps, ornamental knobs, and decorative markings being added. Daniel Harmon, a fur trader, described a pack saddle in use on the Northern Plains early in the 19th century: "On the back of the horse, they put a dressed buffalo skin, on the top of which they placed a pad, from which are suspended stirrups, made of wood and covered with the skin of the testicles of the buffalo."

The first frame saddles were traded from Mexico, and they represented considerable wealth for the owners. It was natural that when the Indians attempted to make their own frames, they followed the Spanish style, then modified it through the years. With the growth of the fur trade, among the principal articles in demand at company posts along the Missouri were saddles. By this time, the Plains Indians were beginning to alter and redecorate the white man's saddle for their own special uses. John C. Ewers noted that a saddle taken from an Indian who participated in the Custer battle had been stripped of its commercial leather rigging and equipped with Indian-made stirrup straps, stirrups, and cinch.

Woman and children of the Stump Horn family (Cheyenne) prepare to relocate to another encampment using a horse-drawn travois to transport their possessions. Photograph by Christian Barthelmess. Courtesy of Montana Historical Society, Helena.

One piece of horse gear created by Plains Indians was the horse-mask. In 1806, Alexander Henry described masks that he saw on the mounts of a band of Cheyenne warriors. The Cheyennes' horses "were masked in a very singular manner, to imitate the head of a buffalo, red deer, or cabbrie, with horns, the mouth and nostrils — even the eyes — trimmed with red cloth. This ornamentation gave them a very fierce appearance." The Blackfeet and Crows also devised elaborate horse-masks, usually fitted with horns and decorated with quills and bright-colored feathers. As late as the 1880's, Frederic Remington saw a mask on a Blackfoot war pony "gorgeous with red flannel, brass tack heads, silver plates and feathers."

These horse masks may have been derived from early observations of Spanish horse armor, but more likely they were a part of the magic which almost every tribe attributed to their mounts. Horses very early became fixed in tribal mythology and were treated as supernatural beings sent to earth by the gods. Costumes and colors held symbolic meanings in all phases of Plains Indian culture; therefore the colors of a horse's coat and its appurtenances were of great significance. Some tribes esteemed white horses, while others preferred blacks or bays or the distinctively marked pintos. Natural colors were often embellished with bright hues painted on the horse's coat or attached to the animal in the form of bits of gay-colored cloth in the tail or mane — or in a horse-mask.

Because they were regarded as sacred animals — just as corn was a sacred plant to agricultural tribes — horses naturally became a part of tribal religions. This belief was so persistent that even after conversion to Christianity, Indians sometimes depicted, on the walls of their churches, horses soaring to Heaven. One of the most common objects of magic carried by medicine men was a horse fetish. This might be a tuft of horse hair or a small stone figurine shaped like a horse and believed to endow its owner with great powers. The wisest of these holy men were walking repositories of vast stores of unwritten *materia medica*, based upon botanical sources, which aided them in healing sick or injured horses. Long before the coming of white settlers and ranchers, they knew which plants on the Great Plains were deadly if eaten by their precious animals.

⟹〉●〈⟸

From birth, Plains Indians were closely allied to horses through tribal rituals. In some tribes it was the custom for mothers to take their sons' umbilical cords and tie them to the tails or manes of favorite ponies; others would bury the cords in horse tracks to insure future harmony with the animals. Through puberty ceremonies and marriage ceremonies and on to death, the horse was a central figure. Horse songs were sung to both males and females at coming-of-age rituals; horses were traditional marriage gifts; unless a dead person's horse was slain, he or she could not ride to the other world.

When one considers what horses brought to the Plains Indians, it is no mystery that they were so highly regarded. From earth-bound pedestrians, the Indians were changed to creatures of the wind. "Without the horse, the Indian was a half-starved skulker in the timber," said ethnologist James Mooney, "creeping up on foot toward the unwary deer or building a brush corral with infinite labor to surround a herd of antelope, and seldom venturing more than a few days' journey from home. With the horse he was transformed into the daring buffalo hunter able to procure in a single day enough food to supply his family for a year, leaving him free to sweep the plains with his war parties along a range of a thousand miles."

In a way the change was comparable to what mechanization of industry and agriculture did to free the white man from long hours of labor so that he might indulge his fancy for sport, travel, art, and meditation. With horses available to carry their travois and their tipis, tribes no longer had to wait for migratory buffalo to come to them. They could follow the seasonal movements of herds. The semi-nomads became nomads, which brought them into more frequent contacts with other tribes. Except in cases of long-standing tribal enmities, this led to exchanges of goods, foods, crafts, and knowledge. Thus was created an era of prosperity for the Plains Indians — a brief period of less than a century during which few tribes wanted for food, shelter, or clothing, when there was leisure to practice the arts, enjoy the natural world of sky, earth, water, plants, and animals. In that time the Plains Indians became poets, and their contemporary speeches that have survived read like poetry.

The buffalo, of course, was the other necessary element in the golden age of the Great Plains, teeming herds in the hundreds of thousands roaming from Canada south into Texas. "There is such a quantity of them," reported one of Coronado's men, "that I do not know what to compare them with, except with the fish of the sea . . . there were so many that many times when we started to pass through the midst of them and wanted to go through to the other side of them, we were not able to, because the country was covered with them."

A Franciscan friar accompanying that same band of exploring Spaniards was probably the first white man to recognize the economic importance of the buffalo to the people of the Plains. "With the skins they make their houses, with the skins they clothe and shoe themselves, of the skins they make rope, and also of the wool; from the sinews they make threads, with which they sew their clothes and also their houses; from the bones they make awls; the dung serves them for wood, because there is nothing else in that country; the stomachs serve them for pitchers and vessels from which they drink; they live on the flesh; they sometimes eat it half roasted and warmed over the dung, at other times raw; seizing it with their fingers, they pull it out with one hand and with a flint knife in the other they cut off mouthfuls, and thus swallow it half chewed; they eat the fat raw, without warming it; they drink the blood just as it leaves the cows, and at other times after it has run out, cold and raw; they have no other means of livelihood."

Even so, the friar's list omitted numerous other uses made by Plains Indians of the buffalo. From the bones: saddle trees, shovels, knives, From the sinews: cinches, bowstrings, and glue. From the bladder: pouches and medicine bags. From the horns: spoons, powderhorns, and cups. From the hair: ropes, saddle pad filler, and headdresses. From the tails: whips and fly brushes. And from the rawhide, an endless list of household articles, horse gear, apparel, and weapons equipment.

Like the horse, the buffalo entered into Plains mythology and religion to become a sacred animal. Almost every important ceremony included some symbol of the buffalo. In the Sun Dance, the figure of a buffalo was usually mounted on the center pole, and the dancers dragged buffalo skulls tied to ropes that were in turn fastened to skewers inserted in their bodies. Buffalo hair was always important in the preparation of medicine bundles. Without the support of the spirit of a buffalo, a warrior was thought unlikely to obtain success in either hunting or war.

—————⟫●⟪—————

Who were the Plains Indians? They consisted of about thirty tribes, the best known of which were the Arapaho, Arikara, Assiniboin, Atsina or Gros Ventre, Blackfoot, Cheyenne, Comanche, Crow, Hidatsa or Minitari, Iowa, Kansa, Kiowa, Mandan, Omaha, Osage, Oto, Pawnee, Ponca, Sioux, and Wichita. In some of their ways the Shoshone Ute, Nez Perce, and Flathead tribes were like the Plains people, but they are usually considered to be Rocky Mountain Indians. The first tribes to occupy the Plains were probably the Arapaho, Cheyenne, Crow, and Blackfoot, moving from east to west, following the streams or using their dog travois for transport.

The largest and most dominant of the tribes during the golden age of the Plains Indians was the Sioux. The nomenclature for these remarkable people, who are often called Dakota, is quite involved. They fall into three major groups, the Santee, Teton, and Yankton. All came from the east, traveling by rivers, and were known as "canoe Indians" when they reached the Minnesota country. The Tetons, who comprised more than half the tribe, were the first to abandon their birch-bark lodges and move out upon the Plains to live in buffalo-hide tipis. They were the first of the Sioux to obtain horses and were among the best riders of the Plains.

The general locations of plains Indian tribes of the late 1830s and early 1840s are shown on this map prepared by John T. Bradway (American History Illustrated staff). Within the next few decades, this pattern would change considerably in part because of inter-tribal warfare, clashes with the military, disappearance of buffalo herds, and the relegation of tribes to designated reservations.

During the period of the 19th century Indian Wars, the six divisions of Tetons were in the forefront of battle and became well-known in history: the Brule, Hunkpapa, Miniconjou, Oglalla, Sans Arc, and Two Kettle. The Yanktons followed the Tetons to the Plains, keeping close to the Missouri River where their early contacts with explorers and fur traders were mostly peaceable. The Santees, sometimes known as woodland Sioux, came late to the Plains, being driven there after their Minnesota lands were taken from them following the so-called Sioux uprising of 1862.

From the time of the American Revolution to the Indian Wars of the 1870's, the Teton Sioux ruled a vast area — from Minnesota across the Dakotas into eastern Montana and Wyoming, and much of western Nebraska. Population figures are unreliable until after the Indian Wars, but at the height of their power, when all the Plains probably contained no more than 200,000 Indians, the Sioux numbered between 30,000 and 40,000, or about one sixth of the total. They were always considered a handsome people, their pride showing in their behavior and their faces, their ways of walking and riding.

Like all peoples, the Sioux varied in their physical appearance from thin to fat, from short to tall, but most of them — both men and women — were tall and lithe until middle age brought heaviness to their bodies. Their strong faces, with wide-spread, deep-brown eyes and aquiline noses gave them a combination of dignity and handsomeness beyond that of most other Indian peoples.

In his study of the Sioux, Royal Hassrick found that their ideals of conduct placed bravery as the highest goal a member of the tribe could seek. From earliest childhood, the courage of a Sioux was constantly tested by older members of the tribe. The stories they were told, the games they played, all held an underlying theme of fearlessness. Next in importance was the ability to endure discomfort and pain without flinching. To cry out from suffering, or even to show too much outward sign of any feeling — even friendship or affection — was considered unworthy of a Sioux. A third ideal was generosity. Members of the tribe who owned material things were expected to share them with those who owned nothing. It was not how much an individual owned that gave him status; it was how much he gave away, especially to orphans, the crippled, and the old.

From the Sioux have come many great names, some as well-known in the history of the West as those of their white adversaries. Among them are Sitting Bull, Crazy Horse, Red Cloud, Spotted Tail, Shakopee, Wabasha, Little Crow, Philip Deloria and later members of that famous family, John Grass, Black Elk the older and the younger, Gall, Hump, American Horse, and many others.

———————

Living always to the west of the Sioux were the Cheyennes. They were already in Minnesota when the Sioux arrived there from the east and drove them out upon the Plains. The enmity between the tribes was short-lived. After the Sioux became Plains Indians, the two tribes made peace and became active allies in the wars of the 19th century.

As well-known as the Cheyennes were, they probably never reached a population of more than 5,000. Although they often camped beside the Sioux and patterned their dress and some of their ceremonies after those of the larger tribe, the Cheyennes were a fiercely independent people and maintained their customs, their unique council of chiefs and military societies, until their civilization was destroyed in the 1870's. Of their six warrior organizations, the Hotamitanio or "dog soldiers" became best known to the white men. No other warriors on the plains equaled the Cheyennes in fighting spirit, determination, or endurance.

Largely because of geography, the Cheyennes split into northern and southern divisions. The northern group lived around the Black Hills and in eastern Wyoming, using Fort Laramie as a trading base, while the southerners roamed the Colorado and Kansas Plains, with Bent's Fort as their trading post. In recognition of their magnificent physical appearance, the Cheyennes at the height of their power were sometimes called "the Beautiful People." After fighting them for many years, Colonel Ranald Mackenzie saluted them: "I regard the Cheyenne tribe of Indians, after an acquaintance with quite a number of bands, as the finest body of that race which I have ever met."

Certainly the Cheyennes had an abundance of imaginative and audacious young men. They were probably the only Indians who tried to stop the progress of the railroad across their hunting grounds by derailing a locomotive and wrecking a freight train. They accomplished this near Plum Creek, Nebraska in August 1867. They and the Kiowas may also have been the only warriors who fancied Spanish armor. Long after the Spanish soldiers in America abandoned its use, an occasional Cheyenne or Kiowa dressed in rusted mail would appear to challenge an enemy.

<hr>

In the 19th century the Cheyennes came near to total extinction. During the days of the fur trade trappers brought in smallpox, which wiped out hundreds. In 1849 the emigrants brought cholera, which killed more than a third of the tribe. In 1864 they suffered heavy losses in the Sand Creek Massacre; in 1868 this was repeated in the Battle of the Washita. In 1877, Colonel Mackenzie's troopers killed many more before compelling submission of the tribe to reservation life in Indian Territory. In 1878-79 the flight from confinement in Indian Territory to Montana left alive only a handful of a once proud and powerful people.

George Bird Grinnell spent many years with the survivors. He came to know them as warm comrades and friends. "While their culture differs from ours in some respects," he wrote, "fundamentally they are like ourselves, except insofar as their environment has obliged them to adopt a mode of life and of reasoning that is not quite our own and which, without experience, we do not readily understand."

From the Cheyennes came these great men of American history: Black Kettle, Dull Knife, Little Wolf, Roman Nose, Tall Bull, George Bent, White Antelope, and Two Moon. Several of them died defending their way of life.

The closest allies of the Cheyennes were the Arapahoes, a friendship that goes back so far into the past that no one can say when it began. Both tribes belong to the Algonquian linguistic stock, and both moved out upon the Plains at about the same time. Like the

Cheyennes, the Arapahoes were divided into northern and southern branches, and the tribes of both divisions hunted and camped with the Cheyennes. Whenever one tribe was in trouble the other always rushed to its aid. After the Cheyennes allied themselves with the Sioux, the Arapahoes followed their example, participating in many of the wars of the 19th century. The high population mark of the Arapahoes was probably around 3,000.

Those who knew them best described the Arapahoes as a brave and kindly people, their customs being similar to those of their neighbors with one main exception: Instead of placing their dead upon scaffolds, they buried them in the ground. Comparing the Arapahoes with their friends the Cheyennes, James Mooney said the Cheyennes were inclined to stand upon their dignity, were difficult to convince, and slow to give their consent to any proposition. "The Cheyennes always want to know what you want to do it for," he said, "while the Arapahoes are naturally accommodating and of a friendly disposition." Little Raven, Left Hand, and Yellow Robe were among the best known of the Arapaho leaders.

⟹⟩◆⟨⟸

The Northwestern Plains was Crow and Blackfoot country. Like the Sioux, the Blackfoot tribe was a loose confederacy of three major divisions, the Siksika, Piegan, and Blood, numbering together close to 30,000 people. Their range was as large as that of the Sioux, reaching from the Yellowstone River on the south to the Saskatchewan in Canada. Today they have two reservations, one in Canada and one in Montana. Because their western territories were mountainous, some bands of the Crow and Blackfoot adjusted to mountain living; in fact a sub-tribe of the Crow broke away and became known as the Mountain Crows.

The Crow and Blackfoot were aggressive tribes, carrying on continual wars with each other and with most of their neighbors. The coming of the horse and the fur trade undoubtedly contributed to their militancy. As soon as the Shoshones obtained horses from their Comanche cousins, the Crows and Blackfeet began raiding for the highly prized animals. With a population of fewer than 5,000, the Crows could not compete with the power of their Blackfoot neighbors, but they managed to acquire enormous herds of horses.

No Indians placed a higher value on horses than did the Blackfeet, who would travel hundreds of miles to raid herds of the fiercest tribes. Nor did any tribe equal them in the quality of their animals and the excellence of their horse gear.

When the British developed their great fur trading posts in the Northwest, the Blackfeet were among the first Indians to be drawn into their sphere of influence. They took furs and buffalo hides north to the Saskatchewan River, trading for cloth, utensils, tools, and flintlocks. With flintlocks they had the power to capture more horses, and soon the Blackfeet were trading horses to fur trappers for better firearms. Because their new power depended upon British fur trade sources, they became allies of the British and served as mercenaries of a sort against rival American trappers and traders. After American fur companies pushed up the Missouri River and established similar relationships with the Crows and other tribes, an accentuation of old enmities naturally followed.

When Maximilian, Prince of Wied, visited the Crows in the 1830's, he was impressed by the number of horses they possessed. He estimated a herd grazing around a village of four hundred tipis to contain about ten thousand animals. "The Crow women," he said, "are very skillful in various kinds of work, and their shirts and dresses of bighorn leather, embroidered and ornamented with dyed porcupine quills, are particularly handsome, as well as their buffalo robes, which are painted and embroidered in the same manner. . . . The men make their weapons very well, and with much taste, especially their large bows, covered with the horn of the elk or bighorn, and often with the skin of the rattlesnake. . . . Long hair is considered as a great beauty, and they take great pains with it. The hair of one of their chiefs, called Long Hair, was ten feet long, some feet of which trailed on the gound when he stood upright."

Perhaps it was their haughty manners which led Maximilian to express the belief that the Crows held all white men in contempt, yet

"Encampment of the Piekann Indians" by Swiss artist Karl Bodmer. An engraving with aquatint and hand colored. Courtesy of Joslyn Art Museum, Omaha, Nebraska; Gift of the Enron Art Foundation.

he admitted that they were always hospitable to him and his companions. Even at that early date, Crows were serving as scouts for white explorers and brigades of trappers, a practice which continued to the days of George Armstrong Custer. Crow scouts led him to battle on the Little Big Horn. Remembered in history are the names of Curly, Plenty Coups, White Man Runs Him, and White Swan.

Because they were located outside the main streams of westward white migration, neither the Crow nor the Blackfoot tribes were drawn into the Indian Wars. Except for their conflicts with American fur trappers, the Blackfeet seemed content to go about their business of enriching themselves with horses, and with the hunting of buffalo and trading for such of the white man's goods as they needed. Their last great battle was fought in Canada in 1870 with a large war party of Crees, and in 1888, when the United States Government ordered them confined to their present reservation in northwestern Montana, they offered no resistance.

"The Blackfeet," said Maximilian, "are robust, generally well made men, and some of the women and girls are very pretty. The men are partly broad shouldered and muscular, partly of middle stature, and thickset." When he visited them, Maximilian was received with hospitality and lodged in the tipi of a chief. "The owner, with his whole family, slept in the open air; nobody dared to molest the guests."

According to George Grinnell, the Blackfeet had a custom of changing their names almost every year, and whenever a warrior counted coup in battle he was entitled to a new name. "A Blackfoot will never tell his name if he can avoid it. He believes that if he should speak his name, he would be unfortunate in all his undertakings." Perhaps this is why history contains so few familiar names of Blackfoot leaders. The great chief Many Horses, for instance, is also recorded in history by three other names — Sits-in-the-Middle, Dog, and Little Dog.

Historians say that there were three great centers of power among the Plains Indians — the Sioux on the Northern Plains, the Blackfeet in the Northwest, and the allied Comanche-Kiowa tribes on the Southern Plains. The Comanche and Kiowa tribes both came into recorded history in the area of the Black Hills and present-day Montana and Wyoming. Culturally and linguistically the Comanches were cousins of the Shoshones. When pressure from the Sioux and other tribes became too great, the Shoshones retreated to the Rocky Mountains while the Comanches moved southward to become Plains Indians. The Kiowas also left the mountains during the 18th century, moved down into Crow country west of the Black Hills, and for a time became allies of the Crows. During this period there was considerable intermarriage of Crows and Kiowas; for example, the grandfather of the famous Kiowa leader, Kicking Bird, was a Crow.

When the Comanches were driven south by the might of the Sioux tribe, the Kiowas followed them. In the beginning, Kiowa and Comanche contacts were often hostile, but eventually leaders of the tribes met and worked out a treaty of peace which was never afterward broken. From the early years of the 19th century, Comanches and Kiowas camped and raided together, although they arranged a division of territories which insured plenty of wild game for both tribes. The Staked Plains and the valley of Red River were Comanche hunting grounds; the Kiowas roamed both sides of the Arkansas River.

For a tribe which probably never passed 3,000 at its highest point of population, the Kiowas certainly made their mark on history during their brief period of glory on the Southern Plains. They equaled the Comanches in their range of horse-raiding, traveling as far west as the Gulf of California and as far south as Durango in Mexico. They resisted fiercely every invasion by hostile red men or white men upon their last domain. James Mooney once said that the Kiowas killed more white men in proportion to their numbers than any other tribe.

One reason that so much is known about the Kiowas and the tribes they associated with is that Kiowa scribes kept elaborate pictographic records of their activities and those of their friends and enemies — annual calendars of events which were originally painted on buckskin or buffalo hides. The calendars were carefully copied and renewed from time to time as they wore out from handling. Some of the calendars that survived at the end of the Kiowa civilization were painted on heavy paper. The pictographs were arranged in a continuous spiral, beginning in the lower right-hand corner and proceeding chronologically to the center. From the winter of 1834 to the 1890's it is possible to trace the movements and activities of these people who had a sense of history and are becoming better known today as a tribe of philosophers, orators, and artists than as hunters and warriors. Among their great men of the past were Dohasan, Satanta or White Bear, Satank or Sitting Bear, White Horse, Stumbling Bear, Woman's Heart, Adoette or Big Tree, Kicking Bird, and Guipago or Lone Wolf.

The Comanches greatly outnumbered the Kiowas, their twelve divisions probably totalling 10,000 before the Red River Wars of the 19th century. "On their feet the Comanches are one of the most unattractive and slovenly-looking races of Indians I have ever seen," said George Catlin, "but the moment they mount their horses they seem at once metamorphosed, and surprise the spectator with the ease and grace of their movements." Captain Marcy admired their "bright, copper-colored complexions and intelligent countenances, their aquiline noses, thin lips, black eyes and hair." Although they acquired a reputation for ferocity and cruelty, the Comanches, like the Kiowas, also had their poets, notably Ten Bears of the Yamparika band. ("I was born upon the prairie where the wind blew free and there was nothing to break the light of the sun.") Other famous Comanches were Ishatai, Tosawi or Silver Knife, Mow-way, and Quanah Parker.

On the Central Plains before the coming of the white men, the Pawnee and Wichita tribes were dominant. Both were of Caddoan stock, with similar languages, and both were semi-agricultural, raising corn and other crops and hunting buffalo.

As we have seen, the Wichitas preferred grass houses to the tipis of other Plains tribes. For their permanent villages the Pawnees used earthen houses, but adopted buffalo-skin tipis when on the move. To begin construction of an earthen house, they first drew a circle on the ground, then excavated for two or three feet. Within the circle, beams were fastened upon forked poles to support a ring of leaning poles braced against the walls of the excavation. Additional supports and reinforcements and a framework of willow and grass thatching completed the shell. Over this the Pawnees laid a heavy coating of sod pieces, cut from the prairie so they could be overlapped like shingles. Under springtime sunshine and rains, the Pawnee houses turned green, and were sometimes brightened with wild flowers. The sod houses of the first white settlers who came to the treeless Plains were variations of the Pawnee earthen houses.

Another distinguishing feature of the Pawnees was the hair style of the warriors. They shaved their heads in a manner similar to that of some Eastern tribes, leaving a small tuft at center. On this they applied a dressing of animal fat mixed with paint which made the hair stand erect in the shape of a horn. A single braid was often worn at the back. The women wore their hair parted in the middle, with two braids hanging over their shoulders in front.

As the principal range of the Pawnees was along the Platte Valley, they came into contact with the first white travelers on the route that came to be known as the Oregon Trail. They were early victims of the white man's diseases. Before the American Civil War, the Pawnees' great confederacy of more than 10,000 people was reduced by half. Although Pawnees raided some of the wagon trains which intruded upon their territory, the tribe never made war against the United States Government. Being long-time enemies of the Sioux, Cheyenne, and other tribes to the north, it was natural for the Pawnees to enlist as scouts for the U.S. Army during the Indian Wars, the most notable group being Frank North's Pawnee Scouts.

The Pawnees remained in the Platte River country until forced to a reservation in Indian Territory during the 1870's, but long before that the Wichitas abandoned their harassed territory along the Big Bend of the Arkansas and drifted southward. Although the population of the Wichita tribe was only about a third that of the Pawnees, at one time their prosperous confederacy extended from Kansas deep into eastern Texas. As in the case of the Pawnees, the white man's diseases rather than his weapons decimated the Wichitas. When they were placed on their Indian Territory reservation, the

Wichita tribe had diminished to 572, and of the thousands of Pawnees only 1,500 remained.

—————➤●◖—————

In addition to those tribes which became well-known through participation in the Indian Wars, the Assiniboin, Gros Ventre, Hidatsa, Mandan, and Arikara also roamed the Northern Plains. Originally the Assiniboins were a division of the Yankton Sioux, many of them moving north into Canada where they formed an alliance with the Crees. At one time they probably had a population of 10,000. The Gros Ventres, or Atsinas, were related to the Arapahoes, ranging from Montana into Canada. The Hidatsas were closely allied with the Mandans; Lewis and Clark found both tribes flourishing along the Missouri River when they made their expedition to the Pacific in 1804. After fur traders brought smallpox up the river in the 1830's, fewer than a hundred Mandans survived the epidemic. These few later joined the Hidatsas who also had suffered severe losses.

The Arikaras were Caddoans, and before the coming of the white men lived with a division of the Pawnees. For some reason they separated and moved northward along the Missouri. Diseases also reduced the Arikara from a strong tribe of three thousand to only a few hundred. During the Indian Wars they were frequently called Rees. Some of them served as scouts for Custer; those most often mentioned in various accounts of the Little Big Horn were Foolish Bear, Bloody Knife, and Bobtailed Bull. Because of his friendly relations with Lewis and Clark, Shahaka or Big White of the Mandans is also of historical importance.

On the central Plains, the Ponca, Oto, Omaha, and Iowa tribes lived along the eastern fringe of the great prairie in country that was partly wooded. The Ponca and Omaha were related, having the same language, but the tribes separated after moving westward from the Ohio River country. The Oto and Iowa were also related tribes, moving often, probably because they were small in numbers and could not compete with their more numerous and warlike neighbors. From the Poncas came Standing Bear, the famous leader who was involved in

"The Interior of the Hut of a Mandan Chief" by Karl Bodmer. An engraving with aquatint, hand colored; completed after the return of the 1832–34 North American Maximilian/Bodmer expedition. Courtesy of Joslyn Art Museum, Omaha, Nebraska; Gift of the Enron Art Foundation.

the civil rights case in 1879 which resulted in Indians becoming "persons within the meaning of the law." Among his chief supporters were members of the La Flesche family, well-educated Omaha Indians — Francis, Joseph, and Susette (who became popularly known as Bright Eyes).

Farther south were the Kansa and Osage, both related to the Omaha and Ponca tribe. The Kansas, often known as the Kaws, lived along the river in the state that was named for them. The Osage was the largest of this group of tribes, all of whom can be traced back to the Ohio and Wabash river regions east of the Mississippi. When they came out of the woodlands in the 18th century, the Osages had already earned a reputation as a military power and continued their warlike ways after reaching the Plains. At one time they claimed all the territory in present-day Oklahoma north of the Arkansas River, and parts of present-day Missouri and Arkansas. The Kansa tribe lived west of the Osage. Both tribes signed treaties of peace with the United States early in the 19th century, and because of their frontier locations were in frequent contact with fur traders and explorers. When George Catlin visited them in the 1830's, he found both tribes considerably weakened by diseases but still preserving their valor as warriors. "The Osages," he said, "may justly be said to be the tallest race of men in North America, either of red or white skins; there being very few indeed of the men, at their full growth, who are less than six feet in stature, and very many of them six and a half, and others seven feet."

In the 1870's the Osages were removed to a reservation in Indian Territory, the Kansa tribe following them there shortly afterward. Famous among the Osages were Pawhuska or White Hair, and in modern times John J. Mathews, whose books about his people form an important part of the literature of the American Indians. From the Kansa tribe came the mother of Charles Curtis, the first part-American Indian to serve as Vice President of the United States, in Herbert Hoover's administration, 1929-33.

With so many tribes traveling widely over the Great Plains but speaking different tongues and dialects, it was necessary for them to develop a universal sign language. Simple systems of communication by body gestures were used by all North American Indians, but it was on the Plains that this method of exchanging information reached its highest form. Like any other language of a vigorous people it constantly changed and expanded until the Plains Indians' civilization was destroyed.

When Captain William P. Clark (known as White Hat to the Indians) first began his study of sign language in the 1870's, he was surprised at the ease with which members of tribes with entirely different vocal languages could communicate by gestures. "I found that the Indians were wonderfully good and patient instructors, and that the gesture speech was easy to acquire and remember." Clark once asked Iron Hawk of the Sioux how it was that the Plains Indians had become so skilled in sign language. Iron Hawk replied that it was a gift from the Great Spirit. "The whites have had the power given to them by the Great Spirit to read and write," he added. "He gave us the power to talk with our hands and arms, and send information with the mirror, blanket, and pony far away, and when we meet with Indians who have a different spoken language from ours, we can talk to them in signs."

As sign language became more sophisticated, metaphors were added to its single nouns and verbs, and it was Clark's opinion that one could not fully understand what was being communicated without knowing the metaphor signs. It was necessary also to understand the system of word arrangements in a sentence. Articles, conjunctions, and prepositions were omitted, and adjectives followed nouns. For example, to say in sign language *In one month I shall reach my camp,* the arrangement of signs was Moon-die-I-arrive-there-my-camp.

According to James Mooney, the tribes which became most proficient in the use of signs were the Crow, Cheyenne, and Kiowa. "In fluent grace of movement," he said, "a conversation in the sign language between a Cheyenne and a Kiowa is the very poetry of motion."

Mooney also related an experience he had with a young Arapaho who was trying to guide him on horseback to a tribal dance being held somewhere near the Canadian River. The Arapaho was not certain of the exact location for the dance, but upon sighting another Indian a mile or so away across the plain, he raised one arm and made a query in signs. The reply came back across the distance in a few simple motions; the Arapaho dance was a certain distance to the north on the opposite side of the river. "We went and saw the dance," Mooney said.

When Francis Parkman was spending a summer with the Oglalla Sioux west of Fort Laramie, he complained once in his journal of the languor and monotony of a series of inactive days in camp. The summer heat was debilitating, the talk was repetitive, and everyone lay about in the shade doing nothing. It did not occur to young Parkman that his Indian hosts were as bored as he was. What they were waiting for was a report from scouts that a buffalo herd had been sighted nearby. When the report of a sighting finally came in, the village immediately surged to life. In small parties the hunters mounted their ponies and galloped off across the plain as eagerly as 20th century men go to engage in some event which totally involved their skills and endurance.

The three most exciting events in Plains Indian life were buffalo hunts, raids for horses, and Sun Dances. Between these happenings, life flowed along in gentle ups and downs, sometimes as languorous as Parkman found it or as modern man finds it between vacations, journeys, business deals, entertainments, sports, and other pursuits which enliven his existence.

When Parkman followed after his galloping hosts, he said that he did so with a philosophic resolution to remain a quiet spectator of the hunt. "But amid the rush of horses and buffalo, the uproar and the dust," he added, "I found it impossible to sit still." As four or five buffalo ran past him in a line, he lashed his horse in quick pursuit. For the remainder of the day Parkman became a part of one of the most glorious experiences of his life — an Indian buffalo hunt.

Before the advent of the horse, buffalo hunting was work of the hardest kind, but with gradual improvement in horse gear and the acquisition of firearms, the Plains tribes converted this necessary quest for food into an organized sport. Individual hunting was discouraged, in fact was forbidden by some tribes because a single hunter might be able to kill two or three animals yet at the same time frighten the herd out of an area, forcing the entire tribe to move its camp in search of buffalo.

When scouts brought in reports of a herd in the vicinity, the tribal leaders would gather to decide the method of hunting to be used and the time of departure. While artist Rudolph Kurz was living with the Hidatsas in 1851 he noted that preliminary to a buffalo hunt the "soldiers" or warriors of the tribe would gather in their assembly lodge, and after final decisions were made they were announced throughout the village by a crier. "Nobody is allowed to take his own course contrary to the decision of the 'soldiers' on the buffalo hunt, because, according to the rules of the sport, everyone is to enjoy equal opportunities."

Each hunter usually took along two horses, leading the faster mount so as to save its strength for the buffalo chase. After the hunt, the horse ridden out from camp was used as a pack animal to bring in the meat. As the hunting party neared the herd, extraordinary precautions were taken to avoid frightening the buffalo. The approach was always from the downwind direction so the animals would not pick up the scent of the hunters, and if a hill, canyon, or other natural landform was nearby it would be used for cover. As soon as they were near enough to charge the herd, the hunters stripped to breechcloth and moccasins, transferred to their swifter mounts, lined up, and at a signal from their leader, swept out across the plain, each man eager to make the first kill. William Hamilton, who was with the Cheyennes during the 1840's, said that their hunters divided into two parties, each attacking a different section of a herd simultaneously to insure larger kills.

Although mounted Plains Indians sometimes surrounded a herd and set the animals to milling in a circle — a method used in the old days when they hunted on foot — they generally preferred the chase on horseback, each man choosing an animal and riding alongside at close quarters until it was brought down. Some hunters quickly adapted the white man's firearms to buffalo hunting, but others believed the bow-and-arrow was a more effective weapon. "One arrow was sufficient to bring a buffalo to its knees," said Hamilton. "They shot behind the shoulder, sending the arrow deep enough to strike the lungs." Francis Parkman saw an Oglalla Sioux hunter drive an arrow so deep into a buffalo that only the notch at the end was left protruding. And according to Major H. H. Sibley, a Yankton Sioux chief named Waneta "on one occasion discharged an arrow with sufficient force entirely to traverse the body of a female buffalo, and kill the calf by her side."

A feast usually followed a big hunt. If the animals were killed a considerable distance from a village, the tipis would be moved near the slaughter grounds; if the hunt was close by, women and children and old men would come out to help with the skinning. By nightfall huge fires would be burning and as soon as sufficient embers were ready, the roasting of the choicest cuts of meat began — calves' heads, tongues, and ribs. A buffalo feast might last for three days, but while it was in progress the work of salvaging every scrap of meat, hides, and bones also continued. Hides were stretched out and meat was stripped for drying. Nothing was wasted, and when a Plains tribe moved on after a buffalo hunt, very little was left behind for the coyotes and the wolves.

———◦———

Preparation for a horse raid — which frequently developed into a fight between the raiders and the raided — was more elaborate than the preliminaries for a buffalo hunt. Most horse-raiding parties or war parties were made up of young men in their late teens or early twenties who were eager to obtain horses to increase their wealth and social standing in the tribe. Sometimes they would invite an older and more experienced warrior to lead and advise them. Usually on the night before a raid, members of the party would assemble to chant war songs to the accompaniment of a drum, and the celebration often attracted other young men to join the expedition — provided it was still open to additional members. Raiding parties were generally limited to a dozen participants or fewer, except when attempts were made to seize entire herds from a strong enemy. In such cases, fifty or more warriors might ride together, and parties of this size often ended up battling with the raided Indians.

As in all societies of men, some spokesmen in a tribe favored peace, others were warlike — the age-old division of doves and hawks. To illustrate these opposing attitudes, Edwin Denig recorded for the Bureau of American Ethnology the speeches of two Assiniboin leaders in council after they had received an offer of peace from the Crows:

OLD ASSINIBOIN CHIEF: *My children I am a mild man. For upward of twenty years I have herded you together like a band of horses. If it had not been for me, you would long ago have scattered like wolves over the prairies. Good men and wise men are scarce; and, being so, they should be listened to, loved, and obeyed. My tongue has been worn thin and my teeth loosened in giving you advice and instruction. I am aware I speak to men as wise as myself, many braver, but none older or of more experience. I have called you together to state that our enemies (the Crows) have sent tobacco, through the medium of the whites at the big fort, to me and my children, to see if they could smoke it with pleasure, or it tasted badly. For my part I am willing to smoke. We are but a handful of men surrounded by large and powerful nations, all our enemies. Let us therefore by making peace reduce this number of foes and increase our number of friends. I am aware that many here have lost relatives by these people, so have we by the Gros Ventres, and yet we have peace with them. If it be to our interest to make peace all old enmities must be laid aside and forgotten. I am getting old, and have not many more winters to see, and am tired seeing my children gradually decrease by incessant war. We are poor in horses — from the herds the Crows own we will replenish. They will pay high and give many horses for peace. The Crows are good warriors, and the whites say good people and will keep their word. Whatever is decided upon let it be manly. We are men; others can speak. I listen — I have said.*

YOUNG ASSINIBOIN CHIEF: *I differ from all the old chief has said concerning our enemies. He must be growing old and childish to advise us to smoke the tobacco of our enemies, the Crows. Tell the whites to take it back to them. It stinks, and if smoked would taste of the blood of our nearest relations. Our old father, the chief, should make a journey to the banks of the Yellowstone, and speak to the grinning skulls of thirty lodges of his children, and hear their answer. Would they laugh? Would they dance? Would they beg for Crow tobacco or cry for Crow horses? If horses are wanted in camp, let the young men go to war and steal and take them as I have done — as I intend to do as long as a Crow Indian has a horse. What if in the attempt they leave their bones to bleach on the prairie? It would be but dying like men! For my part it always pleases me to see a young man's skull; the teeth are sound and beautiful, appearing to smile and say "I have died when I should and not waited at home until my teeth were worn to the gums by eating dried meat." The young men will make war — must have war — and, as far as my influence goes, should have war. I have spoken.*

To insure success in capturing horses or securing victory in battle, members of the raiding parties carried some special object as a protective power, a sacred war medicine. Among the Cheyennes, feathers from a bald eagle or a blue hawk were believed to possess the strongest medicine because they came from the strongest birds of the Plains. Old Whirlwind of the Cheyennes was convinced that he owed much of his success as a warrior to hawk feathers. In one fight every feather in his warbonnet was shot away, but he was not touched by a bullet.

Even when protected with the best of war medicines, however, experienced raiders were not inclined to be reckless in their actions. They usually rode at night and kept under cover during daylight. Before taking final action, the raiders carefully scouted enemy camps and horse herds, the terrain, and escape routes. A favorite time for attack was in the first gray light of dawn when the enemy was sleeping. With knives ready, the raiders would creep into the herd, each man choosing two or three horses. As soon as picket lines were cut, they would mount one and lead the others out quietly. If there was sign of alarm, the raiders went out in a fast gallop, trying to gain as much distance as possible before the enemy could pursue.

With each fleeing raider in possession of one or two extra horses, they were able to switch from one mount to another as the animals tired. This gave them an advantage over their pursuers, who in the excitement of the chase seldom took along a spare horse. It was not often that members of a carefully planned raid were overtaken, but when this occurred a fight of some kind was certain to ensue.

Upon reaching its home village, a successful raiding party was welcomed with joyous shouts and songs. Distribution of captured horses followed. A young man who was courting a girl might ride up to her father's lodge and leave one there. Other animals might be given to medicine men, to poor families, or widows in need of horses. Drums were brought out, and an all-night dance would begin. If there had been a victorious fight, the dancing might continue through another day and night.

One of the vows often made by young men before going on a horse raid was to undergo self-torture at the next tribal Sun Dance. No aspect of Plains Indian life was more often misinterpreted by white observers than Sun Dance rituals. Explorers, soldiers, and missionaries who were given an opportunity to view the dance seldom understood its meanings, and only a few recognized it as a spiritual ceremony, joyous in some aspects, penitential in others. The Sun Dance was confined mainly to Plains tribes and its variations followed linguistic lines — Siouan, Caddoan, Algonquian, and Shoshonean groups organizing their dances in slightly different ways. It was an annual ceremony, usually held in late spring or early summer, and abounded in religious symbols marking the rebirth of the tribe. About four days were spent in preparation, and about four days in rituals which included chanting and dancing, feasts of mourning, fasting, self-torture, and revelations through visions.

One of the few explanations of the Sun Dance ever recorded by a contemporary Plains Indian was that of George Bushotter, a Teton Sioux, who also drew a series of illustrations to depict various stages of the event. The Teton name for the dance, he said, was "They Dance Looking at the Sun." Preparations for it began in the spring, and invitations were always sent to neighboring tribes. "The visitors from the different nations begin to come together," Bushotter said, "each visiting tribe forming its separate camp. Though some of the visitors are hereditary enemies, it matters not during the Sun Dance; they visit one another; they shake hands and form alliances. In this manner several weeks are spent very pleasantly." The immense gathering of tribes along the Little Big Horn in 1876 followed a Sun Dance in which Sitting Bull danced "looking at the sun" and saw in a vision hundreds of blue-coated soldiers falling from the sky right into the Indian camp.

When the Sioux and their neighbors gathered for a Sun Dance, they pitched their tents in the form of a circle, and usually spent two days in preparing the inner grounds. "On the third day," Bushotter said, "some men are selected to go in search of the mystery tree, out of which they are to form the sun pole." (The Sisseton and Wahpeton divisions customarily sent two young boys.) The warriors participating in the search dressed themselves in warbonnets and other regalia. On the fourth day an excavation for mounting the sun pole was made in the center of the circle, and upon the raw earth they placed sweet grass, wild sage, and a buffalo skull. That same day, at the eastern edge of the inner ground, they set up a large tipi for the use of those who had made vows to participate in the dance. In the back of this tipi was placed a row of buffalo skulls, one for each participant. Within this shelter the participants fumigated themselves with smoke from sweet-smelling leaves and grass, painted their bodies, and prepared for the ordeal.

On the fifth day, a large party composed of both sexes of all ages went out to the previously selected mystery tree. Along the way they laughed, sang, and shouted, but as they neared the tree they fell silent or talked in whispers. After a series of ceremonies in which the tree cutters told of their past exploits, the work of felling the tree began, with both men and women taking part in the chopping. After the tree was cut down, all limbs except those at the very top were removed. The log was then carried back to the camp circle and there it was raised by the most distinguished men of the tribe. It was now a sun pole. On the top limbs left by the cutters were mounted a medicine bundle, a scarlet blanket, and two figures cut from dried buffalo hide. One figure was shaped like a buffalo, the other like a man — each equipped with a large phallus to represent the essence of life, the fertility of the summer season. Firmly attached to the top of the pole were also a dozen rawhide lariats reaching to the ground. These were to be used by the young Indians waiting in the preparation tipi to fulfill their vows of self-torture.

Around the sun pole, two concentric circles of forked posts were set in the ground. Poles and brush were used to roof this outer ring thus formed, but the center of the dancing lodge was kept open so that the dancers might see the sun and moon.

Participants in the first ceremony were the chiefs and old men who marched around the pole. With dramatic flourishes they would spend several minutes shooting at the figures at the top. At this point the official crier for the tribe would sometimes announce a give-away, urging everyone to present gifts to widows, orphans, and poor families. Young men would bring ponies into the ring and turn them loose for those who needed them. Blankets, bolts of cloth, beads, and jewelry would be piled at the foot of the pole for anyone to take.

After the give-away was ended, mounted warriors would enter, racing their horses circus fashion around and around, shooting into the ground until the dancing lodge was filled with powder smoke. As the day ended, young men and women riding in pairs circled the sun pole, singing back and forth to each other until the sun set.

The remaining days of the Sun Dance were given over to the young men who endured self-torture to satisfy their vows. After going through rituals which varied from tribe to tribe, about a dozen participants (naked except for a breech-cloth) would present themselves to medicine men who made incisions in their breasts and then passed wooden skewers behind the pectoral muscles. Buckskin thongs laced to the skewers were fastened to the end of one of the lariats hanging from the sun pole. Each dancer then backed away until his lariat was taut. Raising his arms to the sun and blowing upon an eagle-bone whistle which had been placed in his mouth, the young man would now begin the Dance Looking at the Sun. The whistling of the eagle-bone symbolized the breath of life and the cry of the thunderbird, that awesome bird which hurled arrowheads from the sky in the form of lightning.

Drummers kept up a steady beat while the dancers pulled at the lariats until blood streamed from the incisions in their bodies. One by one the young men broke loose by forcing their own weight to tear away the incised flesh, and then the medicine men wrapped their bleeding bodies in blankets and led them away to the preparation tipi for restoration. Among the variations mentioned by some observers was scarification of the back muscles as well as the front. Sometimes a buffalo skull would be fastened to the skewers, the weight of it break-ing the flesh when the dancing began.

At the conclusion of the last dance, the vow keepers ended their fasts, tipis were taken down, visitors returned to their homes, and the camp was broken up. Only the sacred pole was left standing until sun and rain and wind brought it finally back to earth.

―――――――――▶◆◀――――――――――

Participation of women in many of the sun dance ceremonies sur-prised white observers who were under the impression that Indian women were always kept in the background during the most im-portant ceremonies of the Plains tribes. According to George Bushotter, women not only joined in the ceremony of cutting the mystery tree, they aided the dancers during their ordeals and some-times participated in the Sun Dances themselves. "She suffers as the male candidates do, except in one respect — her flesh is not scarified. This woman wears a buckskin shirt, and lets her hair fall loosely down her back."

Plains Indian women were not the slaves and drudges so often depicted by casual observers of the 19th century. They did have their special duties just as men were expected to perform certain tasks. The arrangement was based upon a division of economic responsibilities necessary for tribal survival in a primitive society. The male's first responsibility was to see that child-bearing women and young children survived all dangers — war, famine, cold, storms. If the seed of the tribe died, the tribe died. Numerous accounts of attacks upon villages during the Indian Wars tell of how warriors sacrificed themselves in efforts to insure the escape of women and children. The role of protector required the male to bear arms, to keep always alert to repel enemies, unhampered by anything except his weapons. "Chiefly for this reason, the men commonly went ahead," George Grinnell observed, "and the women, following behind, looked after the children, bore the burdens, or cared for the animals which transported the camp property."

The men were also expected to hunt for and kill animals necessary for sustenance, to manufacture weapons and utensils, and to provide materials for construction of tipis and other lodges. While the males were engaged in these vigorous and often dangerous pursuits, the women were busy converting the products of the hunts into edible food and useful objects. Sometimes, as in all societies, there were overlappings of duties. Men could do work around the lodges, and women could fight in battle, but the pressures of economics tended to keep the duties of the sexes distinct.

Although women did not hold positions of political leadership in Plains tribes during the period when white men knew them, there are traditions from earlier days of female chiefs, of women who possessed mysterious powers and showed great wisdom in tribal councils. Perhaps the rapid changes that followed the coming of the white man and his horse accentuated the division of responsibilities between women and men, leaving the women little time to participate as tribal leaders. Nevertheless they continued to have great influence, as Grinnell found when he lived with the Cheyennes. He said the women acted as a spur to the men if they were slow in performing their duties, and often held them back from hasty, ill-advised actions. "They discuss matters freely with their husbands, argue over points, persuade, cajole, and usually have their own way about tribal matters. They are in fact the final authority in camp."

In the training of children, men and women both played important roles, advising their young sons and daughters together. When the children began nearing their teens, usually a grandfather or an uncle would join in counseling the boys, while an uncle or an aunt might assist in the instruction of the girls. It was the father's duty to prepare the wooden frame for the cradle of a newborn child, the mother or grandmother covering it with dressed skin and adding ornaments of beads, quills, and fringes. Sometimes toy trinkets for amusement of the children were attached.

Babies were not usually fastened to cradleboards until they were two or three months old, or until their mothers believed they were strong enough to endure the exposure of the cradle. From that time until they learned to walk, children were carried on cradleboards upon their mothers' backs, being attached by broad straps fastened around the mothers' foreheads or breasts. This left the women free use of their hands for work around the tipi. When the tribe was travel-ing, cradleboards might be swung from the pommel of a saddle, or fastened to a travois. As often as possible during the day, children were taken from their cradles and allowed to lie or roll about on a blanket.

Until a child was able to walk and talk and understand, it was called only by a pet name. Then, in an important family ceremony, the boy or girl was given a formal name. It was often bestowed by a grandfather who might pass along his own name or that of a respected ancestor. Methods of choosing names varied greatly from tribe to tribe.

Discipline began at a very early age. As tribal life and family life in village or camp kept people very close to each other, babies were taught to be quiet, and if they persisted in crying their mothers were expected to take them out of earshot of older people in a lodge. Children also were discouraged from interrupting their elders when they were talking, but the severest punishment given a child for mis-behaving was usually only a mild shaking. Promises of rewards for good behavior, or threats of punishment for bad behavior were seldom made. Parents taught their children to follow courses of conduct which would bring them respect and approval of their associates in the tribe, and they expected them to follow their advice.

The first present given a young boy was usually a bow and arrows; for a young girl it was more likely a doll made of wood or dressed skin. When both grew a little older, they were given puppies for pets. In their games, Indian children imitated their elders just as all children do around the world. They would build little tipis, arranging them in the circular fashion of their camps, and sometimes they fought mock battles, the boys riding sticks for horses, the girls dismantling toy tipis and pretending to flee. On other days they would play at buffalo hunting, some children acting the roles of the animals, others attacking them with toy arrows or with weed-stalk lances.

Because they grew up with horses and became accustomed to the motion of horses, balancing upon them with their mothers from babyhood, boys and girls learned to ride almost as early as they learned to walk. One of the first responsibilities given a young boy was the care of a certain number of horses. "These were his special charges," George Grinnell said, "and he must watch them, never lose them, and see that they had water always."

The boy's father or some older man would instruct him in the ways of buffalo hunting — how to approach the animals, how to aim at and strike the most vulnerable parts of their bodies. As soon as he reached his teens, the boy was allowed to join a buffalo hunt, and if he made a kill on his first hunt a celebration of some kind was held in his honor.

"I was taught to ride horseback alone when I was four years old," recalled a Cheyenne woman who was a child during the golden age of the Plains Indians. "When I became an older girl this was my greatest sport. I even rode untamed ponies. My mother taught me how to put a pack on a pony." But she did not ride a horse out to hunt buffalo; that was for the young boys. "My mother taught me everything connected with the tipi, such as cooking and tanning hides for different purposes. The first pair of moccasins I made were for my father."

The tipi was the center of women's activities, their ruling base. They performed most of the work of making a tipi, fleshing down the buffalo skins and tanning them. Somewhat in the manner of a frontier family inviting neighbors for a barn-raising, a lodgemaker would invite her friends to a feast and after it was ended, she would give each one a buffalo hide and several strips of sinew thread. Thus in one day all the skins for a tipi could be spread on the ground and sewed together in a semi-circular shape.

To make an average-sized tipi covering, fifteen to nineteen buffalo skins were required, an odd number being traditional. Cheyenne lodgemakers believed that a covering would fit better if made from an odd number of hides. The tipi framework consisted of about twenty trimmed poles, preferably cedar, set firmly in the ground in a circle about fifteen feet in diameter, and brought together about four feet from the top so that the pole ends would project above the covering. When the framework was properly arranged, a special pole at the back of the tipi was used to lift the covering in place, and then the two ends were brought around to the front and fastened with wooden pins. The bottom flare of the tipi — which required considerable skill to shape properly — was then pegged tightly to the ground. Where pegs were not available or the ground was rocky, heavy stones might be used to hold the bottom down. Even into the 20th century, sites of abandoned Plains Indian villages were often identifiable by rings of tipi stones.

A dressed skin stretched over a willow frame served as the tipi doorway. In the center of the interior was a fire-pit where coals were always kept alive, the smoke escaping through the smoke-hole at the top. Movable flaps of buffalo hide fastened to each side of the smoke-hole were used to regulate the smoke outlet whenever the wind direction changed. The age of a skin covering could usually be determined by the amount of soot collected around the smoke-hole.

Ordinarily a tipi would accommodate three low platforms which were used as seats by day and beds by night. They were covered with buffalo robes or blankets, and waterproof skin curtains might be stretched above the platforms to keep off any rain that might fall through the smoke-hole during a storm. Although tipis appeared to be perfect cones, they were not exactly so. The back sides were made shorter than the eastward-facing entrances in order to provide greater resistance to the strong west winds that prevailed on the plains.

According to legend, the idea for the tipi came from an old Indian who had emigrated from the woodlands to the Plains and was dissatisfied with the poor earthen shelters his people had to live in. One day while he was idly folding a large poplar leaf, he chanced to shape it into a cone. He saw it as a shelter, and shaped one like it from buffalo skins. The old man was probably a Sioux, *ti* in that language coming from the root word "to dwell," and *pi* from "used for" — tipi meaning in Sioux "used for to dwell."

The tipi, which became the best-known symbol of the Plains Indians, vanished with the buffalo. By the hundreds of thousands that sacred animal — the sustainer of life for all the tribes — was slaughtered by white hide hunters until only a few small herds remained. During the bitter Indian Wars of the 1870's, almost every victorious Army unit systematically rounded up the defeated Indians' horses and slaughtered them. Without the buffalo and the horse, there were no more Plains Indians. Dismounted, disarmed, and confined to reservations, the survivors of the once free and mighty tribes were dependent upon an indifferent government which had taken their land and now doled out to them in exchange for it miserly amounts of food and clothing.

To comprehend what happened to the Plains Indians, a modern non-Indian American should try to imagine that his work activity and travel are abruptly forbidden, that all his food stores, building materials, and clothing manufactures are taken away from him, leaving him totally dependent upon the will of his conquerors. Then a horde of strangers speaking a different language descends upon him, compelling him to abandon his religion, his customs, and his language, and to adopt those of his conquerors. At the same time he is repeatedly told that he is of an inferior race, and that everything he represents or believes in is inferior to that of his conquerors.

That descendants of the Plains Indians have survived into the late 20th century is evidence enough of their fortitude and vitality. Today the survivors of three generations of ignominious treatment and exploitation are struggling to break out of the poverty trap that was imposed upon their forebears. There is a surge of pride among them in being Indians, a renaissance of the spirit, a renewal of belief in their roots and their native earth, a determination to restore the best of their heritage, and to share as well in the best of 20th century American life.

Several women in this Sioux camp sit in front of buffalo meat that was cut into thin strips and hung on pole frames to dry in the hot sun. Some of this meat was then preserved as pemmican for the winter months. Courtesy of Montana Historical Society, Helena.

15

The Day of the Buffalo

"As far as the eye could reach the country seemed
blackened by innumerable herds."

From the middle of the 16th century until late into the 19th,
travelers upon first seeing buffalo on the Western plains were
struck with amazement, if not disbelief, at the immensity of
the herds. "There is such a quantity of them that I do not
know what to compare them with," wrote one of Coronado's men in
1541, "except with the fish of the sea. . . . Many times we started to
pass through the midst of them and wanted to go through to the other
side of them, we were not able to because the country was covered
with them."

While the fur trader Alexander Henry was spending the winter
of 1801 in Manitoba, he was awakened one morning by the bellowing of a buffalo herd which covered the level plain at every point of
the compass. Not until three days later did he record in his journal
that the herd, passing at full speed, finally ended with a few lagging
old bulls bringing up the rear. Six years afterward, while Lewis and
Clark were passing through the Dakota country, they sighted a herd
which darkened the whole plain, so many that they found it impossible to calculate the numbers. In 1832, while Captain Benjamin
Bonneville was traveling along the North Fork of the Platte, he reported: "As far as the eye could reach the country seemed blackened
by innumerable herds."

One of George Catlin's most dramatic paintings depicted a buffalo herd crossing the Missouri as he and his companions were coming down the river in a boat. "We were actually terrified at the immense numbers that were streaming down the green hills on one side of the river and galloping up and over the bluffs on the other. The river was filled, and in parts blackened, with their heads and horns."

While crossing the Platte Valley in 1834, J. K. Townsend was astounded by a herd which he sighted from a hilltop. He estimated that he could see for at least ten miles down an eight-mile-wide plain between bluffs and river bank, the whole of it covered with buffalo. "It was truly a sight," Townsend recorded, "that would have excited even the dullest mind to enthusiasm."

When surveyors for a Pacific railroad in 1853 came upon a herd covering several square miles near the Cheyenne River, various members of the party used their instruments to estimate the numbers. Their calculations varied from 200,000 to half a million. In this same area ten years later Nathaniel Langford, who was to become the first superintendent of Yellowstone National Park, heard the rumbling of a herd half an hour before it appeared on the horizon. Observing the mass of animals through his field glass, Langford estimated the herd to be five miles wide. "They were running as rapidly as a horse can go at a keen gallop, about 12 miles an hour . . . the whole space, say 5 miles by 12 miles, as far as we could see, was a seemingly solid mass of buffaloes."

In 1868 William Blackmore started across the plains on the then uncompleted Kansas Pacific Railroad. West of Ellsworth for more than a hundred miles the train passed through an almost unbroken herd of buffalo. Several times the locomotive was forced to stop to allow them to cross the track. As late as the 1870's there were reports of herds extending over many miles. In 1871 Colonel Richard Irving Dodge, commander at Fort Dodge, passed a twenty-five-mile-long migration in western Kansas. A year or so later an Army post trader traveled for 200 miles across Montana and was never out of sight of buffalo.

No one knows of course how many buffalo there were in North America when the first Europeans arrived. Some sources say 60 million, but estimates based upon forage requirements indicate that there probably could not have been more than 30 million. By the time official exploring expeditions began to make estimates, the buffalo were largely confined to the Great Plains. Most sources agree that in the years immediately preceding the great buffalo slaughter of the 1870's, about 4 million animals ranged south of the Platte River, and about a million and a half north of it. These figures are based on recorded shipments of hides during the years of slaughter.

To be zoologically proper one should call the American buffalo a bison, but general usage long ago superseded scientific usage, and in the historical record the animal is almost universally known as the buffalo. French explorers used the name first, but it probably did not appear in print in English until publication of *A Relation of Maryland* in 1635. Most authorities believe that the buffalo came to North America over the same Bering Strait land bridge crossed by ancestors of American Indians. In the folklore of the Indians, however, the buffalo was a culture hero and originated in various supernatural ways. Some tribes said the buffalo came from the underworld when a large stone was magically moved; others said herds appeared suddenly one day from the four directions, arriving just in time to save the tribes from starvation; still others believed they came from a deep cave far to the north.

Although the buffalo is most closely associated with the Great Plains, there is evidence that herds once ranged to the Atlantic states, and that there was a "woods buffalo" somewhat different in appearance from the plains buffalo. In 1540 the Cherokees of Georgia presented De Soto with a buffalo skin, the first ever seen by Europeans. Occasional references to buffalo in Pennsylvania can be found in contemporary accounts of the 18th century, and during the middle of that century Daniel Boone was still hunting buffalo in the southern

Appalachians. In 1780 Delaware Indians hunted buffalo along the Kanawha River of West Virginia, selling the meat to the commander at Fort Pitt, and at least two buffalo were killed in that same valley during 1815. In 1803 the last buffalo was seen in what is now the limits of Buffalo, New York, and by 1820 the animals were practically extinct everywhere east of the Mississippi River.

The paramount importance of the buffalo in the lives of Plains Indians as well as tribes that lived contiguous to the plains is indicated by the way in which it permeated their culture and religion. It was the king of the animals, the central figure in the tribes' myths of creation, in numerous folk tales, in art works, songs, and dances. Elaborate ceremonies were held in honor of the buffalo; it was the chief symbol on sun dance altars and poles. February was the "Moon When the Hair Gets Thick on the Buffalo"; March was the "Moon When the Buffalo Cows Drop Their Calves"; June and July were the "Moons When the Buffalo Bulls Bellow and Hunt the Cows." Tatanka Yotanka meant "sitting buffalo bull," the name of one of the greatest of the Plains Indian leaders — Sitting Bull.

Before the coming of the horse, buffalo hunting was a tedious task, consuming most of the time of male Indians. The herds first had to be located by individual searchers on foot. When a searcher sighted a herd, he made no effort to kill an animal; in fact, individual hunting was forbidden to the point that if any one disobeyed this tribal law he was usually severely beaten, tipi destroyed, and his horses slain. Upon sighting a herd, a searcher hastened back to the main camp and informed the chiefs, who sent criers through the camp ordering the warriors to prepare for a hunt. Armed with bows and arrows, the hunters would then follow the search back to the herd, often running for long distances.

As they approached the herd, they spread out, moving cautiously until they completely encircled a number of animals. Methods of attack varied, depending upon the size of the herd and the lay of the land. If a sharp cliff was in the vicinity they might try to stampede the herd off the edge; the fall would kill or disable the buffalo so that they could easily be tracked down. If there was a deepening coulee with a dead end, they might try to drive the herd into it, slaying the animals as they milled around at the end. Near good grazing grounds to which buffalo repeatedly returned, the Indians sometimes built permanent V-shaped entrapments of rocks or logs with a fenced corral at the end. More often that not in the days before the horse, the hunters simply encircled the herd, closing in until the buffalo began running in a panic circle, arrows bringing them down one by one.

The arrival of horses in large numbers during the 18th century changed the buffalo hunt from drudgery to an exciting event. No longer did the tribes have to wait for buffalo to come to their camping areas. On horseback a hunter could ride right into the herd, choosing the best specimens for the kill.

The main hunting season was during the summer moons when the animals were in their prime, the hair thin and the flesh best suited for cutting into strips and drying in the sun. When the hunt ended, the work of the women began. It was they who attended to the drying of the meat and the dressing of the hides. They pounded a considerable amount of meat into pemmican for storage into the winter months, and saw that every edible portion was consumed, from the flesh to marrow and gristle.

That the buffalo was the staff of life for numerous Western tribes is evident from the long list of uses made of each butchered animal. During his field work with the Blackfoot tribes, John C. Ewers of the Bureau of American Ethnology compiled with the help of informants a list of eighty-seven non-food items, the basis of the tribes' material culture, all originating from the buffalo. Among them was clothing — from coats to caps to moccasins, as well as winter underpants for women. The buffalo furnished shelter in the form of tipis and tipi furnishings, including the beds. Shields, bowstrings, arrowhead fastenings, powder flasks, knife sheaths were warrior accouterments that came from the buffalo. From buffalo horns came cups and spoons, from the hoofs came glue, from the fat came polishing and paint-mixing materials. Buffalo rawhide and hair were the materials

for more than a dozen necessary items for riding and transport —
saddles, saddlebags, stirrups, bridles, lariats, travois hitches, and horse-
shoes. From bones and rawhide and hair came sleds and hoops and
balls for games. For sun dance altars — the skull; for dance rattles —
hoofs and rawhide; for headdresses — hides and hair. And for fuel to
cook and to keep warm by — buffalo chips.

It was no wonder the buffalo was considered a sacred being, and
no wonder that when it vanished so did the culture and power of the
Western tribes. The end came with dramatic suddenness, precipitated
by the building of railroads across the West. Processions of wagon
trains along the Oregon and Santa Fe trails during the 1840's and
1850's had frightened the nervous herds away from those travel
routes, but offered little of the threat to their numbers that the railroads did.

By the time the Union Pacific construction crews began laying
rails west across Nebraska in the late 1860's, buffalo herds kept so far
away from the Platte Valley that the contractors had to buy beef cattle
herds, driving them along with the tracklayers, to furnish meat for the
workers. The Kansas Pacific Railroad, building west from Leavenworth about this same time, did not follow an overland trail route but
drove through the heart of the Southern herds' finest grazing grounds.
Its contractors could supply buffalo meat for their construction camps,
using hired buffalo hunters for this purpose. Their most noted hunter
was a 21-year-old marksman, William F. Cody.

For $500 a month young Cody guaranteed to bring in twelve
buffalo a day, butchered and dressed. One day a hunting party of Army
officers from Fort Harker sighted a small herd on the plain ahead of
them, but before they could bring their rifles into action, a lone
hunter came up at a gallop and with a series of rapid shots slew the
entire herd. According to legend, the amazed officers nicknamed
the Kansas Pacific's meat hunter "Buffalo Bill" and so created one of
the American West's most enduring folk heroes. By his own account,
he killed 4,280 buffalo during the few months that he hunted for the
railroad contractors.

Within a short time the presence of the two parallel railroads and the towns which sprang up along them separated the Southern herds from the Northern herds. The greatest threat to the buffalo, however, came from the armies of sportsmen and professional hunters from the East, who now had easy access by rail to the once remote grazing grounds.

Before the vast herds of Kansas retreated from the constant commotion along the Kansas Pacific, that railroad organized special excursions for buffalo hunters, distributing broadsides and other advertisements throughout the East. One such excursion announced for October 27, 1868 promised that ample time would be allowed for *A Grand Buffalo Hunt On The Plains*. "Buffaloes are so numerous along the road that they are shot from the cars nearly every day. On our last excursion our party killed twenty buffaloes in a hunt of six hours. All passengers can have refreshments on the cars at reasonable prices." And whether an excursionist shot a buffalo or not, the 400-mile run across the plains from Leavenworth to Sheridan was a bargain at ten dollars for a round trip ticket.

Randolph Keim, who joined one of these excursion parties, persuaded the engineer to let him ride on the cowcatcher of the locomotive. (Keim called it a buffalo-catcher.) "After proceeding about ten miles, we struck a large herd crossing the track. . . . Approaching the herd rather rapidly, I did not favor the idea of receiving a buffalo in my lap, a fact growing momentarily more probable. One animal planted himself in the middle of the track, with his head down as much as to say, 'Come on, who ever you are, and we'll try.'" Keim retreated to the locomotive's steam-chest and failed to get his buffalo, which leaped off the track when the engineer sounded the whistle.

Sometimes large herds of buffalo endangered trains. According to Colonel Dodge, if a train was in the way of a herd in rapid motion, "each individual buffalo went at it with the desperation of despair, plunging against or between locomotives and cars, just as its blind madness chanced to direct it. . . . After having trains thrown off the track twice in one week, conductors learned to have a very decided respect for the idiosyncrasies of the buffalo, and when there was a possibility of striking a herd . . . the train was slowed up and sometimes stopped entirely."

With buffalo ranges accessible by rail, buffalo hunting quickly became a fad among wealthy Easterners and British noblemen. They traveled in luxurious parlor cars accompanied by servants and all the trappings of the Victorian age. Buffalo Bill Cody became a popular guide for these parties and found his income rising and his fame spreading.

The most widely publicized of the "royal hunts" was that of the Grand Duke Alexis of Russia, who came over for a buffalo shoot in 1872. General Phil Sheridan and Colonel George Custer joined the Grand Duke's special train at Omaha, and they went speeding across the Nebraska plains with American and Russian flags flying from the locomotive. At a specially prepared camp named Alexis in honor of the guest, Buffalo Bill was waiting, and he and Custer took the Grand Duke out to show him how to hunt buffalo. Spotted Tail and some of his warriors also had been drafted to entertain the visiting royalty. When a Sioux hunter named Two Lance demonstrated how his people killed buffalo with the bow by driving an arrow into the heart of a running animal, Alexis was so impressed that he presented the Indian with a twenty-dollar gold piece. On the second day of a fifty-mile hunt, the party killed fifty-six buffalo, but this did not seem to satisfy the hosts. They insisted that the Grand Duke journey on to the more thickly populated plains of Kansas where they shot fifty more animals.

The exploits of the Grand Duke made good newspaper copy back East, but some Westerners were beginning to tire of the constant procession of wealthy young men who seemed determined to slaughter every buffalo on the plains. "Men come from London — cockneys, fops and nobles — and from all parts of the Republic to enjoy what they call sport," grumbled a Kansas editor in 1872. "Sport! when no danger is incurred and no skill required. I see no more sport in shooting a buffalo than in shooting an ox nor so much danger as there is hunting Texas cattle."

Actually the "cockneys, fops and nobles" contributed only in a minor way to the decline in the buffalo population. It was another class of hunters — the professionals who killed for profit — that brought doom to the great buffalo herds and came very near extinguishing the species entirely between 1872 and 1882.

In 1872 the tracks of the Atchison, Topeka & Santa Fe Railroad pushed up the valley of the Arkansas River, just about the time that a huge market was opening for buffalo hides. Tanners in Eastern cities and in Europe were demanding thousands of hides, and dealers in Kansas City and Leavenworth began offering prices that appealed to professional hunters. Both Wichita and Dodge City on the Santa Fe became bases for hide hunters, turning into boom towns even before Texas cattlemen began driving their Longhorns up the trails for shipment on the new railroad. In 1873 two-thirds of the population of Dodge City was engaged in hunting, skinning, or shipping buffalo hides, and during the next four years the chief industry of the area around that frontier town was killing buffalo.

Using one of the new Sharps or Remington breechloaders, even an unskilled hunter could kill large numbers of buffalo in a day. Because hunting was much easier than skinning or curing, everyone wanted to be a hunter, and the first years of slaughter were marked by reckless waste. Colonel Dodge estimated that as the result of careless skinning and curing, each marketable hide shipped east on the railroad represented three to five dead buffalo.

The profit motive, however, soon led to more efficient methods. Hide dealers in the railroad towns were so eager for first-class buffalo pelts that they began outfitting hunting parties. A typical expedition consisted of one expert marksman, two skinners, and one man to stretch and dry the skins. As each member of the party received a percentage of the value of the hides, they were inclined to be less wasteful and more careful in the conservation of hides.

During 1873 hundreds of camps established by such hunting parties extended for miles along the river valleys adjacent to the Kansas Pacific, Santa Fe, and Union Pacific railways. By summer's end of that year, thousands of square miles of the Southern Plains were filled with decaying carcasses. "The air," said one traveler, "was rendered pestilential and offensive to the last degree." Except for the tongues, which were considered a delicacy and could be preserved with salt in barrels, very little of the meat was utilized.

According to records kept by the Santa Fe Railroad, 1873 was the year of greatest slaughter along that route. A statistical table compiled by William T. Hornaday of the National Museum indicated that three million buffalo were killed by white hunters in 1872 and 1873, so diminishing the Southern herds that only 42,000 hides were taken in 1874. Significantly, during those three years only an estimated 390,000 buffalo were killed by the Plains Indians for their food, shelter, and clothing.

Nevertheless, the slaughter continued until the great Southern herds — whose numbers had amazed travelers in the West for three centuries — ceased to exist by the end of 1875. A few thousand survivors drifted off to the Staked Plains of Texas where they were hunted for several more years from Fort Griffin, with Fort Worth serving as the railroad shipping point. Until well into the 1880's scattered stragglers were occasionally sighted in unsettled parts of Kansas and Nebraska. By that time they were almost curiosities of the past, yet anyone sighting a buffalo seemed to have a compelling urge to kill it.

After virtually annihilating the Southern herds, the professional hunters moved into Montana and the Dakotas to begin slaughtering the Northern herds. Although the total number of animals in the North was only about one-third that in the South, these remaining buffalo roamed over a much larger area and served as the commissary of populous Plains tribes from the North Platte to well beyond the Canadian border. Here the Northern Pacific Railroad was building westward, furnishing transport for hides, and if the railroad was not handy, the Missouri River was still filled with steamboats.

Because of the sudden scarcity of hides after the decimation of the Southern buffalo, prices rose sharply, and by 1880 an excessive number of hunters were tracking the Northern herds. 1881 was the peak year of slaughter. "The past severe winter caused the buffalo to bunch themselves in a few valleys where there was pasturage, and there the slaughter went on all winter," a Sioux City newspaper reported in May of that year. "There was no sport about it, simply shooting down the famine-tamed animals as cattle might be shot down in a barnyard. To the credit of the Indians it can be said that they killed no more than they could save the meat from. The greater part of the slaughter was done by white hunters, or butchers rather, who followed the business of killing and skinning buffalo by the month, leaving the carcasses to rot."

This incredibly rapid destruction of millions of buffalo — the entire economic base of the Plains tribes — had a shattering effect upon them. Within a decade their source of food, shelter, clothing, and numerous other objects used in their daily lives was wiped out. It was no accident that the Southern Plains Indians chose to make their last great assault upon the invading white men at Adobe Walls, for this was the main base used by buffalo hunters in the last big year of slaughter in the Southwest. In June 1874 a force of Kiowa, Comanche, and Cheyenne warriors tried to overrun the buffalo hunters at Adobe Walls, but repeating rifles with telescopic sights were too much for the galloping warriors. They had to withdraw, and the hunters continued to kill buffalo on ranges reserved by treaty for the exclusive use of the tribes.

Buffalo played a large part in the Ghost Dance religion, which had its most ardent followers among the Northern Plains tribes during the late 1880's — the period immediately following the destruction of the Northern herds. The passing of the buffalo had not only destroyed their material culture, but also had forced them to live as wards of the government on reservations. Their religion and spiritual lives, so completely interwoven with the buffalo, were now threatened. For many, the only escape from despair was through the new Ghost Dance religion which promised to bring back the buffalo:

> *The Eagle has brought the message to the tribe.*
> *Over the whole earth they are coming.*

The buffalo are coming, the buffalo are coming.
The father says so, the father says so.

The dream ended in the bloody affair at Wounded Knee Creek, December 1890. In that year there were probably fewer than a hundred wild buffalo left alive in the United States.

"The disappearance of these millions of buffalo in the space of a few years," wrote James Mooney in his study of the Ghost Dance religion, "has no parallel in the annals of natural history." And even after the great herds were obliterated, the extermination of single individuals continued. In the autumn of 1883 Sioux Indians at Standing Rock — including Sitting Bull — were permitted to leave the reservation for their last buffalo hunt. After that, what few animals remained were more or less reserved for white hunters from the East and Europe who came in numbers far greater than those of the buffalo they sought to kill.

A contest, whipped up by newspapers, developed out of this pursuit of the last herd on the Plains. The nearer the species approached extermination, the more eagerly some hunters strove for the fame that would be theirs for killing the last wild buffalo. In the late 1880's, after the estimated number of surviving animals dropped to four in Dakota, ten in Montana, and twenty-six in Wyoming, the Associated Press began chronicling the kills as they did the deaths of old Western gunfighters.

Had it not been for a handful of dedicated conservationists, the American buffalo (bison) might well have vanished with the billions of passenger pigeons which passed out of existence when the last of the species died in a Cincinnati zoo in 1914. During the closing years of the 19th century, while an army of bone-pickers was gathering bones from the Plains for shipment to fertilizer factories, zoologists from the National Museum and the American Museum of Natural History suddenly discovered that buffalo were so rare that they could not obtain representative specimens for their collections.

William Hornaday of the National Museum compiled a census of free-ranging buffalo in 1889; the only sizable herd was in Yellowstone

National Park. It numbered less that 200 and was under constant threat from poachers who reduced its size to twenty by 1894. In that year Congress enacted a law forbidding the killing of buffalo, and efforts somewhat similar to those being made today to restore the population of whooping cranes began for the buffalo in Yellowstone Park. In seven years the depleted herd was increased to only twenty-five. Alarmed over the possibility that the Yellowstone herd might die out completely, the Federal Government in 1907 established a protected reserve in the Wichita Mountains of Oklahoma. The only source for stocking the range was the New York Zoo, and fifteen specimens were transported from there to Oklahoma. When the animals arrived in the heart of Kiowa-Comanche country, they were the first buffalo seen by these Indians for a generation.

In the meantime the American Bison Society had been formed to save the buffalo, and several interested individuals were struggling to build up private herds. With two bulls and two calves, a Pend d'Oreille Indian named Walking Coyote started a buffalo herd on the Flathead Reservation in Montana. He sold ten of his calves to rancher Michel Pablo, who by 1906 developed a herd of 700 which were purchased by the Canadian Government for a reserve in Alberta. In Texas, Charles Goodnight, starting with two wild calves in 1878, built a herd of more than 200. Charles J. (Buffalo) Jones, Gordon (Pawnee Bill) Lillie, the Dupree family of South Dakota, Charles Allard of Montana, and several other ranchers also worked to save the buffalo. Goodnight, Jones and others experimented with crossbreeding cattle with buffalo, naming the hybrid "cattalo," but it was never widely accepted.

Today the buffalo seems to be safe from extinction; about 35,000 descendants of the millions that once darkened the Plains thrive on wildlife refuges and ranches and in parks and zoos across North America. Once a sacred token of the mighty Plains tribes, the buffalo has become one of the most popular images in the iconography of America. We use the buffalo on our coins, our stamps, currency, flags, and medals. It appears in our art, our songs, on emblems of numerous organizations, on logos for thousands of products. The

Department of the Interior, which is responsible for the welfare of the buffalo, used the animal on its seal. Many athletic teams proudly bear its name. One cannot travel across America without passing through towns, crossing streams and mountains, and seeing berries, fruits, grass, and even insects which have been given its name. The eagle may be the national emblem, but the buffalo has come out of history as the most truly representative of America's symbols.

Buffalo or "Crook-Backed" Ox, by Gomara in 1553, is perhaps the earliest appearance of an engraving of the buffalo. From A History of the American People *by Woodrow Wilson.*

16

━━━━━▷●◁━━━━━

Day of the Longhorns

*"Theirs was the era of cowboys, long cattle drives, and rip-roaring trail
towns — the hard-riding, colorful West they helped to create."*

When Coronado marched northward from Mexico in
1540, searching for the mythical golden cities of Cibola,
he brought with his expedition a number of Spanish cattle. These were the first of the breed to enter what is
now the United States. Over the next century other Spanish explorers
and missionaries followed, most of them bringing at least "a bull and
a cow, a stallion and a mare." From these seed stocks, Longhorns and
mustangs and cowboys and ranching slowly developed in the Southwest, the Spanish cattle mutating and evolving, the vaquero
perfecting his costume and the tools of his trade.

The Longhorns, which also came to be known as Texas cattle,
took their name from their wide-spreading horns which sometimes
measured up to eight feet across, and there are legends of horn spreads
even more extensive. From their mixed ancestry of blacks, browns,
reds, duns, slates, and brindles the Longhorns were varicolored, the
shadings and combinations of hues so differentiated that, as J. Frank
Dobie pointed out, no two of these animals were ever alike in appearance. "For all his heroic stature," said Dobie, "the Texas steer
stood with his body tucked up in the flanks, his high shoulder-top
sometimes thin enough to split a hail stone, his ribs flat, his length
frequently so extended that his back swayed."

233

Ungraceful though they were, the Longhorns showed more intelligence than domesticated cattle. They were curious, suspicious, fierce, and resourceful. After all, by the mid-19th century they were the survivors of several generations which had lived under wild or semi-wild conditions. They possessed unusually keen senses of smell, sight, and hearing; their voices were powerful and penetrating; they could survive extreme heat or cold; they could exist on the sparest of vegetation and water; they could out-walk any other breed of cattle. It was this last attribute that brought the Texas Longhorns out of their native habitat and onto the pages of history to create the romantic era of the cowboys, the long drives, and riproaring trail towns of the Great Plains.

The drives began even before Texas became a state. A few enterprising adventurers occasionally would round up a herd out of the brush and drive them overland to Galveston or Shreveport where the animals were sold mainly for their hides and tallow. After the California gold rush of 1849 created a demand for meat, a few daring young Texans drove herds all the way to the Pacific coast. W. H. Snyder put together an outfit that moved out of Texas into New Mexico, and then crossed Colorado, Wyoming, Utah, and Nevada. After two years Snyder finally got his Longhorns to the miners. Captain Jack Cureton of the Texas Rangers followed a southern route across New Mexico and Arizona, dodging Apaches all the way, but from the meat-hungry goldseekers Cureton took a profit of $20,000, a considerable fortune in those days.

In the early 1850's a young English emigrant named Tom Candy Ponting probably established the record for the longest trail drive of Longhorns. Ponting was engaged in the livestock business in Illinois when he learned of the easy availability of Longhorns in Texas. Late in 1852 he and his partner traveled there on horseback, carrying a small bag of gold coins. They had no trouble assembling a herd of 700 bawling Longhorns at nine dollars or less a head. Early in 1853 they headed north for Illinois. It was a rainy spring and Ponting and his partner had to hire Cherokees to help swim the cattle across the Arkansas River. "I sat on my horse every night while we were crossing through the Indian country," said Ponting. "I was so afraid I could not sleep in the tent, but we had no stampede." Missouri was still thinly settled, and there was plenty of vegetation to keep the Longhorns from losing weight. At St. Louis the animals were ferried across the Mississippi, and on July 26 Ponting and his cattle reached Christian County, Illinois.

There through the winter months he fed them on corn, which cost him fifteen cents a bushel. He sold off a few scrubs to traveling cattle buyers, and then in the spring he cut out the best of the herd and started trail driving again, this time toward the East. At Muncie, Indiana Ponting found that railroad cars were available for livestock transport to New York. "We made arrangements and put the cattle on the cars. We unloaded them at Cleveland, letting them jump out on the sand banks. We unloaded them next at Dunkirk, then at Harnesville, and then at Bergen Hill." On July 3, 1854, from Bergen Hill in New Jersey, Ponting ferried the much-traveled Longhorns across the Hudson to the New York cattle market, completing a two-year journey of 1,500 miles on foot and 600 miles by rail. They were the first Texas Longhorns to reach New York City.

"The cattle are rather long-legged though fine-horned, with long taper horns, and something of a wild look," reported the New York Tribune. "The expense from Texas to Illinois was about $2 a head, the owners camping all the way. From Illinois to New York, the expense was $17 a head." To the New York buyers the Longhorns were worth $80 a head. Tom Ponting had more than doubled his investment.

About this same time another young adventurer from Illinois, Charles Goodnight, was trying to build up his own herd of Longhorns in the Brazos River country. As a young boy Goodnight had journeyed to Texas with his family, riding much of the way bareback. When he was 21, he and his stepbrother went to work for a rancher, keeping watch over 400 skittish Longhorns and branding the calves. Their pay for this work was one-fourth of the calves born during the year. "As the end of the first year's branding resulted in only thirty-two calves for our share," Goodnight recalled afterward, "and as the value was

The Kansas Pacific Railroad advertised its advantages to Texas cattlemen.

about three dollars per head, we figured out that we had made between us, not counting expenses, ninety-six dollars."

Goodnight and his partner persevered, however, and after four years of hard work they owned a herd of 4,000. Before they could convert many of their animals into cash, however, the Civil War began. Goodnight soon found himself scouting for a company of Confederate mounted riflemen, and spent most of the war disputing control of the upper Brazos and Red River country with Comanches and Kiowas instead of with blue-coated Yankees. At the war's end his makeshift uniform was worn out, his Confederate money was worthless, and his Longhorn herd had virtually disappeared. "I suffered great loss," Goodnight said. "The Confederate authorities had taken many of my cattle without paying a cent. Indians had raided our herds and cattle thieves were branding them, to their own benefit without regard to our rights." He was 30 years old and financially destitute.

Almost every other Texan returning from the war found himself in the same situation. When rumors reached the cattle country early in the spring of 1866 that meat was in short supply in the North, hundreds of young Texans began rounding up Longhorns. Huge packing houses were being constructed in Northern cities, and on a 345-acre tract where nine railroads converged, the Chicago Union Stock Yards was opened for business. A Longhorn steer worth five dollars in useless Confederate money in Texas would bring forty dollars in good U.S. currency in the Chicago market.

From the brush country, the plains, and the coastal regions of Texas, mounted drivers turned herd after herd of cattle northward across Indian Territory. Their goal was the nearest railhead, Sedalia, in west-central Missouri. Following approximately the route used by Tom Ponting thirteen years earlier, the trail drivers forded Red River and moved on to Fort Gibson, where they had to cross the more formidable Arkansas. Plagued by unseasonable cold weather, stampedes, and flooded streams, they pushed their Longhorns on into southeastern Kansas.

Here they encountered real trouble. From Baxter Springs northward to the Sedalia railhead, the country was being settled by small farmers, many of them recent battlefield enemies of the Texans. The settlers did not want their fences wrecked and their crops trampled, and they used force in stopping the Texans from driving cattle across their properties. By summer's end, over 100,000 stalled cattle were strung out between Baxter Springs and Sedalia. The grass died or was burned off by defiant farmers. Dishonest cattle buyers from the North bought herds with bad checks. The unsold cattle died or were abandoned, and the great drives of 1866 came to an end. For many of the Texans it had been a financial bust.

A less optimistic folk might have gone home defeated, but not the cattlemen of Texas. By the spring of 1867 many were ready to drive Longhorns north again. And in that year, thanks to an enterprising Yankee stockman, a convenient shipping point was waiting to welcome their coming. At the end of the Civil War, Joseph McCoy, of Springfield, Illinois had started a business of buying livestock for resale to the new packinghouses in Chicago. Appalled by the Baxter Springs-Sedalia debacle of 1866, McCoy was determined to find a railroad shipping point somewhere at the end of an open trail from Texas. He studied the maps of new railroads being built westward, and chose a town in Kansas — Abilene, near the end of the Kansas Pacific Railroad.

"Abilene in 1867 was a very small, dead place," McCoy admitted. But it met all the requirements for a cattle-shipping town. It was west of the settled farming country; it had a railroad, a river full of water for thirsty steers, and a sea of grass for miles around for holding and fattening livestock at the end of the drives. And nearby was Fort Riley, offering protection from possible Indian raids.

Within sixty days McCoy managed to construct a shipping yard, a barn, an office, and a hotel. From the Kansas Pacific he wheedled railroad ties to build loading pens sturdy enough to hold wild Longhorns. Meanwhile, he had sent messengers southward to inform the cattlemen of Texas that Abilene was "a good safe place to drive to, where they could sell, or ship cattle unmolested to other markets."

Over what soon became known as the Chisholm Trail, thousands of Texas cattle began moving into Abilene. Although the 1867 season got off to a late start and rail shipments did not begin until September, 36,000 Longhorns were marketed that first year. In 1868 the number doubled, and in 1870 the Kansas Pacific could scarcely find enough cars to handle the 300,000 Longhorns sold to Northern packing houses. Abilene in the meantime had grown into a boom town of stores, hotels, saloons, and honkytonks where Texas cowboys celebrated the end of their trail drive and engendered the legends of gunmen, lawmen, shootouts, and exotic dance hall girls.

One Texas cowman who did not make the long drive north to Abilene was Charles Goodnight. Back in the spring of 1866 when most of his neighbors were driving herds across Indian Territory for the Sedalia railhead, Goodnight was still trying to round up his scattered Longhorns. By the time he was ready to move out, he suspected that there was going to be a glut of cattle in Kansas and Missouri. Instead of heading north, he combined his Longhorns with those of Oliver Loving and they started their herd of 2,000 west toward New Mexico. Cattle were reported to be in great demand there by government agents who bought them for distribution to reservation Indians.

To reach New Mexico, Goodnight and Loving followed the abandoned route of the Butterfield Overland Stage along which waterholes and wells had been dug by the stage company. For this arduous journey, Goodnight constructed what was probably the first chuckwagon. Obtaining an old military wagon, he rebuilt it with the toughest wood he knew, a wood used by Indians for fashioning their bows — Osage orange or *bois d'arc*. At the rear he built a chuckbox with a hinged lid to which a folding leg was attached so that when it was lowered it formed a cook's work table. Fastened securely in front of the wagon was a convenient spigot running through to a barrel of water. Beneath the driver's seat was a supply of necessary tools such as axes and spades, and below the wagon was a cowhide sling for transporting dry wood or buffalo chips to be used in making cooking fires. A generation of trail drivers would adopt Goodnight's chuckwagon for long drives and roundups, and variations of it are still in use today.

Goodnight's and Loving's first drive to New Mexico was un-eventful until they began crossing the lower edge of the Staked Plains, where the water holes had gone dry. For three days the rangy Longhorns became almost unmanageable from thirst, and when they scented the waters of the Pecos they stampeded, piling into the river, some drowning under the onrush of those in the rear. The partners succeeded, however, in driving most of the herd into Fort Sumner, where several thousand Navajos confined in the Bosque Redondo were near starvation.

A government contractor took more than half the Longhorns, paying Goodnight and Loving $12,000 in gold. By the standards of that day they had suddenly become prosperous. While Loving drove the remainder of the cattle to the Colorado mining country, Good-night returned to Texas to round up another herd of Longhorns.

⸺━⊰●⊱━⸺

In the years immediately following the disruptions of the Civil War, thousands of unbranded Longhorns roamed wild in the Texas brush country. The cowboys soon discovered that the easiest way to round up these cattle was to lure them out of the chaparral with tame de-coys. James H. Cook, an early trail driver who later became a leading cattleman of the West, described such a wild Longhorn roundup:

"About sunrise we left the corral, taking with us the decoy herd, Longworth leading the way. After traveling a mile or more he led the herd into a dense clump of brush and motioned us to stop driving it. Then, telling two men to stay with the cattle he rode off, signaling the other men and myself to follow him . . . in the brush ahead I caught a glimpse of some cattle. A few minutes later I heard voices singing a peculiar melody without words. The sounds of these voices indicated that the singers were scattered in the form of a circle about the cattle. In a few moments some of the cattle came toward me, and I recognized a few of them as belonging to the herd which we had brought from our camp. In a few seconds more I saw that we had some wild ones, too. They whirled back when they saw me, only to find a rider wherever they might turn. The decoy cattle were fairly quiet, simply milling around through the thicket, and the wild ones were soon thoroughly mingled with them." Cook and the other cowboys now had little difficulty driving the combined tame and wild Long-horns into a corral where they were held until time to start an overland drive to market.

The work of rounding up Longhorns gradually developed into an organized routine directed by a man who came to be known as the range boss. During a roundup, his authority was as ironclad as that of a ship's captain. At the beginning of a "gather" the range boss would assemble an outfit of about twenty cowhands, a horse wrangler to look after the mounts and, most important of all, a camp cook. Roundups began very early in the spring because every cattleman was eager to be the first to hit the trail before the grass was overgrazed along the route to Kansas.

On the first morning of a roundup the men would be up before sunrise to eat their breakfasts hurriedly at the chuckwagon; then in the gray light of dawn they would mount their best ponies and gather around the range boss for orders. As soon as he had outlined the lim-its of the day's roundup, the boss would send his cowhands riding out in various directions to sweep the range. When each rider reached a specified point, he turned back and herded all the cattle within his area back into the camp center.

After a herd was collected, the second operation of a roundup began. This next step was to separate the young stock which were to be branded for return to the range from the mature animals which were to be driven overland to market. "Cutting out" it was fittingly called, and this performance was, and still is, the highest art of the cowboy. Cutting out required a specially trained pony, one that could "turn on a dime," and a rider who had a sharp eye, good muscular re-flexes, and who was an artist at handling a lariat. After selecting an animal to be separated from the herd, the rider and his horse would begin a quick-moving game of twisting and turning, of sudden stops and changes of pace.

Roping, the final act of the cutting out process, also required close cooperation between pony and rider. Forming an oval-shaped noose six or seven feet in diameter, the cowboy would spin it over his head with tremendous speed. A second before making the throw, he would draw his arm and shoulder back, then shoot his hand forward, aiming the noose sometimes for the animal's head, sometimes for its feet. As the lariat jerked tight, the rider instantly snubbed it around his saddle horn. At the same moment the pony had to be stopped short. The position of the pony at the moment of throw was important; a sudden jerk of a taut lariat could spill both horse and rider.

As soon as the unbranded animal was roped, it was immediately herded or dragged to the nearest bonfire where branding irons were kept heated to an orange red. In Texas, all branding was done in a corral, a legal requirement devised to prevent hasty and illegal branding by rustlers on the open range. The first brands in Texas were usually the initials of the owners, and if two cattlemen had the same initials, a bar or a circle distinguished one from the other. Law required that brands be publicly registered by counties in Texas; other western states had state brand books. In the early years when ranches were unfenced and land boundaries poorly marked, friction over unbranded cattle caused many a gunfight. To discourage rustlers who could easily change a "C" to an "O," an "F" to an "E," a "V" to a "W," ranchers designed unusual brands, some of the more famous being Stirrup, Andiron, Scissors, Frying Pan, and Dinner Bell.

As soon as the work of branding was completed, preparations for the trail drive began in earnest. The owner of the cattle was responsible for food and other supplies, but each cowboy assembled the personal gear he would need on the journey. Every item he wore or carried was designed for utility. Tents were seldom taken along, two blankets being considered sufficient shelter from the elements. If the weather was warm, the cowboys shed their coats, and if they wore vests they rarely buttoned them because of the rangeland belief that to do so would bring on a bad cold. Most wore leather chaps to protect their legs from underbrush and weather. They put high heels on their boots to keep their feet from slipping through the stirrups, and they wore heavy leather gloves because the toughest palms could be burned raw by the lariats they used constantly in their work. They paid good money for wide-brimmed hats because they served as roofs against rain, snow, and sun. They used bandannas for ear coverings, as dust masks, as strainers when drinking muddy water, for drying dishes, as bandages, towels, slings for broken arms, to tie hats on in very windy weather, and for countless other purposes.

<hr>

Getting the average trail herd of about 3,000 cattle underway was as complicated an operation as starting a small army on a march across country. Each rider needed several spare mounts for the long journey, and this herd of horses accompanying a cow column was known as the remuda — from a Spanish word meaning replacement. A trail boss, sixteen to eighteen cowboys, a cook and chuckwagon, and a horse wrangler for the remuda made up the personnel of an average drive.

It was necessary to move slowly at first until the restive Longhorns grew accustomed to daily routines. To keep a herd in order a wise trail boss would search out a huge dominating animal and make it the lead steer. Charles Goodnight had one called Old Blue which he considered so valuable as a leader that after every long drive he brought the animal back to the home ranch. Two or three quiet days on the trail was usually long enough to calm a herd of Longhorns. After that the cattle would fall into place each morning like infantrymen on the march, each one keeping the same relative position in file as the herd moved along.

Cattleman John Clay left a classic description of an early trail herd in motion: "You see a steer's head and horns silhouetted against the skyline, and then another and another, till you realize it is a herd. On each flank is a horseman. Along come the leaders with a swinging gait, quickening as they smell the waters of the muddy river." The pattern of trail driving soon became as routinized as that of roundups — the trail boss a mile or two out in front, horse herd and chuckwagon following, then the point riders directing the lead steers, and strung along the widening flow of the herd the swing and flank riders, until at the rear came the drag riders in clouds of dust, keeping the weaker cattle moving.

Not many trail drivers had time to keep diaries, that of George Duffield being one of the rare survivors. From it a reader can feel the tensions and weariness, the constant threats of weather, the difficult river crossings, and dangers of stampedes.

May 1: Big stampede. Lost 200 head of Cattle.

May 2: Spent the day hunting & found but 25 Head. It has been Raining for three days. These are dark days for me.

May 3: Day spent in hunting Cattle. Found 23. Hard rain and wind. Lots of trouble.

May 8: Rain pouring down in torrents. Ran my horse into a ditch & got my Knee badly sprained — 15 miles.

May 9: Still dark and gloomy. River up. Everything looks Blue to me.

May 14: Swam our cattle & Horses & built Raft & Rafted our provisions & blanket & covers. Lost Most of our Kitchen furniture such as camp Kittles Coffee Pots Cups Plates Canteens &c &c.

May 17: No Breakfast. Pack & off is the order.

May 31: Swimming Cattle is the order. We worked all day in the River & at dusk got the last Beefe over — I am now out of Texas — This day will long be remembered by me — There was one of our party Drowned today.

George Duffield made his drive along the eastern edge of Indian Territory in 1866. Ten years later the drives were still as wearisome and dangerous, but the trails had shifted much farther westward and there had been a swift succession of trail towns. A new railroad, the Santa Fe, pushed sixty-five miles south of Abilene in 1871, and Newton became the main cattle-shipping town. Newton's reign was brief, however; it was replaced by Ellsworth and Wichita. Although the advancing railroad tracks were a boon to cattlemen seeking shorter routes to markets, they also brought settlers west by the thousands. By 1876 the life of the Chisholm Trail was ending and the Western Trail, or Dodge City Trail, had taken its place.

———————

Dodge City was the king of the trail towns, the "cowboy capital," a fabulous town of innumerable legends for a golden decade. The names survive in history: Long Branch Saloon, the Lady Gay, the Dodge Opera House, Delmonico's, Wyatt Earp, Doc Holliday, Boot Hill, Bat Masterson, Clay Allison, Luke Short, and Big Nose Kate. But it was Longhorns and cattlemen that made Dodge City, and it was during Dodge's long reign that the Longhorns came to the end of their day of glory.

One of the men responsible for the change was Charles Goodnight. In the year that Dodge opened as a cow town, 1875, Goodnight found himself financially destitute for the second time in his life. He had made a fortune with Texas cattle, bought a ranch in Colorado, become a banker, and then lost everything in the Panic of 1873. All he had left in 1875 was a small herd of unmarketable Longhorns, and he decided it was time to return to Texas and start all over again.

He chose an unlikely region, the Texas Panhandle, an area long shunned by cattlemen because it was supposed to be a desert. Goodnight, however, recalled the immense herds of buffalo which had roamed there for centuries, and he reasoned that wherever buffalo could thrive so could Longhorns. He found a partner, John Adair, to furnish the capital and drive his Longhorns into the heart of the Panhandle, to the Palo Duro Canyon, where he discovered plenty of water and grass. There he founded the JA Ranch. Soon after starting operations, Goodnight began introducing Herefords and Shorthorns, cross-breeding them at first with Longhorns so that his cattle produced more and better beef, yet retained the ability to flourish on the open range and endure long drives to Dodge City.

Other ranchers soon followed his example, and "White Faces" instead of "Longhorns" gradually became the symbol of trail cattle. After a continuing flood of homesteaders, brought west by the proliferating railroads, made it necessary to close the trail to Dodge City, one more overland route — the National Trail to Wyoming and Montana — saw the last treks of the Longhorns.

As the 19th century came to an end, so did open range ranching and trail driving. There was no longer any place for rangy Longhorns. Until the day he died, however, Charles Goodnight kept a small herd of them to remind him of the old days. A few specimens survive today in wildlife refuges and on larger ranches as curiosities, or for occasional use in parades and Western movies. But most of these animals are descendants of crossbreds. The day of the genuine Texas Longhorn — with his body tucked up in the flanks, his high shoulder-top thin enough to split a hail stone, his ribs flat, his back swayed, his ability to outwalk any other breed of cattle — now belongs to history.

"The head was thrown on the trail and driven away to the west without rest or halt." A cattle drive in motion as depicted in illustrations by Maynard Dixon which appeared in Mc Clure's Magazine, *November 1908, as part of the article, "Loving's Bend— A Reminiscence of the Texas Ranchmen," by Edgar Beecher Bronson.*

17

———⟫❦⟪———

The Pony Express

"His mailbags saddled to a spirited horse, a solitary rider galloped out of St. Joseph, Missouri on the first mission to California with . . ."

S hortly after noon of April 3, 1860, a special messenger carrying mail — which had been collected in several Eastern cities — crossed the Mississippi River to Mark Twain's town of Hannibal, Missouri. There he boarded a train consisting of an eight-wheeler locomotive and a single car waiting on the tracks of the Hannibal & St. Joseph Railroad. That day the engineer set a new speed record by crossing the state of Missouri and bringing the messenger into St. Joseph in less than five hours.

As the train steamed into the station, a booming cannon announced its arrival, and while a brass band played stirring music and the people of St. Joe waved flags and cheered wildly, the contents of the mail pouch from the East were quickly transferred to a specially made rectangular saddlebag. Known as a *mochila* (Spanish for knapsack) it was designed with four pouches and two slits in the leather so that it would fit tightly over cantle and pommel of a saddle. A rider mounted upon it would have a pouch in front of and behind each leg. As soon as the pouches were padlocked, the mochila was thrown across the saddle of a horse waiting in front of the St. Joseph livery stable, and a jockey-sized rider leaped upon the animal's back.

Recorded details of that first departure of the Pony Express for San Francisco vary considerably. Some observers described the horse as a bay; others said it was black. Some accounts reported that the rider left on schedule at 5 p.m., others said he was delayed until 6:30 or possibly 7:15. As for the rider's name, at least four have been recorded, but Johnny Frey (sometimes spelled Frye or Fry) is most often given credit.

Regardless of whether the rider was Johnny Frey, there seems no doubt that he left at a gallop, and that he was dressed in fancy regalia — red shirt, blue pants, a wide-brimmed hat, and shiny, high-topped boots. At the beginning of service, all the riders were presented with a red shirt and a pair of Levi Strauss's indigo-blue denim pants, but most of them preferred plain buckskins. At any rate, that first rider was soon clattering aboard a Missouri River Ferry and a few minutes later rode off the boat into Elwood, Kansas to gallop away on the first section of the 1,966 miles to Sacramento that he and thirty or more other young men were determined to traverse during the next ten days.

<hr/>

The route cut across northeastern Kansas into Nebraska, following the Platte Valley to Fort Kearney, Julesburg, and Fort Laramie. From there it ran through the famed South Pass of the Rocky Mountains to Fort Bridger, crossed the Wasatch Range to Salt Lake City, skirted the south edge of Great Salt Lake, and took a tortuous route across the alkali flats of Nevada to Carson and Lake Tahoe, climbed through the high passes of the Sierra, and descended to Sacramento where an easy boat ride to San Francisco completed the journey.

At about the same hour that the first westbound Pony Express was leaving St. Joe, an eastbound rider was leaving San Francisco. Although three different riders have been given credit, the best evidence indicates that James Randall made a "show" ride from the San Francisco Pony Express office to the local boat landing, and that Billy Hamilton rode the first horse east out of Sacramento. This confusion of names is comparable to the modern difficulty in remembering functions and names of the first moon-bound astronauts. It was the event rather than the participants that intrigued everybody's imagination.

The grandest celebration of this event occurred in San Francisco about midnight of April 14. A few hours earlier San Franciscans had learned by telegraph from Sacramento that the first Pony Express rider from the East had arrived there and was already aboard the steamboat Antelope bound for the Golden Gate. When Billy Hamilton rode his horse off the boat a festive crowd carrying torchlights was waiting for him. A brightly costumed band began playing "See the Conquering Hero Comes" and led a noisy parade beneath street-wide banners proclaiming a welcome to the Pony Express. At the corner of Montgomery and California streets the celebrants lighted a huge bonfire, the tumult awakening the city fire department which came rushing to extinguish the blaze, but then joined in the merrymaking. The reason for this riotous celebration was the demonstrated proof that mail delivery to California from the East could be accomplished in ten days.

The mail carried on that first run weighed less than fifteen pounds — about eighty-five pieces including letters, telegrams, bank drafts, newspapers from Eastern cities printed on thin paper, and a message of congratulations from President James Buchanan to the governor of California. But the important thing was that the Pony Express had cut in half the regular delivery time of the Butterfield Overland Mail.

A hope of capturing the Butterfield Overland's $600,000 government-subsidized mail contract was indeed the sole reason for the existence of the Pony Express, and the man chiefly responsible for its creation was William Hepburn Russell. He was a partner in the West's largest wagon-freighting operation — Russell, Majors & Waddell. Early in 1860, when delays in collecting bills and a costly venture into a stagecoach line to Colorado brought the company into financial difficulties, Russell journeyed to Washington in search of contracts and funds. There he met Senator William Gwin of California, whose constituents were constantly demanding faster mail service from the East. Since 1858 the Butterfield stage company had been carrying the mail from St. Louis to San Francisco, but its route ran far south by way of El Paso (partly for political reasons, partly to avoid winter blizzards), and its 2,800 miles required three weeks for passage.

Russell assured Gwin that his company could cut the time in half by taking a more direct central route and carrying the mail on horseback. What Russell wanted to prove was that the central route could be used as a permanent thoroughfare throughout all seasons of the year. He believed that if he could do this, he would have no difficulty in winning the lucrative government mail contract away from Butterfield Overland Mail; its trail crossed Texas, and when that state joined the Confederacy in February 1861 all service would be suspended.

In January 1860 Russell and Gwin made a mutual agreement: Russell pledged to organize a Pony Express mail service from the Missouri River to California, and Gwin promised to obtain a subsidy from Congress to insure its success. On January 27 Russell telegraphed his partners from Washington that he was arranging to start the ten-day Pony Express on April 3. On January 30 the Leavenworth News hailed the glamorous project with headlines: *Great Express Adventure From Leavenworth To Sacramento In Ten Days. Clear The Track And Let The Pony Come Through.*

When Russell returned to Leavenworth he found his partners firmly opposed to the Pony Express. Their freighting company was already deeply in debt, and the proposed new operation would only add to the burden. Russell admitted that the stakes were high, but he was confident that if the Pony Express was a success, the company was bound to win millions of dollars in mail contracts.

"Mr. Russell strenuously insisted that we stand by him," Alexander Majors, one of the partners, later wrote, "as he had committed himself to Senator Gwin before leaving Washington, assuring him that he could get his partners to join him, and that he might rely on the project being carried through, and saying it would be very humiliating to his pride to return to Washington and be compelled to say the scheme had fallen through from a lack of his partners' confidence."

Majors and the third partner, William Waddell, eventually agreed to proceed with the undertaking, although reluctantly, and Russell was authorized to use notes of credit to organize the Pony Express. He had only sixty days to assemble 500 horses and employ station-keepers, stock-tenders, and riders. He estimated that 190 stations would have to be stocked and manned. The company already operated a freighting and stage line to Salt Lake City, but many new stations would have to be added for the pony riders, and the route lengthened to Sacramento. He chose St. Joseph, Missouri for the eastern terminus because it was the farthest westward point then reached by both telegraph and railroad.

To find the riders he wanted, Russell placed advertisements in newspapers along the frontier:

WANTED — Young, skinny, wiry fellows not over 18. Must be expert riders willing to risk death daily. Orphans preferred.

From the numerous applicants he selected eighty, none weighing more than 130 pounds, and before each rider was hired he was required to take a solemn oath not to use profane language, nor get drunk, nor gamble, nor to treat his mount with cruelty, nor interfere with the rights of citizens or Indians. He was then presented with a copy of the Holy Bible "to defend himself against more contaminations" and a pair of Colt's revolvers and a rifle "to defend himself against warlike Indians." The rifles were afterward recalled, being too cumbersome to carry on swift-moving ponies across the West.

Late in March Russell announced through newspapers in California and in the East the departure times for Pony Express mail from major cities to connect with San Francisco or St. Joseph, where on April 3 the riders would be leaving on their first runs east and west. The charge for letters was set at $5 per half ounce plus the regular ten cents postage for U.S. mail.

Although it was organized in great haste, the Pony Express proved to be one of the most dependable mail services ever operated in the United States. The logistics of intermeshing riders, horses, stations, and supplies into a tight schedule across hundreds of miles without direct communication from a headquarters was incredibly difficult. Yet somehow the system worked efficiently most of the time in spite of bad weather and one dangerous period of Indian harassment.

The 190 stations were separated into five divisions, each under a hard-driving superintendent whose responsibility was to see that the riders and stationmasters performed their duties and kept to their schedules. Within each division was a series of swing stations and relay stations. The Pony Express riders began and ended their rides at swing, or home, stations which might be forty to more than a hundred miles apart, depending upon the terrain. At intervals of ten, fifteen, or twenty miles between the home stations were relay stations, consisting usually of a small shelter with a stable beside it containing perhaps two horses. The home stations were considerably larger, being furnished with bunks and dining facilities; they frequently served also as stagecoach stops. The stations were built of timber or logs where available, sod across the Plains, and adobe in the desert country.

To supply stations between St. Joe and Salt Lake City, Russell, Majors & Waddell bought grain from Midwestern farmers and hauled it in wagons for hundreds of miles at transportation costs of ten to twenty cents a pound. Grain was very important for Pony Express horses; the Indian-fighting army had already discovered that a grain-fed horse could outrun and outdistance the Indians' grass-fed mounts. For the section west of Salt Lake City, the company depended upon the Mormons to supply grain, hay, and food-stuffs. Across the arid wastelands to the Sierra, barrels of water also had to be hauled long distances to supply the stations. At each of the home stations, either the stationmaster or an assistant was required to be on duty at all times, and at least one man was assigned to each relay station.

One of the most dramatic performances designed to save time was the changing of mounts at relay stations. The company allowed only two minutes for the transfer. At first it furnished the riders with a horn to blow, in the manner of approaching stagecoach drivers, but this was quickly abandoned as unnecessary. The drumming of hoofs and the hallooing of the rider gave the stationkeeper time enough to saddle and bridle a mount. As soon as the rider dropped from his saddle, the stationkeeper handed him a cup of water, or sometimes hot coffee and a bite of bread with meat. While the rider was gulping food and drink and stamping the stiffness out of his legs, the station-keeper was quickly transferring the mochila to the waiting horse. In two minutes or less, the rider was mounted again, spurring his fresh pony away for another ten- or twenty-mile run. At the home stations, of course, another rider would be waiting to take the mochila across the next section of the route.

———————

Operating on the theory that the lighter the load the faster the horse, the far-sighted William Russell ordered saddle-makers to manufacture about a hundred special Pony Express saddles that would weigh a third less than regular saddles. They had no skirts and were fitted with single cinches and lightweight stirrups. The same saddle-makers designed the mochilas to fit the low, sloping cantles and shortnecked pommels.

En route the mail was handled with great care. Letter bundles were wrapped in oiled silk to protect them from weather damage. Three of the four mochila pouches bore locks which could be opened at only five points along the route by division superintendents or military officers for removal or addition of letters. The fourth pouch was used to carry mail, company orders, and the time card of the rider. All stationmasters had keys to fit its lock, and they were required to note and initial the times of arrival and departure of the rider on his card.

At the beginning of service a limit of twenty pounds was set for each mail, a weight that was rarely exceeded as the average number of letters carried was about one hundred, hardly comparable to the average 6,300 carried on the slower Butterfield Mail coaches. In hopes of increasing the volume of letters, the Pony Express on July 1, 1861 reduced its rates from $5 per half ounce to $1, and although the number of letters increased, the monetary returns dropped. At that time the service had only four months remaining before completion of the first transcontinental telegraph ended its life and virtually proved that the most urgent messages carried by the Pony Express were news dispatches. So eager were Eastern newspapers to receive news from the Far West that several of them employed part-time correspondents at St. Joseph to receive messages on the Pony Express and then telegraph them to the newspapers.

To make certain that enough riders were always available to carry the mail, William Russell gradually added about forty more to his original eighty, replacing a few who departed to join one of the contending armies in the Civil War, and stationing extra men on the more rugged and dangerous sections of the route. These riders became romantic figures in the American imagination, and for a contemporary description of one of them as seen by a stagecoach traveler we are indebted to Mark Twain:

> *Away across the endless dead level of the prairie a black speck appears against the sky, and it is plain that it moves. Well, I should think so! In a second or two it becomes a horse and rider, rising and falling, rising and falling, rising and falling — sweeping toward us nearer and nearer — growing more and more distinct, more and more sharply defined, nearer and still nearer, and the flutter of the hoofs comes faintly to the ear — another instant a whoop and a hurrah from our upper deck, a wave of the rider's hand, but no reply, and man and horse burst past our excited faces, and go winging away like a belated fragment of a storm!*

For this arduous work under burning summer skies and rains and winter blizzards, the riders received about $125 a month, according to Alexander Majors — who recalled that they were the highest paid employees after superintendents, and this included bed and board. The stationkeepers received between $50 and $100, depending upon their locations. In terms of today's purchasing power, Pony Express riders probably earned what would be equal to $15,000 a year.

The horses which these young men rode cost Russell, Majors & Waddell about $200 each, or four times the price of an average riding horse. Most of them were tough, undersized mustangs, sure-footed and fast, and were branded upon the right flanks with the company brand XP. The upkeep of these horses, the maintenance of stations, payrolls for more than 500 employees, and losses of equipment during an unexpected Paiute Indian uprising soon ran the operating costs to more than $30,000 a month. William Russell had never expected to make a profit from the Pony Express, but he had hoped to break even. After a few months' operation, however, expenses were exceeding income by at least two-thirds, and the future of the Pony Express was obviously in jeopardy.

In the meantime the brave young men in the saddles were performing heroic feats and establishing remarkable endurance records. The two who became most famous were Robert (Pony Bob) Haslam and William F. Cody, later known as Buffalo Bill.

Pony Bob probably set the record for endurance with a series of rides made during the so-called Washoe County War — an uprising of Paiutes against miners invading their territory in Nevada. On May 11, 1860 Haslam started out on his regular seventy-seven-mile run from Friday's Station near Lake Tahoe to Buckland's Station (Fort Churchill), but at Carson he found that all spare ponies had been seized by miners pursuing the Paiutes. After resting his horse, Pony Bob continued to Fort Churchill, where wild rumors of Paiute raids had so frightened the relief rider, Johnson Richardson, that he refused to carry the mochila over the next 115-mile section. When the division superintendent offered Pony Bob $50 to take Richardson's run, he accepted and rode to the next home station without incident. After sleeping a short time, Haslam was awakened and told that the westbound mail had arrived and he would have to take Richardson's run back to Fort Churchill. At Cold Springs, however, he found the smoking ruins of the relay station and the dead body of the station-keeper. The Paiutes had taken the spare horses, and Pony Bob had to ride his tired mount on to Sand Springs. Upon reaching Fort Churchill, he found no relief rider, and had to mount up again for his regular run to Friday's. He rode into his home station on May 13, after covering 384 miles on horseback in thirty-six hours of riding.

———————

As for Bill Cody, because of the numerous myths surrounding his career some skeptical writers have questioned whether he ever was a Pony Express rider. He would have been only 14 or 15 years old at the time, yet Alexander Majors testified that during 1861 Cody was the regular rider on the 116-mile section between Red Buttes and Three Crossings in central Wyoming. According to the legend, Cody was working as a messenger for Russell, Majors & Waddell, and when he asked for a job as a Pony Express rider, William Russell recommended him to division superintendent Jack Slade (who later became an outlaw and was hanged by vigilantes). On one occasion young Cody reportedly replaced a rider killed by Indians, taking the mail over a double section as Pony Bob Haslam had done, riding for 322 miles. In later years after he became Buffalo Bill, either he or his ghost writer lengthened the distance to 388 miles, or four miles farther than Pony Bob's ride, so that he could claim the record.

<hr/>

Among other Pony Expressmen who performed astonishing feats were Jack Keetly, who rode 340 miles in 31 hours; Jim Moore, who rode 280 miles in and out of Julesburg in 14 hours and 46 minutes, which was probably the speed record; and Richard Egan, who replaced a fellow rider (who wanted to go courting) and stayed in the saddle for 330 miles. Undoubtedly the handsomest of the Pony Expressmen, Egan in later life became a Mormon bishop. One of the unproven legends concerns Johnny Frey, whose girl friend on his Kansas route baked cookies for him. It is said that she invented the doughnut so that Johnny could spear one on a finger as he galloped past.

Records of casualties among the riders are incomplete. The name of Burt Riles was listed in a frontier newspaper as having died of wounds at Cold Springs Station on May 16, 1860 during the Paiute uprising, and early accounts tell of an unnamed rider who was killed and scalped along the Platte River, his horse escaping to bring the mail safely to the next station. In Nevada seven stations were listed as burned by Paiutes, and the number of stationkeepers recorded as killed varies from seven to sixteen. Yet during its nineteen months of existence only one mochila was lost, that one being a casualty of the Indian disturbances.

Among the important letters and messages carried by the Pony Express were the reports of Lincoln's election, his inaugural speech in which he warned the seceding Southern states that they could not lawfully leave the Union, startling dispatches telling of the firing upon Fort Sumter, military messages requesting the California state government to raise five regiments, and then orders as to their disposition in the Southwest. For important messages special efforts were made to speed the ponies: Lincoln's inaugural crossed the West in seven days and seventeen hours, news of Fort Sumter in eight days and fourteen hours. In addition to newspapers, heavy users of the express were businessmen and government officials. One of the most expensive letters contained a file of detailed dispatches sent by a British official

Some Pony Express riders (clockwise from top left): Richard Erastus "Ras" Egan; Jack Keetley (Courtesy of Pony Express National Memorial, St. Joseph, Missouri); and William F. Cody as he appeared in a tintype taken circa 1864 only three years after the mail delivery experiment ended. (Courtesy of Buffalo Bill Historical Center, Cody, Wyoming)

notifying his government of movements of its Asiatic fleet; the letter cost the sender $135.

Throughout most of its existence, the Pony Express was engaged in a race across the continent with the first transcontinental telegraph line. Two months after mail service began, Congress appropriated funds to build a telegraph line to California, the contracts stipulating that it must be completed by July 1, 1862. As was done a few years later in the building of the first transcontinental railroad, one company built westward from Omaha and another eastward from California. By November 1860 the line out of Omaha was completed to Fort Kearney, and telegrams to California went into the mochilas there instead of at St. Joseph.

William Russell meanwhile was attempting to shore up the disintegrating financial structure of his company. He and his partners had sunk half a million dollars into the Pony Express, and he knew that it could never compete with the telegraph. Believing that two years would pass before completion of the telegraph line, he continued working toward winning the government mail contract away from Butterfield as well as obtaining a subsidy for the Pony Express. Senator Gwin, however, was unable to aid him with either objective, and to stave off bankruptcy Russell persuaded Godard Bailey, an official in the Interior Department, to lend him some Indian Trust Fund bonds which he took to New York and used as security to pay off his most pressing debts. During the last months of 1860 Russell and Bailey juggled funds secured on nearly a million dollars worth of "borrowed" government bonds until at last on Christmas Eve their illegal activities were discovered and Russell was arrested and jailed.

He was indicted for fraud, but in March 1861 was freed from prosecution on a legal technicality. He stayed in Washington, brazenly continuing to lobby for the Butterfield mail contract, but the nation was exploding into civil war. When the Butterfield route was closed across Texas in March, the old contract was switched to the Central Overland California & Pike's Peak Express Company, which had once belonged to Russell and his partners but during their financial difficulties had come under control of Ben Holladay, the Stagecoach King of the West.

━━━━━━◝◝◝◟◟◟━━━━━━

On October 18, 1861 the telegraph construction crew from the East reached Salt Lake City, and six days later the California crew joined them to connect the wires and establish telegraphic communication between the Atlantic and Pacific. They were more than eight months ahead of the contract schedule. On October 26 brief notices appeared in newspapers in the East and West: "Pony Express Will Be Discontinued From This Date." On that same day the editor of the Sacramento Bee published a farewell salute:

> Our little friend, the Pony, is to run no more . . . Farewell and forever, thou staunch, wilderness-overcoming, swift-footed messenger . . . thou wert the pioneer of a continent in the rapid transmission of intelligence between its people, and have dragged in your train the lightning itself, which, in good time, will be followed by steam communication by rail. Rest upon your honors; be satisfied with them, your destiny has been fulfilled — a new and higher power has superseded you.

Losses incurred by Russell, Majors & Waddell during operation of the Pony Express were at least half a million dollars and perhaps more, hastening bankruptcy for that once powerful company. According to one statistical study, during its brief existence the Pony Express carried 34,743 pieces of mail, and receipts totaled $90,141. "The amount of business transacted," said Alexander Majors in his rueful summing up of the enterprise, "was not sufficient to pay one-tenth of the expenses." By its example, however, the Pony Express proved that the central route across the West was superior to all others, thus determining the route of the first transcontinental railroad. At the same time, by providing swift communication it had helped Lincoln hold California for the Union. And it had forever captured the imagination of the Republic, its brave riders ranking to this day with Western cowboys as symbols of the frontier spirit of individual daring and perseverance.

Members of the Sylvester Rawding family pose in front of their sod house, north of Sargent, in Custer County, Nebraska, 1886. Photograph by Solomon D. Butcher, "a pioneer who photographed pioneers." Solomon D. Butcher Collection. Courtesy of Nebraska State Historical Society.

18

The Settlement of
the Great Plains

*"This whole country is full of persons rushing
hither and thither in search of homes."*

uropeans ventured upon America's Great Plains as early as the
16th century, yet for 300 years these vast grasslands remained
virtually unexplored. After the coming of the horse, Indian
tribes found the plains to be superb hunting grounds for
buffalo, antelope, and elk, and based their economy and culture upon
the mounted pursuit of wild game. The few white men who crossed
the plains during this time followed the rivers westward to the Rocky
Mountains in search of furs.

From the beginning of exploration, the area was regarded as a
spatial barrier, a monotonous, treeless expanse inhabited by savage
Indians and without enough rainfall to supply the necessary water requirements of men and their livestock. The early 19th-century map
makers labeled the area between the 98th meridian and the Rocky
Mountains as the Great American Desert. After the discovery of
California gold in 1848, a flood of adventurers headed west. Both
plains and Rockies were obstacles to be crossed, and if we may judge
from diaries and letters of gold-seeking travelers the big, rolling land
was generally regarded as a wasteland "unfit for cultivation and of
course uninhabitable by people depending upon agriculture for their
subsistence." They undoubtedly saw the plains during one of the

drought periods, which some meteorologists believe occur in cycles of approximately forty years.

By the end of the Civil War, most good farmland east of the Mississippi had been claimed, and a surge of aspiring war veterans and European emigrants poured out upon the plains looking for homes. Fortunately for them, a cycle of normal rainfall had returned. "Thare is good land on the Missouri for a poar man's home," one man wrote back to his Eastern friends, and another declared: "We are in the land of the living and in the place of hope." The settlement of the plains was the settlement of America's last frontier, and it was an epic of courage and greed, of sacrifice and plundering, of man's frailties and his capacities to endure. It was a tragic clash of cultures, and no area so vast was ever so transformed in so brief a time as the Great Plains between the end of the Civil War and the 1890's. The states formed by this settlement include the Dakotas, the western parts of Nebraska, Kansas, Oklahoma, and Texas, and the eastern parts of New Mexico, Colorado, Wyoming, and Montana.

To aid land seekers, Congress passed in 1862 an act enabling settlers to claim without cost homesteads of 160 acres. Permanent title to the acreage could be obtained by living on and improving the land. As the Homestead Act excluded persons who had borne arms against the United States, most Southerners were unable to take advantage of it, although after restoration of citizenship they were eligible to buy land under an earlier act of 1841. This law provided preemption rights to 160 acres of public land at a cost of $1.25 per acre. Settlement of the central and northern plains, however, was accomplished mainly by Union veterans or European emigrants who had applied for citizenship. In 1873, at the height of the Great Plains land rush, a third provision known as the Timber Culture Act enabled settlers to acquire an additional 160 acres by planting specified acres in trees and cultivating them for periods of eight to ten years. Many small groves of oak, maple, walnut, and other trees which can still be found on the plains had their origins in this act.

Another and very important source of acreage for settlement was railroad land. Taking advantage of the national fever for rapid

stoves were developed for use on the plains, but a popular remark of the times was that it required "two men and a boy to keep a hay fire going." The hay-burners consisted of metal cylinders containing coiled springs; the springs were pushed down by packing the cylinders tightly with hay. As the fuel burned, the springs pressed a fresh supply into the fire. Such stoves required constant attention, especially during zero weather.

———⊰⊱———

For those whose homesteads were distant from dependable streams, water supply was also a problem. As soon as a settler marked his claim and set up a wagon-cover tent, he started searching for water. It was not unusual for a plains farmer to haul water in barrels for several miles over a period of a year or more until he could dig a well by hand or hire a professional well driller. The distance from ground surface to water was sometimes as much as 300 feet through hard clay and rock. One Oklahoma plainsman when asked why he persisted in hauling water nine miles instead of digging a well replied: "It's just as near to water one way or the other, and I prefer to get mine along horizontal rather than perpendicular lines."

To illustrate the twin problems of wood and water on the plains, historian Edward E. Dale told a story of an old Tennessean who was visiting the homestead claim of his two nephews. When he arrived at their location beside a sandy arroyo, one of the young men took a pickaxe and began digging in the dry earth for mesquite roots which were used to make a fire. At the same time the other nephew hung a pail over the end of an iron pipe running from their windmill. As there was no wind stirring, he had to climb to the top of the wind-mill tower and turn the wheel with his hands to force water into the pail. When he climbed down, his Tennessee uncle asked: "Is there ever any water in that creek?" "Oh, yes," the nephew replied, "when it rains." "What's the name of the creek?" "José Creek, spelled J-O-S-É, pronounced Hosay." The visiting uncle retorted: "I don't know why you boys want to live in a country where you have to climb for water and dig for wood and spell Hell with a J!"

Not all settlers were able to endure such rugged conditions. One defeated man nailed this sign on the door of his claim shack:

One hundred miles to water
Twenty miles to wood
Six inches to Hell
God Bless our home
Gone to live with the wife's folks.

With no wood to build houses, the plains homesteaders borrowed ideas from the Indians for shelter. Because of the rapid decline of the buffalo, the skin tipi offered no solution to the problem. But from the earthen lodges of the Pawnees, the sod house was soon derived. "We take a prairie plow, set it so that it cuts a sod of even thickness and even width," wrote a newly arrived settler. "With this we break up a piece of ground where the sod is toughest. We then take a spade and measure and cut the sod thus turned into even lengths. . . . They are generally blocks of a foot wide, two feet long and three inches thick. These well laid into a wall make a smooth even wall and furnish a house warmer than any other that can be built in this climate."

Sod houses varied from dugouts constructed against slopes or the banks of excavations to very rare two-story houses. The most difficult part to build was the roof support, which usually rested upon a ridgepole log that formed a gable across a pair of forked tree trunks. If a settler could afford a few rolls of tar paper over the support poles and fitted his sod shingles properly, his roof was leakproof. One-sash window frames furnished light for the interior, and if no lumber was available the doors were made of slatted poles covered with canvas. In areas where wood was extremely hard to come by, barns, sheds, and even the first schools, churches, and courthouses were built of sod. "Sodbusters" was a natural choice for a name for these settlers.

"Well here I am in Nebraska and in a sod house," a woman wrote in 1873. "For the first 24 hours I felt dolefully, but gradually I became used to the strange surroundings, and have not been blue since. These unbounded prairies have such an air of desolation — and the stillness is very oppressive." An oft-repeated remark of newcomers to the plains was: "A man can look farther and see less." It applied to women as well, although most of them were too busy to spend any time gazing at the horizon. Plainsmen who criticized male Indians for letting their women do so much hard work apparently were blind to the endless tasks required of their own wives and daughters.

Keeping food on the table of a frontier home was never easy and at certain times of the year presented problems to baffle the most resourceful. Money was scarce, grocery stores were few and poorly stocked, and present-day methods of preservation unknown. Wild game furnished most of the meat which women preserved by cutting it into strips and drying it in the sun, or by salting heavily and hanging it in a smoke-house or by the fireplace.

Women also had to perform most of the labor attendant upon raising vegetables, and caring for chickens, pigs, and cows. They churned milk for butter, and baked all the bread. They made mattresses of prairie grass, corn shucks, or buffalo hair; they molded candles by melting deer tallow; they carded and spun wool. They dyed, sewed, and knitted most of the clothing for members of the family, including coats, socks, and underwear. They fashioned their own hats from braided straw; they made their own soap and used it to wash dishes and clothes; they concocted medicines from herbs and ministered to ailing members of the family. And while they were performing all these tasks, they endured extremes of cold and hot weather, windstorms, dust, hordes of invading insects, snakes, and other pests — while hungering for such things as music, something to read, and the companionship of other women.

The majority of homesteaders who first came to the plains engaged in agriculture to sustain themselves and their families. Few of them could afford even the crude farming machinery of that time, and many a first crop was put in with hoes, spades, and mattocks. Plowing was extremely difficult where the sod was formed of native buffalo grass which had a dense root mass. Because corn was grown on almost every farm, one of the first "machines" acquired was either a hand or foot corn planter. "This labor saving device," read one advertisement for a hand planter, "is important to the farmers of the West. It is carried or used like a walking stick or cane. It is simple, cheap, accurate and dependable." The foot planter was more complex, being buckled to the farmer's foot and connected by an elastic tube to a bag of seed corn swung at his side. "When the foot is raised to make a step," the manufacturer claimed, "a grain of corn drops into a chamber in the planter. When the foot comes down on the ground, the corn is pressed into the earth."

Harvesting and threshing were laborious and tedious tasks until the sodbusters were sufficiently prosperous to obtain the new machinery which inventors devised especially for rapid expansion of agriculture on the plains. Corn husking, for example, had to be entirely by hand. "A wagon with a deep box and a high bang board on the left hand side and a farmer with a husking peg constituted practically all the equipment needed to husk the crop," recalled a Nebraska pioneer. "The ears would bang against the back of the wagon in a steady stream as the farmer's team pulled the wagon slowly through the field."

⎯⎯⎯⎯⎯⎯⎯⎯⎯⎯⎯

To make a crop, farmers on the plains had to contend with droughts, blizzards, windstorms, hail, grasshoppers, and grass fires. "The prairie fires have raged furiously and the country all about us for miles is black as ink," a homesteader reported in 1872. "We protected our haystacks by plowing several furrows around them, then plowing at some distance again outside these furrows and then burning the space between."

In the summer of 1874, before flying saucers were invented, farmers all across the plains began sighting strange silvery circles in the sunny skies. The puzzled observers soon discovered that the mysterious circles were millions of grasshoppers in flight. For several seasons in succession these grasshopper hordes fell upon plains homesteads, consuming hundred-acre cornfields in a few minutes.

Near Fort Scott, Kansas a descending cloud of grasshoppers stopped a horse race. At Kearney, Nebraska, when masses of them landed upon the tracks of the Union Pacific Railroad, they stopped all trains, grease from the crushed insects setting locomotive wheels to spinning. Tormented homesteaders tied strings around their trousers' bottoms to keep the pests from biting their legs. When the grasshoppers could find nothing else to consume, they ate harness, window curtains, hoe handles, and even each other. At last the grasshopper invasions began to decline, and as was the frontier custom after a major crisis, an anonymous bard of the plains composed a grasshopper ballad — the verses sung to the tune of "Buffalo Gals," with a turkey gobbler as folk hero.

Without laughter, the sodbusters probably could not have prevailed against the hostile elements which surrounded them. As bad as things were, they could always be worse — that was the attitude adopted by most plains settlers. To support this rationale, they created a considerable amount of tall-tale humor. They bragged about blizzards so fierce that lantern flames, spoken words, and even sunshine froze solid. One homesteader claimed that to measure wind velocity he suspended a heavy chain from a post. If the chain hung at a 45-degree angle, a light breeze was up; if it assumed a horizontal position, a plains wind was blowing. After a bad storm a settler declared that the wind drew all the milk from his herd of cows and sprayed it into the air where it became mixed with small hail pellets and fell back to earth as ice cream. Another laughed off disastrous storm damage to his crops by bragging that the hailstones imbedded in his field were so large that water melting from them would water his stock all summer and make fine boating ponds. A Dakota plainswoman took issue with John G. Whittier over his description of a blizzard's "eddying" snowflakes. "Flakes don't eddy here," she said. "They whistle and go straight by as though shot from a cannon. If he were here he might write another *Snow Bound*, but it would have to be on a different plan. I doubt if there is a poet living who possesses enough vim to write a poem about a Dakota blizzard. I guess such a blizzard would knock all the poetry out of a man."

⟝⟞

In the early days of settlement, conflicts occurred with cattlemen accustomed to driving longhorn herds north across the open plains from Texas. The trail drivers resented the fences built by "nesters" (homesteaders) and sometimes cut the wire and drove their herds across cultivated fields. Violent encounters resulted at first, but gradually settlers and cowboys adjusted to the changing West, many of the former becoming cattle raisers themselves. Meetings between the two tended to become friendly, sometimes comical, as related by a trail boss who invited some "nester" families to dine at his chuckwagon. "We camped the last night out in the edge of the 'Nesterments' and the milk pen calves ate the cook's clothes up while he was taking a bath. The only surplus clothes in the outfit was a pair of chaps that one of the boys had in the wagon. The cook climbed into them, got his fire to going and his supper started. He hadn't more than got started when a surrey full of women folks drove up to eat supper at the wagon. You can imagine how that poor boy felt cooking a meal of victuals, tending his fires and all without ever turning his back on them women folk."

The growth of towns or "nesterments" as the cattlemen called them, kept pace with the growth in farm population. Towns usually began as railroad stops. A small hotel, a saloon, a blacksmith shop would be quickly followed by land speculators, lawyers, doctors, and merchants. The town livery stable usually served as a sort of men's club. "Here all commercial transportation was arranged, teams and saddle horses were stabled in bad weather, fancy stallions were kept at stud, and Indian ponies were sold," a Nebraska pioneer said. "Another common meeting place for men was the local blacksmith shop. When the women folks came to town there wasn't much for them to do except to sell their eggs and cream and buy yard goods, clothing and staples for the family. Then they herded the tired kids while the men folks did their business."

The most widely observed holidays were Christmas, Decoration Day, and the Fourth of July. The Fourth was one day of the year when settlers cut loose with joyous celebration and noisy, home-made explosives. They journeyed to the nearest town to watch horse races; they participated in sack and foot races; they climbed greased poles and chased greased pigs; they listened to patriotic oratory; they drank toasts to the Constitution, to George Washington, the Declaration of Independence, the Union, and to whatever state or territory they lived in.

Boosterism, which was rampant in most of the burgeoning towns, was reflected in their newspapers: Come To New Liberty To Live. The Climate Is So Healthy We Had To Shoot A Man To Start Our Graveyard. Editors bragged about the size of cornstalks, potatoes, watermelons, and other crops grown in their counties. "A farmer in the Camp Springs community has raised a stalk of corn so high he was unable to count the number of ears on it. His eldest son was sent up the stalk to ascertain the amount of corn. The stalk grew so fast that the corn, boy and all, disappeared heavenward." Sometimes when Eastern newspapers published exaggerated stories of bad weather on the plains, an editor would counter with an even greater exaggeration: Estelline, Dakota Territory. Snow one hundred feet deep. Stock on western ranges all dead. Railroads will take up all tracks west of Chicago in the Spring. Everybody, including the oldest inhabitant dead, this news being brought by a traveling salesman who was the only person who escaped."

One editor grown weary of boosting, however, announced a new policy to his readers: "Hell is full of newspapermen who killed themselves blowing for some little one horse town, and that too without enough support to fatten a grasshopper. We have decided that it is a sin to lie anyway, and in the future, we'll be found telling the truth."

As soon as schools and churches could be built, they became centers for community gatherings. Respect for education ran high among all settlers, native or foreign and schoolhouses were often first on the list of desired public buildings. One newly arrived sodbuster was so anxious to have a school that he offered the use of his homestead lean-to as a school room. The children brought soap boxes for desks and the teacher used a log plank. "The trying part of the arrangement," the teacher recalled, "was that the classroom was the homesteader's bedroom. Each school morning I'd have to help carry the bed into the yard before the pupils arrived. Each evening it had to be returned."

After literary and debating societies and amateur drama groups were formed, entire families would travel for miles in wagons or buggies to attend the meetings, speeches, debates, and plays. These gatherings were more likely to be concerned with serious subjects rather than with recreation and amusement.

Churches also served as social centers, but the first meeting places were usually as makeshift as those of the first schools. "Last Sunday I preached in the morning in a hall over a drugstore," a plains preacher reported. "The audience sat upon boards the ends of which rested upon boxes and saw-horses. The room was lighted with candles and lanterns." Some of the plains cowtowns which established reputations for lawlessness and sin for the entertainment of visiting cowboys were embarrassed by the arrival of churches. "The wicked city of Dodge," reported that town's newspaper for June 8, 1878, "can at last boast of a Christian organization — a Presbyterian church. It was organized last Sunday week. We would have mentioned the latter last week but we thought it best to break the news gently to the outside world."

In one wicked town on the Texas Plains, the gamblers and toughs warned a certain Parson Potter not to come there to do any preaching. The preacher ignored the warning and found a large crowd of hecklers awaiting his arrival. Parson Potter mounted to the crude pulpit, opened his Bible, pulled out a long-barreled cap-and-ball pistol, and laid it beside the book. "Now," he said, "you fellows sent me word not to come, saying that I couldn't preach here. I've come and I'm going to preach. The first fellow that makes a move while I am preaching, I'm going to shoot him right between the eyes, and I'm a good shot. You are the fellows I mean! You fellows right there!" Parson Potter pointed his finger straight at a group of rowdies sitting on one of the benches and none of them moved a muscle. He said afterward that the congregation was the most attentive he had ever had; not a man stirred during the sermon.

Members of the medical profession also had to adjust to the rugged environment of the plains. Hospitals were non-existent; children were born at home; and surgery was usually performed on the kitchen table of the ailing patient. A typical doctor's office consisted of a rough, pineboard shelf and a table filled with surgical instruments, a few dental tools, splints, the medicines of the day, a stethoscope, a microscope, and possibly a jar of leeches. Some doctors also kept a few bottles of alcohol containing gall bladders, appendices, and other removed bits of former patients.

To answer a call to a sodbuster's cabin, a doctor might have to ride half the night with only a lantern to light his way across a trackless prairie. Many doctors traveled on regular circuits, timing their visits to coincide with expected births. They usually rode in buggies, over roads so bad that in rainy weather the mud would fill the wheels up solid to the hub, and stops would have to be made to clean the sticky, clinging stuff away. A doctor in western Nebraska told of driving for hours, lost in the darkness. When he stopped his buggy and got out with his lantern to search for a landmark, a frightened man with children crowding at his side appeared suddenly out of nowhere. "Get out of here," the man shouted angrily. "What do you think you're doing? Get off my house!" The doctor had stopped his team on the roof of his patient's combination dugout and sod house.

In spite of all the difficulties new settlers kept coming to the plains. Census records of the Dakotas, for example, show a jump from 4,000 in 1860 to 14,000 in 1870, to 135,000 in 1880, to 540,000 in 1890. The other plains states also grew rapidly during that thirty-year span: Nebraska from 28,000 to a million; Kansas from 100,000 1,400,000. In the later years the greatest influx came from northern Europe, with Germans predominating, followed by Swedes, Norwegians, Irish, English, Danes, Russians, and Bohemians. When one nationality established a colony in an area, other settlers of the same origin tended to follow. While the Germans established themselves from Nebraska to Texas, the Swedes favored Minnesota because the terrain and climate were similar to those of their homeland; they later pushed out upon the plains in the western part of the state and entered the Dakotas. Many other Swedish settlers homesteaded on the plains of Nebraska, Kansas, and Colorado. The Norwegians also preferred Minnesota, but their emigration period was late, and many families moved on to the Dakotas to find land. The Irish and English settled mainly in the mid-plains region, with a considerable number of English and Scots taking claims on Montana ranges for ventures in livestock raising. The Danes settled in Nebraska and South Dakota, while the Russians chose the wheatlands of Kansas and the Dakotas.

This diverse army of settlers brought a fascinating mixture of ideals, customs, religions, languages, prejudices, and ambitions to the Great Plains. The combined resourcefulness and inventiveness of these people, and their energy and optimism made failure impossible. By the later 1870's it became obvious to many homesteaders that 160-acre tracts were too small to support a family in most parts of the Great Plains. It was this pressure for larger tracts that forced the Plains Indians to surrender much of their reservation territory from the Dakotas to Oklahoma. Homesteads were enlarged to 320 or 640 acres, and power machinery to plant and harvest these large farms became a necessity.

The inventors responded, turning to steam to perform the tasks. Steam plows, harvesters, and threshers began appearing on the plains. Each year these machines grew more gigantic, moving like prehistoric monsters across the big, rolling land. The machines in turn made possible even larger wheat fields, and railroads such as the Northern Pacific began operating farms as large as 100,000 acres in the Dakotas. Bonanza farming, they called it. "A sea of wheat," wrote an admiring visitor. "The railroad train rolls through an ocean of grain."

During this same period, cattle ranchers were increasing their holdings, overstocking the ranges. In the early 1880's, farmers and livestock raisers prospered from their sales of grain and beef and wool. And then in the winter of 1886-87 the Great Blizzard struck, wiping out the entire herds of many livestock raisers across the plains.

The following summer rainfall was scanty, and then for nine years the Great Plains suffered from one of its periodic dry cycles.

Out of the economic depression that accompanied the long drought came the Populist movement of the 1890's. Colorful leaders such as Sockless Jerry Simpson, Mary E. Lease, and William A. Peffer toured the plains country, attacking mortgage bankers, the railroads, and Wall Street. "Formerly the man who lost his farm could go West," Senator Peffer would shout to his beleaguered audiences. "Now there is no longer a West to go to. Now they have to fight for their homes insteading of making new!" Mary Lease was equally forceful: "The people are at bay. Let the bloodhounds of money who have dogged us thus far beware! What you farmers need is to raise less corn and more hell!"

The noisy campaigning of the Populists was heard across the nation. Although most contemporary newspapers and periodicals were sympathetic toward the plight of plains farmers, few were friendly toward the new third party, which was viewed as a threat to the American political system. The Populists won few victories outside the West.

Through the years of hard times, however, the sturdy plainsmen endured. They considered no defeat short of death as being final, and when the drought years ended and prosperity returned, most of them were still on their land. Neither droughts, blizzards, pestilence, nor "malefactors of great wealth" could drive them from their homesteads. "When you have once set eyes upon the never-ending sweep of the Great Plains," said an Englishman who arrived there during the first years of settlement, "you no longer wonder that America rejects Malthusianism. . . . The impression is not merely one of size. There is perfect beauty, wondrous fertility in the lonely steppe; no patriotism, no love of home, can prevent the traveler wishing here to end his days."

SAILING OVER THE PLAINS

Several 19th century accounts of travelers crossing America's Great Plains mention attempts to harness the continual prairie winds to various modes of transportation. Most of the experiments were failures, but according to a correspondent for the New York *Sun* who was traveling across Kansas in September 1876, at least one sail-car proved its worth.

Finding himself stranded in Ellis, with no train east for 24 hours, the newspaperman decided to walk the Kansas Pacific Railroad track to Fort Hays, a distance of fifteen miles. He had scarcely started when to his astonishment a strange contraption came rattling along behind him. It was a wheeled vehicle bearing a triangular snuff-colored sail attached to a sixteen-foot mast and topped by a red signal flag.

The sail-car braked to a stop, and the two men aboard offered him a ride. He got aboard somewhat dubiously and took a seat on one of the benches. A few seconds later the brown sail billowed in the breeze and they were off, "skimming over the rails like a sage bird."

The "captain" of this machine was a water-tank inspector for the railroad, and he had built the six-foot-long sail-car himself. Rises in the undulating prairie sometimes diminished the wind so that their speed slowed to a crawl. At other times they swept around curves and over bridges so swiftly that the newspaperman feared they would leave the rails.

They covered the distance to Fort Hays in forty minutes, and by this time the New York *Sun's* man was so entranced by wind-powered transportation that he decided to continue to the end of the tank inspector's run. The final thirty miles — to Russell — was across open plains. "The free winds sent us along at a rattling pace, sometimes at the incredible speed of forty miles an hour," he recorded. "Although I pronounce sail-car riding one of the most delightful experiences a person can taste, I wonder if the idea could not be utilized farther east."

PART V

Final Battles

Adrian Ebell, a refugee himself, took the only known photograph of settlers fleeing the Sioux warriors. Courtesy of Minnesota Historical Society.

19

In Pursuit of Revenge:
The Sioux Uprising of 1862

*I*t was a summer Sunday on the Lower Sioux Reserve in Minnesota. Taoyateduta, who was known as Little Crow to the white settlers, attended the Episcopal church that morning. At the conclusion of services he shook hands with friends among the other worshipers and returned to his house two miles up the Minnesota River. The day was August 17, 1862.

Late that night he was awakened by the sounds of excited voices as several members of his tribe entered his room. He recognized the voices of Big Eagle, Shakopee, Mankato, and Medicine Bottle, and knew that something serious must have occurred. Big Eagle told him how four young men of Shakopee's band had crossed the river that afternoon to hunt for wild game because they were hungry.

"They came to a settler's fence," Big Eagle said, "and here they found a hen's nest with some eggs in it. One of them took the eggs, when another said: 'Don't take them for they belong to a white man and we may get into trouble.' The other was angry, for he was very hungry and wanted to eat the eggs . . . and replied: 'You are a coward. You are afraid of the white man. You are afraid to take even an egg from him, though you are half starved. Yes, you are a coward!' The other replied: 'I am not a coward. I am not afraid of the white man, and to show you that I am not I will go to his house and shoot him. Are you brave enough to go with me?' They all went to the house of the white man, but he got alarmed and went to another house where there were some other white men and women. The four Indians followed them and killed three men and two women. Then they hitched up a team belonging to another settler and drove to Shakopee's camp . . . and told what they had done."

On hearing this, Little Crow condemned the four young men for what they had done and then sat silent for a time considering what course of action he should take. As chief of the Mdewakanton subtribe of the Eastern or Santee Sioux, he bore most of the responsibility for the loss of the once vast Sioux woodland that had been ceded to form the state of Minnesota. To avoid the bloodshed of war, he signed two treaties — the first in 1851, the second in 1858 — giving up ninetenths of the tribal lands. In return for this, government agents promised to pay annuities to the Sioux for the purchase of food, clothing, and supplies for farming during a period of fifty years. The tribe also kept a strip of land along the Minnesota River which was divided into Upper and Lower Reserves, Little Crow's Mdewakantons sharing the Lower Sioux Reserve with another subtribe while two remaining Santee subtribes shared the Upper Reserve. Led by their chiefs, they replaced breechclouts and blankets with the clothing of the whites, built houses, joined churches, and started farming.

———————

During the ten years before the Civil War more than 150,000 settlers pushed into the ceded land, and friction between them and the Indians gradually increased. In 1861 the Sioux farm yields were poor, and during the summer of 1862 another crop failure seemed certain. Most of the wild game was gone from the reservation lands, and when the Indians crossed into the Big Woods — their old hunting grounds now claimed by settlers — trouble often followed. Many had to go to the white traders' storehouses at the reservation agencies to obtain food on credit. They had learned to hate this credit system because they had no control over their accounts. When the annuity funds came from Washington, the traders held first claim on the money, and whatever amount the traders claimed in their accounts, government agents would pay them. Some of the Sioux had learned to keep accounts and although their records might be less by many dollars than the traders' accounts, the government agents would not accept them.

On that warm August night when the subchiefs came to tell Little Crow of the killing of the settlers, he tried to find a reason for the violence, blaming it on the broken promises of the white men and the hunger of his people. Annuity funds for purchasing food were more than a month overdue and there were rumors that the government had spent all its gold fighting the Civil War and had no money left for reservation Indians. (In August 1862 Confederate armies were nearing Washington for the second Battle of Bull Run.) Only two days earlier Little Crow had met in council with Agent Thomas Galbraith, asking that food be issued to his starving people. "The money is ours," he said, "but we cannot get it. We have no food, but here are these stores filled with food." He pled with Galbraith to issue the supplies and warned: "When men are hungry they help themselves."

Instead of replying, Agent Galbraith turned to the traders and asked them what they would do. Trader Andrew Myrick answered contemptuously: "If they are hungry, let them eat grass or their own dung." The trader's words spread rapidly among the hungry Sioux. On that Sunday night two days later, Little Crow must have wondered if those words had been heard by the four young men who killed the white people. At last he spoke to the subchiefs who had come to tell him of that grave offense: "The white men are like the locusts when they fly so thick that the whole sky is a snowstorm. . . . Count your fingers all day long and white men with guns in their hands will come faster than you can count."

The other Sioux leaders replied that because of the killings no Sioux life would now be safe. It was the white man's way to punish all Indians for the crimes of one or a few. The Sioux might as well strike first instead of waiting for the soldiers to come and kill them.

"Braves, you are little children, you are fools," Little Crow told them. "You will die like the rabbits when the hungry wolves hunt them in the Hard Moon of January. But Little Crow is not a coward. He will die with you."

After sending runners to summon warriors from the Upper Reserve, Little Crow ordered that the women be awakened to mold bullets and assist in other war preparations. At dawn he led the attack on the agency. They killed twenty men, captured ten women and children, emptied the warehouses of provisions, and set the other buildings afire. Among the dead was Andrew Myrick, who had said "let them eat grass." He lay on the ground with his mouth stuffed full with grass.

After this easy victory, the Sioux decided to march ten miles downriver to attack Fort Ridgely, which had been built by the army to keep watch on the reservation. In the meantime, however, news of fighting at the agency had reached Captain John Marsh, who commanded the force of seventy-six Minnesota Volunteers at the fort. With forty-six men, Marsh started on a rescue march, passing several burning houses and meeting along the way numerous settlers fleeing toward the fort. At Redwood Ferry the Indians ambushed Marsh's soldiers and blocked the return route to the fort. In the fighting, twenty-three soldiers were killed, and Marsh was drowned while trying to cross the river. A 19-year-old sergeant, John Bishop, led the survivors back to Fort Ridgely. The Sioux had lost only one warrior.

━━━━◦▶◦◀◦━━━━

Not until the afternoon of August 20 was Little Crow able to assemble a force of approximately four hundred warriors for an attack upon Fort Ridgely. (On the 19th most of the Indians had spent their time in an unsuccessful attempt to invade the nearby town of New Ulm, where there were stores to loot.) The delay had enabled more than two hundred reinforcements to reach the fort and about the same number of fleeing civilians from the countryside to find refuge there. Among the reinforcements was Lieutenant Timothy Sheehan, who took command from Lieutenant Thomas Gere — who was ailing with the mumps.

In their first assault the Indians attempted to rush the unstockaded square of buildings, but soon were driven back by cannon fire. Then they began shooting at the windows of the two-story barracks.

Little Crow, chief of the Mdewakanton subtribe of the Santee Sioux and leader of the uprising, is depicted in this watercolor by Thomas W. Wood, August 1860. Courtesy of Minnesota Historical Society.

"During the shooting we tried to set fire to the buildings with fire arrows," a warrior named Lightning Blanket later recalled, "but the buildings would not burn, so we had to get more powder and bullets. The sun was about two hours high when we went around to the west of the fort, and decided to go back to Little Crow's village and come and keep up the fight next day."

Heavy rains which had begun falling during the night continued into the first daylight hours, giving the fort's defenders an opportunity to replenish their water supplies and to build barricades of cordwood and grain sacks. Little Crow's force, however, was doubled by the arrival of warriors from the Upper Agency, and this time they approached the fort through gullies and brush. Again they sent showers of fire arrows onto the roofs, but the rain had dampened the shingles and only a few small blazes resulted. Charges of canister shot from the fort's artillery cut down every attempt to rush the buildings, and after Little Crow was wounded, the attack was called off. The fort's defenders suffered the loss of three dead and thirteen wounded. The Sioux lost many more, possibly a hundred.

As usually occurs among loosely disciplined forces, control by Little Crow and the other leaders was now rapidly lost. Wandering bands of armed Indians began spreading out on both sides of the Minnesota River, attacking surprised settlers wherever they found them, either killing all members of a family, or taking some or all of them captive. Because of poor communications during the first days of violence, the settlers were unable to prepare any kind of organized defense. On the Upper Reserve several Indians warned white missionaries of the uprising and joined them in an escape by wagons. Among the possessions taken along by missionary Adrian Ebell was a camera, but only one of his photographs made on the flight appears to have survived, a view of the fugitives during a rest stop.

After abandonment of the attack on Fort Ridgely, dissension arose among the Sioux leaders about what course of action to pursue next. Little Crow, suffering from his wound, denounced those who were killing helpless settlers and opposed those who wanted to attack New Ulm. None of the leaders was strong for an assault against the town, but when they perceived that the more reckless warriors were going to attack anyhow, Mankato, Wabasha, and Big Eagle decided to take part.

⟶⟩⟩⟨⟨⟵

As was the case with Fort Ridgely, the Indians' delay gave the people of New Ulm time to prepare defenses. Charles Flandrau, a former Indian agent, quickly organized an armed force of Frontier Guards and set up barricades of wagons and barrels around a section of New Ulm's main street. Crowded into this small area more than a thousand unarmed citizens of the town awaited the expected attack.

At midmorning of August 23 about 350 warriors attacked New Ulm. They streamed out of the woods in bright sunlight, formed an arc across the prairie, and swept toward the town. When the Sioux came within a mile and a half of the forward line of defenders, the mass of warriors began spreading like a fan. At the same time they started running at full speed toward the houses on the outskirts of New Ulm.

Charles Flandrau later recalled that moment: "Then the savages uttered a terrific yell and came down upon us like the wind." The war cries, he said, "unsettled the men a little," and they abandoned their outer positions to the Indians. Flandrau, however, rallied the Frontier Guards and they retook some of the buildings. "The firing from both sides then became general, sharp and rapid, and it got to be a regular Indian skirmish, in which every man did his own work after his own fashion."

Early in the afternoon the Sioux set fire to several structures on the windward side of New Ulm, expecting to advance under a smoke screen. Sixty warriors, mounted and on foot, charged a barricade, but were driven back by heavy volleys. It was a long and bitter battle, fought in the streets, dwellings, outhouses, and store buildings. During the day and into the night, 140 buildings were set afire and destroyed. Shortly after dawn the Indians fired off a few shots, rounded up a herd of the townfolk's stray cattle, and then withdrew with an unknown number of their dead and wounded.

New Ulm counted its casualties: thirty-four were dead, sixty wounded. As very little ammunition or food remained, Flandrau and the other leaders decided to evacuate the town and seek safety in Mankato, thirty miles to the east. "It was a melancholy spectacle," Flandrau said, "to see 2,000 people, who a few days before had been prosperous and happy, reduced to utter beggary, starting . . . through a hostile country, every inch of which we expected to be called upon to defend from attack. . . . Under Providence we got through."

The Sioux uprising was not yet over, but the stubborn resistance of the defenders of New Ulm and Fort Ridgely had blunted its force, saving other settlements from attack and giving Colonel Henry H. Sibley time to bring 1,400 men of the 6th Minnesota Regiment up-river from St. Paul. After reaching Fort Ridgely on August 28, Sibley sent a combined reconnaissance force of mounted rangers and infantry — about 150 men — forward to the Lower Agency, which had been overrun by Little Crow's warriors on the first day of the uprising. The soldiers buried the bodies of the victims and then camped across the river near the head of Birch Coulee.

At dawn, while many of the soldiers were still sleeping, Big Eagle, Mankato, and Gray Bird led several hundred warriors in a surprise attack, and during the hour of close combat that followed they killed twenty-two and wounded sixty men. Sounds of the Birch Coulee battle reached Sibley's headquarters at Fort Ridgely, and he immediately started four companies to the rescue and prepared his entire command for a general campaign.

Little Crow meanwhile had led his warriors north into the Big Woods, raiding Hutchinson and Forest City and skirmishing with militia at Acton. By mid-September the combined Sioux forces had taken almost three hundred white and half-blood prisoners. In a move to rescue the captives without endangering their lives, Colonel Sibley attempted to open negotiations with Little Crow and some of the other Sioux leaders.

From the beginning, Little Crow had known that his people could not defeat the armies of the white men, but he now hoped that he might save them from exile or perhaps extermination by obtaining favorable terms from Colonel Sibley in exchange for the captives.

Chief Wabasha, however, hoping to save his own band, communicated secretly with Sibley, offering an immediate transfer of the prisoners. Sibley exploited this split between the Indian leaders by sending a messenger to Little Crow, charging him with responsibility for the uprising and demanding an unconditional surrender of the captives.

Believing that there was no hope for peace except by abject surrender, Little Crow decided to fight one more battle. On September 22 his scouts reported that Sibley's soldiers had reached the Upper Reserve and were encamped near Wood Lake. "All our fighting chiefs were present and all our best fighting Indians," Big Eagle said afterward. "We felt that this would be the deciding fight of the War." Big Eagle's supposition proved correct. Although the Sioux devised a perfect ambush, a small foraging party of soldiers unmasked the trap prematurely and started the battle before the main body of Indians could join in. Sibley's Minnesotans quickly put their artillery into action, then charged the Indians and drove them from the field. Mankato and about thirty warriors were killed in this action, the soldiers losing seven killed and thirty wounded.

<hr/>

Little Crow now accepted the fact that the uprising had failed. That evening, several miles north of Wood Lake, he called the chiefs together for a final council. The Sioux of the Minnesota woodlands were finished, he told them. They must either surrender or flee to join their cousins, the prairie Sioux of the Dakota country. Little Crow, Shakopee, Medicine Bottle, and their followers decided to flee to the west. Wabasha and Big Eagle, although they had fought in most of the battles, decided to stay and barter their white prisoners for mercy from Colonel Sibley.

Four days later Sibley marched through the truce flags of the Sioux into their camp north of the Upper Agency. After freeing the captives, the majority of whom were women and children, he placed a cordon of artillery around the camp, informed the Indians that they were prisoners of war, and ordered construction of a huge log building to house all those accused of participating in the uprising until they could be tried by a military court.

Not until early November did Sibley's ponderous "military commission" complete its work of gathering evidence against the Sioux prisoners of war. The commission sentenced 303 to die by hanging; 16 were given long prison terms. The remaining 1,700 were transferred to Fort Snelling, near St. Paul. There under heavy guard, living in crowded conditions, and fed on scanty rations, the remnants of the once proud woodland Sioux awaited an uncertain fate.

Colonel Sibley and his commander, General John Pope of the Military Department of the Northwest, urged prompt execution of those condemned to death, but President Abraham Lincoln — busy though he was with the Civil War — insisted upon reviewing the trial records of the Indians in order to differentiate between murderers and those who had engaged only in battle. On December 6, Lincoln notified Sibley that he should "cause to be executed" 39 of the 303 convicted Sioux, at the town of Mankato on December 26.

That morning the town was filled with crowds of vindictive and morbidly curious citizens. At the last minute one of the convicted Indians was given a reprieve. About ten o'clock the remaining condemned men were marched from the prison to the scaffold. They sang the Sioux death song until soldiers pulled white caps over their heads and placed nooses around their necks. A moment later thirty-eight Sioux dangled lifeless in the air. Without the intercession of Abraham Lincoln there would have been three hundred. Among those whose lives were saved was Big Eagle, who was sentenced to a long term in prison.

The effects of violent uprisings such as that of the Sioux in Minnesota do not quickly die away, but endure for long periods of time. It was one of the bloodiest episodes in frontier history, the deaths probably totaling 750. All Sioux lands in Minnesota were confiscated by the government, and in May of 1863 (while Grant was pounding at Vicksburg and Lee was preparing to invade Pennsylvania) the first shipment of Sioux who had been confined in the Fort Snelling stockade left St. Paul by steamboat. They were bound for Crow Creek on the Missouri River, their new reservation — a place of barren soil, scanty rainfall, sparse wild game, and alkaline water unfit for drinking. Soon the hills around Crow Creek were covered with graves. Of 1,300 Sioux brought there in 1863, fewer than 1,000 survived the first winter.

While these events were occurring, Little Crow and his followers were fleeing to Canada where they hoped to obtain supplies to rebuild their shattered lives. The Canadians gave them food, but little else. In June 1863 Little Crow, with a small party that included his 16-year-old son Wowinapa, returned to the valley of the Minnesota. Wowinapa afterward told the reason for this journey: "My father said he could not fight the white men, but would steal horses from them and give them to his children so they could be comfortable." Little Crow envisioned his family forced to become Plains Indians, which meant that they must have horses to survive.

When the horse-stealing party reached the Big Woods, they made camp in a secluded place and then Little Crow and Wowinapa went out to forage for food. Two settlers returning from a deer hunt sighted them and immediately opened fire. Little Crow was killed and his fleeing son later was captured. The chief's scalp and skeleton were placed on public display, and Wowinapa was tried by a military court. The 16-year-old boy was sentenced to death, but higher authorities reduced the sentence to imprisonment.

Years later, after his release, Wowinapa changed his name to Thomas Wakeman, became a church deacon, and founded the first Young Men's Christian Association among the Sioux. During his lifetime, however, he was never able to obtain the skeleton of his father to give it proper burial. Not until 1971 were the remains of Little Crow turned over to his descendants for interment in the tribal cemetery, an incident that after more than a century closed the books on the Sioux uprising of 1862.

Some of these Confederate prisoners of war, interned at Rock Island, Illinois, in 1864, no doubt enlisted in the 2nd and 3rd U.S. Volunteers for service against hostile Indians on the western frontier. Courtesy of Dee Brown Collection.

20

Galvanized Yankees

"This nickname for those Confederate prisoners who fought Indians in the West for the Federal Government quickly became a term of respect."

s early as 1862 a few captured Confederate soldiers began taking oaths of allegiance and enlisting in the Union Army, but not until 1864 were sufficient numbers available to form regiments. Officially known as the United States Volunteers, six regiments were recruited from prisons at Point Lookout, Rock Island, and Alton, and from Camps Douglas, Chase, and Morton. Some recruits were foreign-born, Irish and German predominating; some were native stock from the hill country of Tennessee, North Carolina, and Kentucky; a few were from the Old South plantation country, from Virginia to Louisiana.

Each man had his own reasons for choosing this dubious route to freedom — desperation from dreary months of ignominious confinement, of watching comrades die by the hundreds in prison hospitals; a determination to survive by any means; disillusionment with the war; a genuine change of loyalty that was as emotional as religious conversion; a secret avowal to desert at the first opportunity; despair, optimism, perhaps cowardice. In that day there were no psychologists to interview these 6,000 Galvanized Yankees, to search their minds and record their inner fears and longings.

Eventually all these regiments were ordered West to serve against

291

hostile Indians. From the autumn of 1864 through most of 1865, the 1st Regiment helped keep hostile Sioux off settlements on the Minnesota frontier. Along the Missouri River the 1st and 4th Regiments manned five forts, were engaged in numerous skirmishes, and fought gallantly in one bloody battle. In the autumn of 1865, four companies of the 1st marched out upon the Kansas plains to open a new stage route, and endured a winter of Indian attacks, starvation, and blizzard marches.

———————

During the spring and summer of 1865, the 2d and 3d Regiments restored stage and mail service between the Missouri River and California, continually fighting off raiding hostiles. They escorted supply trains along the Oregon and Santa Fe trails; they rebuilt hundreds of miles of telegraph line destroyed by Indians between Fort Kearny and Salt Lake City. They guarded the lonely, dangerous stations of the telegraphers. In the autumn of 1865 and through most of 1866, the 5th and 6th Regiments assumed these same hazardous duties. Sometimes they personally carried the mail through. Two companies of the 5th escorted Colonel James Sawyer's wagon road expedition to Wyoming; six companies of the 6th were strung out across 500 miles of trails between Fort Kearny and Salt Lake City.

Galvanized Yankees were in Patrick Connor's Powder River Expedition; they fought on the Little Blue, the Sweetwater, at Midway, Fort Dodge, and Platte Bridge. They guarded surveying parties for the Union Pacific Railroad; they searched for and recovered white women captured by hostile Indians. They knew Jim Bridger, Wild Bill Hickok, Buffalo Bill Cody, Spotted Tail, and Red Cloud when the outside world had scarcely heard these now celebrated names. In the course of their military duties they found time to write poetry and to publish two post newspapers. And at least one Galvanized Yankee achieved legendary fame in later life — Henry M. Stanley, who found Dr. Livingstone in Africa.

Probably no one can say for certain when they were first called "Galvanized Yankees." Evidence indicates that the term was used originally to designate any captured Union soldier who turned Confederate. Warren Lee Goss and Melvin Grigsby, who wrote of their experiences in Andersonville prison, both used the term with this meaning. As the expression came into general use, however, it was applied more often to Confederates who took the oath of allegiance to the Union, and even to Union sympathizers in the South.

In most of the early official communications the U. S. Volunteers were described simply as "rebel prisoners" or "deserters," terms which soon became inapplicable and were resented by the men themselves. When they first arrived on the frontier, the phrase "white-washed Rebels" was sometimes used by their fellow soldiers from the Western state regiments.

It was Samuel Bowles who defined with exactness the present meaning of Galvanized Yankees and made it stick by dispatching a story to his widely quoted newspaper, the Springfield (Mass.) *Republican*. From Fort Kearny, Nebraska, May 24, 1865, Bowles wrote: "Among the present limited number of troops on the Plains are two regiments of infantry, all from the rebel army. They have cheerfully re-enlisted into the Federal service. . . . They are known in the army as 'white-washed rebs,' or as they call themselves 'galvanized Yankees.'" During the remaining year and a half they served in the West, the Galvanized Yankees were referred to in common speech not only by that name but as galvanized infantry, enlisted prisoners, Rebels, former Rebels, and of course U. S. Volunteers. In all official communications they were U. S. Volunteers, and the longer the regiments served, the fewer were the references to their origin.

Late in 1863, Brigadier General Gilman Marston, commandant at Point Lookout prison in Maryland, conceived the idea of enlisting Confederates in the U. S. Navy. Secretary of War Edwin M. Stanton

considered this proposal for several weeks, consulted with the Secretary of the Navy, and at last on December 21, 1863, issued
instructions to prison camp commanders to arrange to enlist into the
Navy prisoners willing to take the oath of allegiance. There was no
great rush of prisoners desiring Navy service. Not many of them had
any sea experience, and in at least one camp, Rock Island, loyal
Confederates organized themselves to block the efforts of the camp
commandant to so enlist them.

Meanwhile, Major General Benjamin Butler, Marston's department commander, became interested in the plan, and suggested
to Stanton that many more prisoners would be willing to enlist in the
Army than in the Navy. When Stanton brought the matter to
Lincoln's attention, the President became so enthusiastic that he drew
up a list of questions to be asked all prisoners at Point Lookout and
ordered his secretary, John Hay, to make arrangements with Butler
for recruiting.

The interrogation of some 8,000 prisoners individually was a slow
process, and it was late in March 1864 before Butler could inform Stanton that he had "more than a minimum regiment of repentant rebels,
whom a friend of mine calls *transfugees*, recruited at Point Lookout.
They behave exceedingly well, are very quiet, and most of them I am
certain are truly loyal, and I believe will make as efficient a regiment
as there is in the service. I should like to organize and arm it at once."

Four days later Butler received his final authorization "to recruit
and organize a regiment at Point Lookout, Maryland, to serve for three
years or during the war." Officers, with few exceptions, would be
drawn from the Union Army. On March 28, the regiment was officially designated as the 1st U. S. Volunteer Infantry.

Thus far nothing had been said about sending the 1st Regiment
to the frontier to fight Indians. The regiment was assigned to routine
police duties at Norfolk, but under the hard driving of young
Colonel Charles Dimon and his eager New England officers, the 1st
U. S. Volunteers quickly became a first-class body of soldiers. It was
inevitable that Butler and Dimon would want to test them in the field,
and on July 27 the regiment was marched down to Elizabeth City,

North Carolina. The mission was of little military consequence; they seized a few horses and some bales of cotton, fired a few shots at some fleeing guerrillas, and returned to Norfolk.

When General Grant heard of the incident, however, he was disturbed. He had no enthusiasm for recruiting from prison camps. Very likely he viewed the experiment as an extremely unmilitary business conceived by three civilians — Lincoln, Stanton, and Butler — who were too much inclined to meddle in matters which none of them understood.

On August 9 Grant, as general-in-chief of the armies, informed the War Department that he was ordering the 1st Regiment U. S. Volunteers to the Northwestern frontier. "It is not right," Grant explained, "to expose them where, to be taken prisoners, they must surely suffer as deserters." From that date to the end of the war, Grant was firmly opposed to using former Confederates against Confederates; in fact, he was opposed to using prisoners for any kind of military service.

General Grant's order transferring the regiment to the West specified Milwaukee, Wisconsin, as point of destination. "They will proceed via New York . . . reporting on their arrival to Major General John Pope, commanding Department of the North West."

Most officers and men received the news with enthusiasm, and on August 15, 1864 the regiment, 1,000 strong, boarded the transport ship *Continental*.

This vessel was to play a romantic role in the history of the West; less than two years later the *Continental* would carry more than 100 unmarried women, known as Asa Mercer's belles, around Cape Horn to Seattle as prospective brides for lonely male settlers.

Only one woman was aboard with the 1st Regiment — Elizabeth Cardwell, a 21-year-old wife of Private Patrick Cardwell, Company E. Patrick had married her before he shouldered a musket and marched away from his Virginia farm to be captured and sent to Point Lookout. After he had taken the oath and gone with the regiment to Norfolk, Elizabeth joined him. Patrick and Elizabeth evidently were a winsome pair; when they asked Captain Alfred Fay if she might go West with the regiment, the captain recommended to his colonel that permission be granted. Colonel Dimon was a strict disciplinarian but he was only 23 years old himself and filled with romantic notions. He granted permission, and so began a journey of youthful lovers; the Cardwells became the darlings of the regiment.

In New York, Colonel Dimon received a change of orders. Six companies were to proceed to St. Louis, four to Milwaukee. Arriving in Chicago on August 21, the regiment was divided, Dimon continuing with the six companies to St. Louis where further orders awaited him: "Immediately take boat up Missouri River, destination Fort Rice, Dakota Territory. On arrival at Fort Rice, Colonel C. A. R. Dimon will report himself and command to Brigadier-General Alfred Sully, commanding Northwestern Indian Expedition."

On August 27, Dimon led his six companies aboard the *Effie Deans,* and thus in little more than a fortnight after General Grant decided to send them West, they were well on their way into the heart of the hostile Indian country of Dakota.

———————

Within a week after the *Effie Deans* splashed away from its landing at St. Louis, the soldiers aboard grew restless from close confinement and lack of activity. One night near Independence, Missouri, several men deserted, and from that time Dimon began to worry about possible wholesale mutiny and desertion. He knew that for days at a time as they moved farther up the river the *Effie Deans* would be as isolated as a ship at sea, with only the boat's crew and a handful of officers against almost 600 former enemies.

Dimon ordered his officers to be doubly alert, to keep their eyes and ears open for any sign or rumors of sedition. On the evening of September 5, Captain Alfred Fay of E Company was informed by one of his corporals that Private William C. Dowdy had threatened to desert.

The outcome of this incident was a court-martial on board the boat before a court of inexperienced officers barely out of their teens. Private Dowdy was sentenced to death and executed, in complete disregard of the Articles of War which forbade execution without approval of the President. This was only the first of a series of blunders by Colonel Dimon.

On September 27, because of low water in the Missouri, the *Effie Deans* settled into a sand bar and the captain announced he could proceed no farther. Fort Rice was 272 miles to the north, and the next day the regiment began a long overland march. Ten days later they met General Sully and his returning expedition, obtained wagons from him, and continued northward. After a number of minor adventures with Indians, they reached Fort Rice on October 17.

Fancying himself an authority on Indians, Colonel Dimon now began meddling in disputes between warring tribes, and before the men could complete construction of winter quarters they were engaging in skirmishes with prowling hostiles.

Company descriptive books of the 1st U. S. Volunteers indicate that North Carolinians made up about 40 percent of the regiment, Virginians 15 percent, and foreigners 10 percent. The remainder came from almost all the other Confederate states. For the most part they turned out to be good soldiers, operating regular patrols so that their presence served as a deterrent to Indian attacks on the Minnesota frontier settlements. Because of a lack of vegetables in their diet and a shortage of medicines, they suffered an epidemic of scurvy, and about 10 percent of the command died before spring. Among the dead was Elizabeth Cardwell.

The Galvanized Yankees at Fort Rice published a newspaper, *The Frontier Scout*, a complete file of which still survives and in its columns can be found a fascinating record of these six companies of Southerners transplanted to what one described as "the wild, barren, bell-shaped hills of fruitless Dakota." After twelve months of frontier service, he could still "think with unmeasured delight of the fair damsels of Winchester, of the Old Dominion."

Their young commanding officer, Colonel Dimon, meanwhile was still meddling in Indian matters. He committed his final blunder on July 16 by firing off a howitzer salute just as General Sully was arranging a peace parley with the Hunkpapa Sioux. The suspicious Sioux took this as a gesture of hostility and fled back to their hunting grounds to organize a great war party under a then obscure medicine man named Sitting Bull.

Luckily for the Galvanized Yankees, before Sitting Bull and his warriors reached Fort Rice, General Sully dispatched Colonel Dimon to Washington on a pretext of official business and gave the fort's command to Lieutenant Colonel John Pattee, a veteran Indian fighter. Sully also reinforced the garrison with two companies of a recently arrived Galvanized Yankee regiment, the 4th U. S. Volunteers.

⟫⟩●⟨⟪

Sitting Bull's force of more than a thousand swooped down on Fort Rice on the morning of July 28, 1865, surprising the mounted guards and totally surrounding the stockade before the defenders could retaliate. Pattee calmly surveyed the situation, then ordered four infantry companies outside on the plain, rolled his two 12-pounders out the gate, formed his command into two wings and ordered his men to hold their positions and keep firing as the Indians galloped in. Along a line that at times stretched for two miles, the Battle of Fort Rice raged for three hours, a fight between superb horsemen inspired by Sitting Bull, and dismounted ex-Confederate soldiers who refused to yield an inch of ground. As Pattee had known it would, firepower made all the difference. Not even the strong medicine of Sitting Bull could prevail, and by late morning the Sioux had withdrawn from musket range. For three more days small bands remained in the vicinity of the fort, showing themselves on distant hills, but there was no more fighting.

During their stay at Fort Rice, detachments of the 1st Regiment also were assigned duties farther up the Missouri, at Forts Berthold,

Union, and Benton. In October 1865 they were brought together
again with orders to report to Fort Leavenworth for mustering out.
In the last issue of their post newspaper someone contributed a poem:

> We are going home, o'er Missouri's foam
> While the ruddy sunlight flashes.
> To the sunny South, from the land of drouth,
> For Rebellion's burned to ashes.

Meanwhile the other four companies of the 1st Regiment which
had been manning forts in Minnesota were transferred to Kansas for
a long winter of guarding stagecoach stations and fighting for their
lives against Indians and blizzards.

As for the other five regiments of Galvanized Yankees, the 4th
continued through the winter of 1865-66 along the Missouri, while
the 2d, 3d, 5th, and 6th (recruited from Ohio, Indiana, and Illinois
prisons) were spread out along stagecoach and wagon train trails and
telegraph lines from Fort Leavenworth to Fort Douglas, Utah.

One of the most dangerous and exciting assignments was that of
Companies C and D of the 5th Regiment, serving as escort to the
Sawyer's wagon road expedition across Nebraska and Wyoming in the
summer of 1865. Constantly harassed by Indians, they finally had a
showdown with George and Charley Bent and their Cheyenne Dog
Soldiers, then ended up at lonely Fort Reno for a monotonous winter.

The most peripatetic group of Galvanized Yankees was H Company
of the 5th Regiment. Organized from a group of Georgia and Alabama
prisoners at Camp Douglas, Chicago, in April 1865 with a strength
of ninety-seven men, H Company operated in five different army
districts, and one of its detachments had the distinction of being the
only Galvanized Yankee unit to serve in New Mexico — as escort to
a wagon train. With I and K Companies of the 5th, H Company was
also the last of the U. S. Volunteers mustered out, on November 13,
1866. On its last day of service H Company could muster only thirty
of its original ninety-seven men. (By modern standards desertions

were high among Galvanized Yankee companies in the West, but the rate was only one percent greater than the 13 percent estimate for Union Army desertions during the Civil War.)

Their delayed discharges enabled them to benefit from a recent War Department ruling. They could keep their knapsacks, haversacks, and canteens — all for free. If they wanted to retain their well-used Springfield rifles they had to put $6 on the line. Revolvers were $8; swords, $3. Those who elected to stay in the West, and many of them did, probably chose revolvers.

21

Beecher's Island

" 'All hell broke loose'. . . Roman Nose and his Cheyenne warriors thought they could drive the white man from the Western Plains. A handful of desperate soldiers, trapped on an island in the Arickaree River, taught them different in a nine-day battle in September 1868."

n the summer of 1868 several bands of Cheyenne, Sioux, and Arapaho began assembling in eastern Colorado along the Arickaree fork of the Republican River. This was good hunting country for buffalo and antelope. It was also an ideal base from which to raid ranches or small settlements, and to attack railroad construction crews or isolated platoons of U.S. cavalry.

Among the leaders of this loosely organized group of hostile Indians was Roman Nose, a tall, muscular Cheyenne warrior whose nose was hooked like the beak of a fierce bird of prey. Roman Nose was determined to drive all white invaders from the Plains country south of the Platte River. He had good reason to believe in the success of his dream. For three years he had been allied with the Sioux leader, Red Cloud, in a guerrilla war against the U.S. north of the Platte, winning victories at Fort Phil Kearny, Platte Bridge, and against Patrick Connor's Powder River expedition.

When the U.S. offered peace, the hostiles refused to negotiate until all troops were withdrawn and all forts abandoned north of the Platte. In the spring of 1868, the U.S. treaty makers had agreed to Red Cloud's demands but insisted that the hostiles remain north of the river, leaving the country below open for settlement and railroad construction, and for unharassed operation of stage and freight routes. Roman Nose, however, with Pawnee Killer of the Sioux and several minor chieftains of the Cheyenne and Arapaho, believed that if U.S. soldiers could be driven out of the north they also could be driven out of the south. They would use Red Cloud's methods of terror raids against civilians, attacking soldiers only when they heavily outnumbered them, avoiding battle when faced by superior forces.

———⟫⟪———

During the previous two summers, Roman Nose and Pawnee Killer had tested these tactics in Kansas, successfully closing the stage routes by ambushing coaches and burning stations. They outfoxed Brevet Major General George Custer in raids near Fort Wallace in 1867, wiping out Lieutenant Kidder's ten-man detachment south of the Forks of the Republican. Now in this summer of 1868, their strikes were being directed against construction crews of the Kansas Pacific railroad. Roman Nose was determined to stop that most hated forerunner of the white man's encroaching civilization — the Iron Horse.

To counter these hostile forces, General Philip Sheridan had 1,400 infantrymen strung out in forts across western Kansas and 1,200 cavalrymen who were responsible for courier duties, patrolling, guarding wagon trains, pursuing raiders, and seeking out the hostile camps. When the first raids in the summer of 1868 began, Sheridan asked for more troops, but Congress had reduced Army strength to a point where no men could be spared from occupation duties in the recently defeated Confederacy. Sheridan was aware that even if he had obtained reinforcements most of the troopers would have been green recruits from the East who would have been of little use to him in finding or fighting elusive Indians. The War Department's refusal thus gave him an opening to try out a plan he had devised for using veteran frontiersmen against the hostiles.

It was customary for Western cavalry units going into the field to employ one or two civilian scouts who knew plains craft and Indian warfare. Sheridan admired their skill, their tenacity, and their marksmanship, and his plan was to employ fifty scouts at one dollar per day (about twice as much as a soldier in the ranks received), assemble them under command of an Army officer, and assign them to searching out and destroying the enemy.

To lead this scouting company, Sheridan chose Major George A. Forsyth, a trusted aide who was with him on his famous ride from Winchester to the Battle of Cedar Creek. Forsyth's lieutenant was Frederick Beecher, a nephew of the famous Henry Ward Beecher and a Civil War veteran who still limped from wounds received at Gettysburg. For his sergeant, Forsyth enlisted a former brevet brigadier general who had come west to make his fortune but was temporarily down on his luck; his name was William McCall. Forsyth, Beecher, and McCall were the only members of the command who wore regulation uniforms. A fourth man with command responsibility was the chief of scouts, Abner (Sharp) Grover, a swarthy veteran of the plains who had lived with the Sioux and was considered the best scout in the area. Grover was recovering from a wound received while on a recent scouting mission for Lieutenant Beecher.

⟹⟸

In early September 1868, Forsyth assembled his fifty scouts at Fort Wallace. On September 10, the post commander received a telegraphed report of a Cheyenne raid against a wagon train a few miles east of the fort. As this offered an excellent opportunity for Forsyth's Scouts to pick up a fresh trail, they immediately hurried to the scene of attack. Before the end of that day, with Grover and Beecher scouting in advance, they covered twenty miles of the raiders' trail. It pointed straight northward toward the hostiles' stronghold in Republican River country.

The men who made up Forsyth's Scouts were a cross-section of those adventurous Americans who lived on the frontier in that restless postwar period. About half of them were Civil War veterans, seventeen having served with the Union Army, seven with the Confederate Army. One was an Irishman, Martin Burke, who had fought in India for the British Army. Some were middle-aged or older.

Eli Zigler, the youngest, was 17; Jack Stillwell was 18; Sigmund Schlesinger, a Jewish boy from New York City, was 19.

As Grover and Beecher had feared, the Cheyenne raiders soon discovered they were being pursued, and tried various ruses to throw the scouts off their trail. "The Indians were dropping out here and there, one by one," Major Forsyth recorded, "wherever the ground hardened and their individual trails could not be easily followed." For three or four days the Scouts searched the grassy plain, and then at last on September 15 they struck the trail again and followed it until sundown, camping on one of the branches of the Republican. On the following day, Scout John Hurst noted: "The trail kept enlarging and becoming more and more distinct. Some of us became concerned as to the wisdom of following such a large party of Indians with such a small force of men. We made known our anxiety to Major Forsyth, and he asked us if we 'did not enlist with him to fight Indians?' That ended the discussion."

⟵⟶

Late in the afternoon of the 16th, Forsyth's Scouts camped on a grassy swale beside the drying bed of the Arickaree fork. After searching the area, Sharp Grover warned Forsyth that a strong force of warriors was in the vicinity, and that the Scouts should be prepared for surprise attacks. Forsyth was confident that his men, armed with Spencer repeating rifles (carrying six cartridges in the magazine and one in the chamber) could meet any Indian assault. He ordered guards doubled, however, and walked across the shallow bed of the Arickaree to inspect a small island in the middle of the almost dry stream. This sandy island, about 100 yards long and 50 yards wide, was overgrown with high grass and shrubs, and if necessary could serve as a defense position. Later in the evening, Sigmund Schlesinger made a single notation in his diary: "Seen signal fire on a Hill, 3 miles off in evening late."

That signal fire was also observed in the hostile Indian camps a few miles downstream. During the day, Cheyenne and Sioux scouting parties had been watching the approach of the white "soldiers."

The fire seen by Schlesinger and his comrades was a prearranged signal to the war chiefs, marking the location of the Scouts' camp.

———⟫◎◎⟪———

Among the Indians there was considerable disagreement over how to deal with these white men who were invading their base of operations. Some of the older chiefs wanted to break camp and flee northward to the sanctuary above the Platte. Some of the younger warriors — eager for scalps, horses, and glory — wanted to ride out in small parties, set up decoys, and pick off their enemies one by one. Roman Nose and other leaders argued for a mass attack — six hundred warriors charging in formation against the fifty scouts.

Roman Nose had one strong supporter, a white squaw-man who was called Kansas. (His real name was probably John Clybor, a former member of Custer's 7th Cavalry who had been found wounded on the prairie by an Arapaho squaw who nursed him back to health.) Kansas, or Clybor, owned an army bugle and had taught his new Indian brothers how to drill, charge, fire, and re-assemble to the notes of the instrument.

Although Roman Nose's counsel for a massed attack won out, he regretfully declined to lead the charge. His medicine was bad. Recently he had attended a feast in the Sioux camp, and had been served food taken out of a pot with an iron spoon. This was taboo for Roman Nose; he could eat only food handled with a wooden stick. His medicine man warned him that he would be killed if he went into battle before performing certain purification ceremonies. Roman Nose had already begun the ceremonies, but two or three more days must pass before they could be completed. None of his followers questioned this, of course; they all lived under the laws of good and bad medicine.

———⟫◎◎⟪———

During the evening of September 16, six hundred warriors prepared for a dawn attack on Forsyth's camp, and that night with their war bonnets, shields, lances, rifles, and all their protective medicine they moved up the valley of the Arickaree. Just before daybreak of the

17th, eight young [warriors] in the advance party could not restrain their impatience. They charged Forsyth's camp, hoping to stampede the horses. They came in waving blankets and rattling dried hides, but the alert guards drove them off with a loss of only seven mules.

This alarm probably saved the Scouts from annihilation. It gave them time to saddle, load pack mules with ammunition, and prepare for another attack. The attack came only a few minutes later, announced by a pounding of hooves from down the valley. Through a haze of dawn mist Grover sighted them first — hundreds of Indians charging in a line front, urged on by the notes of a bugle.

"The ground seemed to grow them," was the way Major Forsyth described the onrushing Indians. "They seemed to start out of the very earth." Almost immediately he ordered the Scouts to cross over to the island and form a defense ring. "Had we not done so," John Hurst said afterward, "the fight would not have lasted fifteen minutes and not a man would have been left to tell the tale, for out in the open we would have immediately been surrounded and cut down."

The swiftly executed shift to the island also disconcerted the Indians, who were riding in bands under various subchiefs. Without a war chief whom all would follow, they were thrown into confusion when the Scouts moved out of position. Ignoring the blasts of their frantic bugler, they divided — the Sioux keeping mainly to the west bank, the Cheyennes to the east. "By the time the Indians got in range," George Oakes later recorded, "we were busy making breastworks of our saddles and packs and tying our horses in a circle to the brush around us."

When the Indians tried to ride over the island, intensive fire from Forsyth's men quickly broke the assault. They withdrew out of range to dismount and run forward again, taking cover in reeds along the river banks. For about twenty minutes, firing was heavy from both sides, then gradually died away.

During this brief lull, Forsyth ordered his men to dig pits in the damp sand, using knives, tin plates, or their bare hands. They worked in pairs, alternating between digging and standing ready with their carbines. Dr. John H. Mooers, the Scouts' surgeon, alternated with Major Forsyth.

When the Major left the pit to make a cautious observation of the enemy's movements, he became the Scouts' first casualty. A bullet smashed into his right thigh, striking a nerve. "For a moment I could not speak, so intense was the agony." Before he could crawl into the shallow pit another bullet shattered the shin bone of his left leg, and Surgeon Mooers had to pull him to safety.

By this time several Indians had reached the island on foot, concealing themselves in high grass. They opened a concentrated fire upon the ring of horses and mules, and the animals began rearing and plunging, screaming with pain, or falling dead in their tracks. When the last horse fell, one of the concealed attackers (probably Clybor the squaw-man) shouted in English: "There goes the last damned horse anyhow!" The time now was about 9 o'clock in the morning, and Major Forsyth informed Sharp Grover that he was to take command should the major lose consciousness.

⟝⟞

For most of the remainder of the morning, the frustrated hostiles pressed the fight. Concealed sharpshooters fired at any Scout who exposed himself above the rim of his pit, and small war parties made slashing mounted attacks, circling the defense ring. The warriors rode on the outer sides of their ponies, hanging by one hand and a loop of mane, firing under the necks of their mounts.

In one of these attacks Surgeon Mooers was severely wounded in the head. Not long afterward, a bullet tore into Lieutenant Beecher's spinal cord. He dragged himself across the sand to Major Forsyth's pit, where he collapsed. Meanwhile two Scouts, William Wilson and George Culver, had been killed. Several others were wounded.

Early in the afternoon, Roman Nose interrupted his purification ceremonies and rode to one of the hills overlooking the battlefield. As soon as the other Cheyenne leaders learned that he was there, they came to report on the fighting. From stories told afterward by surviving Indians, it is evident that his tribesmen convinced Roman Nose that he was the only leader whom all the warriors would follow into battle, the only one who could lead them to victory.

Although his medicine man, White Bull, warned him that he had no protection against the white men's bullets, Roman Nose decided that he could not stand aside while his tribesmen were dying in battle. After studying the terrain, he announced a plan of attack against the island, and then began painting himself for battle. Wearing the magic war bonnet that White Bull had made for him, Roman Nose rode slowly along the line of hills until he turned a bend in the Arickaree just below the island.

Around this bend and out of view of the island, Cheyenne, Sioux, and Arapaho warriors were already assembling. Roman Nose formed the mounted Indians into seven or eight ranks with a front of about sixty men, knee to knee. He told those who had no horses to go back toward the island, conceal themselves in grass along the banks and serve as sharpshooters. He was sure that when his mounted force charged the white men, they would rise out of their pits; then the sharpshooters could pour a withering fire of bullets and arrows into them.

Perhaps the reason why Roman Nose assembled his warriors around the river bend was to startle his enemies when they saw the massive force appear unexpectedly in the dry river bed. Instead of coming out at a gallop, he led the perfectly aligned horsemen in a slow trot so the white men could see one rank after another wheeling into view. His medicine man, White Bull, rode beside him, scattering magic dust from a pouch, exhorting the spirits to have pity upon the brave Roman Nose.

Roman Nose lifted his rifle and twirled it lightly in a signal to the bugler to sound the charge. "On they came at a sweeping gallop," Forsyth later reported, "rending the air with their wild war whoops . . . keeping their line almost perfectly . . . with their horses' bridles in their left hands, while with their right they grasped their rifles at the guard and held them squarely in front of themselves, resting lightly upon their horses' necks."

Scout George Oakes put it in more colloquial language: "All hell broke loose. The snipers poured in a hail of bullets and arrows into the island, and with a whoop from Roman Nose, the fun began. Forsyth gave us orders not to fire until he gave the word. When he gave the word we pumped all our rifles empty, then used our revolvers. I took two shots at Roman Nose but didn't hit him. He was shot off his horse by the scouts hidden in the grass. I thought sure they would ride over us, but when they saw their leader fall they sort of lost heart. Roman Nose, when he fell, lay still for awhile, but he had strength enough to crawl into the tall grass. He died toward evening. Two young Indians sneaked over after dark and carried him away."

After the Indians broke off the fighting at dusk, Forsyth held an informal council of war. Sergeant McCall led off with a report of casualties, informing those who did not already know that Lieutenant Beecher had died during the afternoon, bringing the total killed to three. Surgeon Mooers and two Scouts were mortally wounded. Nineteen others had received wounds ranging from slight to severe. In one day of fighting, Forsyth's Scouts had taken 45 percent casualties, most of them occurring before the men could dig their sand pits.

Sharp Grover guessed that the hostiles would make no more assaults on the entrenchments, but he warned that they would continue the siege until the Scouts were starved out or had expended all their ammunition. Forsyth estimated that the Scouts could sustain themselves for several days on horse meat if they could keep it from spoiling. He also announced that Martin Burke had discovered that water could be obtained by digging deep in the sand; ammunition was sufficient to last another week if none was wasted; some medical supplies were in Surgeon Mooers' bag.

Hopes of survival, however, depended upon a rescue force from Fort Wallace, which was about a hundred miles to the south. To summon this relief, Forsyth asked for two volunteers. Eighteen-year-old Jack Stilwell and a gray-haired French trapper named Pierre

"Pete" Trudeau immediately responded. Sharp Grover protested that Stilwell was too young and Trudeau too old, and offered to go along. Forsyth refused Grover permission, saying he needed him on the island.

Near midnight in a drizzling rain, Stilwell and Trudeau moved silently out into the darkness. Seven days would pass before their comrades would know whether they had failed or succeeded in their mission.

"In the night," Sigmund Schlesinger wrote next day in his diary, "I dug my hole deeper. Cut meat off of the Horses & hung it upon Bushes. Indians made a charge on us at Day brake, but retreated. Kept shooting nearly all day."

By the third day of the siege, September 19, the stench of butchered horses surrounding the pits became almost unbearable. The seriously wounded men, including Forsyth, were delirious at times. On the night of the 19th Forsyth asked for two more volunteers to make a try for Fort Wallace. There was no way of knowing, he said, whether Stilwell and Trudeau had escaped the watchful Indians. Late in the night, Jack Donovan and Al Pliley crept away from the defense circle and started for Fort Wallace.

A record kept by Civil War veteran Chauncey Whitney graphically depicts the desperate plight of the besieged Scouts during the next five days:

20th — Sunday, and all is quiet. No attack this morning. Last night I slept for the first time in three nights. Our surgeon, Doctor Mooers, died this morning about daylight. He was shot in the head. He did not speak from the time he was shot until he died. We have twenty men killed and wounded; four dead.

21st — No Indians seen today; all dined and supped on horse meat.

22d — No Indians today. Killed a coyote this morning which was very good. Most of the horse meat gone. Found some prickly pears, which were very good. Are looking anxiously for succor from the fort.

23d — Still looking anxiously for relief. Starvation is staring us in the face; nothing but horse meat.

24th — All fresh horse meat gone. Tried to kill some wolves last night, but failed. The boys began to cut putrid horse meat. Made some soup tonight from putrified horse meat. My God! have you deserted us?

On the 22d, Major Forsyth released all the uninjured Scouts from any obligation to remain on the island. By escaping at night and keeping together, he told them, they might reach Fort Wallace; the wounded including himself would remain behind and take their chances on a relief party arriving in time to save them. Not one Scout accepted the proposal. Sergeant McCall spoke for all: "We've fought together," he declared, " and if need be we'll die together."

<hr>

Late on the morning of the ninth day, September 25, Major Forsyth was lying on a piece of canvas that had been stretched for him across a sand pit. Weakened by the pain of his festering wounds and from lack of food, he was barely able to raise his head when he heard a cry: "Indians!" From the pits around him men sprang to their feet, staring at distant hills to the south. Sharp Grover took the major's field glass and studied the moving objects. "There comes our relief party!" he shouted, and as soon as the Scouts saw blue uniforms and the glitter of sabers and carbines they broke into cheers. Sigmund Schlesinger recorded that he "jumped up and joined in a lunatics' dance that was in progress all around."

In a few minutes they could recognize the wind-whipped guid-on of Captain Louis Carpenter's Troop H, 10th Cavalry, and the friendly black faces of the Negro troopers. Private Reuben Waller, a former slave and servant to his master in Bedford Forrest's Confederate cavalry, told about it afterward: "What a sight we saw — thirty wounded and dead men right in the midst of fifty dead horses that had lain in the hot sun for ten days. And these men had eaten the putrid flesh of those dead horses for eight days."

Both pairs of Scouts — Stilwell and Trudeau, Donovan and Pliley — after several narrow escapes had reached Fort Wallace. Jack

Donovan then had galloped to find Carpenter's patrolling troopers near Cheyenne Wells; it was he who had guided them to the island. A surgeon was with them, and as soon as the troopers could move the wounded men off the reeking island, a temporary hospital was established. The surgeon lost only one man, Lewis Farley, bringing the total of dead to five.

So ended the Battle of the Arickaree, known also as Beecher's Island in memory of the brave young veteran of Gettysburg who died there. Indian losses were difficult to estimate; probably thirty-five killed and more than a hundred wounded. The nine-day stand of Forsyth's Scouts forced the hostiles to abandon their secure base and ended the dream of Roman Nose to drive the white man from the southern plains.

An attempt by Cheyenne warriors to ride over the island on the morning of September 17 was repulsed by Major Forsyth's Scouts during twenty minutes of intense fire on both sides. From a drawing by American artist Rufus Fairchild Zogbaum in Harper's New Monthly Magazine, *June 1895.*

22

Geronimo

*"As white men claimed more and more western lands for themselves,
Geronimo's reputation grew. His exploits had legendary qualities, and the
American press rushed to make the warrior a legend. . . . in the autumn
of 1881, for the second time, Geronimo and a few of his followers began
slipping away from the reservation to seek freedom across the border."*

Late in the afternoon of April 20, 1877, a young white man
led twenty-two Apache policemen into the Ojo Caliente
Indian agency in southern New Mexico. The agency was
in the process of being closed, and some of the buildings had
already been abandoned. Camped nearby along the Alamosa River
were 435 Apaches classified by the U.S. Army as renegades because
they had resisted efforts to remove them to the San Carlos reservation in Arizona. Among them was a small band of Chiricahuas, and
one of their shrewdest and most resolute leaders was a man about 50
years old. At that time few white Americans had heard of him. His
name was Geronimo.

The young white man in command of the Apache police was
under orders to arrest the renegades and remove them by force if
necessary to San Carlos, several days' journey to the west. He was John
P. Clum, 24 years old, seemingly a most unlikely candidate for capturing Geronimo and introducing him to the white man's world. Of
Dutch descent, Clum grew up in the Hudson River Valley, went to
Rutgers College where he played football, joined the U.S. Signal

Corps after graduation, and was sent to Santa Fe in 1871 to make meterological observations. In 1874 he was offered the post of Indian agent at the San Carlos Apache reservation, and with youthful enthusiasm set about a reform program. Among his first actions was the establishment of an Apache court to try offenders and the organization of a company of Apaches to police their own agency.

When Clum received orders to bring in the recalcitrant Apaches from Ojo Caliente, he was assured by the Army that three companies of cavalry would join him there to assist in the removal. Clum started from San Carlos with about a hundred of his Apache police, but on the day of rendezvous he made a forced march with only twenty-two police, expecting to meet the cavalry at Ojo Caliente. To his dismay, the soldiers had not arrived, and he knew that if he waited for military assistance the Apaches he had come for would most likely vanish into the mountains. Clum immediately sent a courier to bring up his main force of police, and as they came in silently during the night he concealed them in one of the empty supply buildings. At dawn he sent one of his trusted Apache policemen to the camps along the Alamosa to ask the renegade leaders to come into the agency for a parley.

Believing that Clum had only twenty-two police with him, they responded willingly, bringing their women and children with them. Years afterward Clum told what happened next, exaggerating the role played by Geronimo because by that time the Chiricahua leader had become the most famous of all Apaches. With six of his policemen, Clum stood on the porch of the main agency building, facing the renegades on the parade ground. Fifty yards away was the supply building where his hidden reserve force of police waited to rush out, if necessary, at Clum's signal.

Clum said that he directed his remarks to Geronimo. "You and your followers have been killing white men and stealing their cattle," he accused. "A year ago . . . you promised me you would come to live with me at San Carlos . . . but you spoke with a split tongue; you did not tell the truth. So now we have come to take you back with us. . . . We do not want to have trouble with you, and if you and your people

This is the earliest photograph of Geronimo known to exist. Courtesy of the Arizona Historical Society/Tucson AHS #20602.

will listen to me, with good ears and good hearts, no harm will come to you."

"You talk very brave," Geronimo supposedly replied, "but we do not like that kind of talk. We are not going to San Carlos with you, and unless you are careful, you and your Apache police will not go back to San Carlos, either. Your bodies will stay here at Ojo Caliente to make food for coyotes."

During the next few moments, according to Clum, he and the assemblage of renegades tried to face each other down. Geronimo's thumb moved to within an inch of the hammer of his Springfield rifle. Clum casually raised his left hand to the brim of his hat — the signal for the doors of the supply building to spring open and release his hidden force of eighty Apache policemen. With his right hand, Clum touched the butt of his revolver. He watched Geronimo's thumb move closer to the hammer of his rifle, and then as the swarm of police with rifles at the ready encircled the group on the parade ground, Geronimo's thumb hesitated and fell back to its original position. Geronimo and his comrades stood motionless and silent.

"Tell all your men to lay their guns on the ground," Clum said quietly, "out here in the open, where my police can gather them up and keep them for you."

For the first and what was to be the only time in his life, Geronimo had been captured. Several times later in his life he would surrender on his own terms to Army officers who pursued him, but never afterward did he let himself be entrapped and forced into surrender.

This occasion also marked Geronimo's entrance into that mythical world of Indian villains which was created mainly by imaginative journalists of the boisterous 19th century American press. In his official reports of the capture, John Clum spelled his captive's name "Eronemo" and "Heronemo" and gave him no more prominence than several other leaders now long forgotten. Geronimo, however, had appeared at a propitious moment for the journalists who covered the Wild West. Crazy Horse was dead, Red Cloud had retired to his agency, and Sitting Bull was a fugitive in Canada. If Clum had not found

Geronimo, he or some other Indian villain would have had to be invented. During the next decade, Geronimo the Apache would replace the great Sioux villains in the pages of the sensational press, and eventually he would learn to cooperate in the creation of his legend.

Although Geronimo may have been virtually unknown until the late 1870's to the white men who invaded his country, he had earned a considerable reputation among his own people — during the 1850's as a raider into Mexico, and in the 1860's as a warrior with Cochise's Chiricahuas. Born in 1829, or possibly earlier, into the Bedonkohe band somewhere on the Gila River in southern Arizona, he was named Goyathlay, the One Who Yawns. In the 1830's while he was still a child, the Mexican states of Sonora and Chihuahua offered considerable monetary rewards for the scalps of Apaches of both sexes and all ages, and this set off a guerrilla war along what is now the Arizona border. In 1850 Geronimo's band was ambushed by Mexican scalp hunters. He lost his mother, wife, and three children, barely escaping with his own life, and ever afterward he regarded all Mexicans as his personal enemies. It was during his retaliatory strikes against them that the Mexicans came to know his fierceness. They called him Geronimo, crying the name as a warning when they saw him leading his warriors in an attack. Soon his own people were using the name, shouting "Geronimo" as a battle cry.

Mainly for strength in numbers, Geronimo's band joined forces with other small groups of Apaches, including the Mimbrenos of Mangas Coloradas and the Chiricahuas of the famed Cochise. With the passage of time they all became known as Chiricahuas, with Cochise as their leader.

Near Apache Pass late in the summer of 1851, Geronimo met a group of Americans who were surveying the U.S. boundary line following the Mexican War. "They were good men," he said in his dictated autobiography, "and we were sorry when they had gone on into the west. They were not soldiers. These were the first white men I ever knew." From the surveyors Geronimo also received the first money he had seen, payment for wild game. "We did not know the value of this money, but we kept it and later learned from a Navajo

Indian that it was very valuable." After that, Geronimo regarded money highly. When he died more than half a century later he had several thousand dollars deposited in an Oklahoma bank.

During the twenty years that followed this meeting, Geronimo continued as an unknown to most Americans, but he gradually rose in the ranks of the Chiricahuas, participated in numerous raids into Mexico, and was wounded several times. He came to believe that no bullet could kill him. In 1858, soon after the Butterfield Overland Mail began operations on its southwestern route from St. Louis to San Francisco, the U.S. Indian agent to the Apaches, Dr. Michael Steck, met with Cochise and his warriors and secured a promise from them to permit the stagecoaches to run unmolested through their country. Geronimo was among those who shook hands with Steck to seal the agreement, but apparently he made no particular impression upon the agent.

The peace that followed this meeting came to an abrupt end in 1861 when Cochise was wrongly accused of kidnapping a white child. At the request of an Army officer, Cochise and five of his warriors agreed to meet a detachment of soldiers at Apache Pass. Although under a flag of truce, Cochise was arrested and was badly wounded when he made a successful escape. Because three of his warriors still remained in Army hands, Cochise captured three white men and offered to exchange them. The Army officer replied that he would do so when Cochise returned the kidnapped child. Angry over the implication that he was a liar, Cochise killed his prisoners, the Army officer hanged the warriors, and a bloody war broke out between Apaches and whites.

In the raids against settlers and travelers, Geronimo was a leading warrior, and in 1862 he almost certainly was one of the Apaches who battled several hundred California Volunteer soldiers at Apache Pass until artillery forced the Indians to withdraw. To guard the pass and keep the connecting trails open, the Army built Fort Bowie there in the heart of the Chiricahua Mountains. Although the Chiricahuas were forced to retreat deep into the Dragoon Mountains, they continued their raids through the Civil War into the postwar years, never abandoning their determination to repel the white invaders.

At last in 1871 the Army sent General George Crook to Arizona to round up all Apaches and confine them on reservations. At this time Cochise was still the best known Apache leader and he was also believed to be the least likely to consent to reservation life. In the autumn of 1872, General Oliver O. Howard was sent to arrange a meeting with Cochise in his mountain stronghold. After several days of discussions, Howard realized that the only peaceful way to make reservation Indians of the Chiricahuas was to let them stay where they were, with Cochise's trusted white friend Tom Jeffords as their agent and with Fort Bowie as their agency. During these councils, Geronimo met Howard and liked him. "He always kept his word with us and treated us as brothers," Geronimo said long afterward.

During the four years that followed, the Chiricahuas kept the peace, even though clothing and rations that had been promised them were often slow in reaching their agency. After Cochise died in 1874, Agent Jeffords wanted to resign his post, but as he noted in his report for that year "the head-men of the tribe declared they would only keep the treaty . . . on condition that I remained." A year later, however, when the Office of Indian Affairs halted deliveries of beef cattle to the agency, forcing the Chiricahuas to leave their reservation to hunt for food, the raiding of ranches resumed. Dissension over leadership also arose among various bands of Chiricahuas, and Jeffords found it impossible to draw the various factions together again.

In the meantime the United States Government had concentrated most of the other Apache sub-tribes on the San Carlos reservation. The first agents assigned there were dismissed for either incompetency or dishonesty, until in 1874 young John Clum arrived to take charge.

The government's policy of concentrating all Apaches on one reservation was the result of pressures from white settlers, speculators, and miners who wanted free use of land previously assigned to different sub-tribes, and it caused much of the turmoil that followed during the next ten years. Had the Chiricahuas been left in their homeland, we probably never would have heard of Geronimo. General Crook, whose soldiers had to force most of the Apaches to move to San Carlos, opposed the concentration policy, but in March 1875 he was transferred north to fight the Plains Indians. Seven years later he would be called back to Arizona to deal with the then seemingly indomitable Geronimo.

After capturing Geronimo at Ojo Caliente in the spring of 1877, John Clum put him and twelve other leaders in shackles, and with the assistance of the U.S. Cavalry he conducted the renegades to San Carlos. There the shackled leaders were confined to a guardhouse while their people were settled on a desolate arid flat along the Gila. Geronimo remained in the guardhouse until Clum was replaced by another agent a few weeks later. The forced confinement had a profound effect upon this man who valued his freedom above all else, and it explains much of his later behavior.

For several months after his release from the guardhouse, Geronimo lived the quiet life of a reservation Indian. He promised the new agent who had freed him, Henry L. Hart, that he would not attempt to leave, and Hart made him "captain" of the Ojo Caliente band. Conditions grew steadily worse, however, rations and clothing being inadequate to feed and clothe the recent arrivals. Accustomed to living in the mountains, the Chiricahuas sickened, several dying in a smallpox epidemic or from malaria contracted from the swarms of mosquitos which infested the Gila flatlands that had been assigned them for a new homeland.

On the night of April 4, 1878, with his family and several members of his band, Geronimo fled from San Carlos. The Chiricahuas headed straight for Mexico, plundering a wagon train along the way for food and ammunition, and killing the drivers. A few days later, after beating off an attack by pursuing soldiers, they were safe in a hideout deep in the Sierra Madre of Mexico. During the months that followed this first in a series of breakouts from San Carlos by Geronimo, another Apache leader named Victorio also used a base in

Mexico for making daring thrusts into New Mexico to kill settlers and ambush cavalry forces. Because Geronimo's name was now known by the military and the press, he was blamed for some of Victorio's ruthless forays.

Perhaps because of this, perhaps out of fear of becoming a hunted outlaw like Victorio, or from a desire to see friends and relatives left at San Carlos, or a yearning for a more peaceful life, Geronimo late in 1879 moved his small group of followers into New Mexico and arranged a meeting with an Army officer and the Chiricahuas' old friend, Tom Jeffords. As a result of this council, Geronimo was allowed to take his people back to San Carlos.

Not long after their return to the reservation, a medicine man far up on Cibicu Creek, west of Fort Apache, began preaching an early form of what was to become the Ghost Dance religion a decade later. After rumors spread that the medicine man was raising warriors from the dead through a ceremonial dance, many Apaches became believers. Unfortunately, the white settlers and the military reacted too strongly to the prophet's predictions that the whites would soon be driven from the Apaches' lands, and soldiers were sent to arrest him. As was to be the case a dozen years later in South Dakota when an attempt was made to arrest Sitting Bull during the Ghost Dance excitement, the medicine man was killed and bloodshed between soldiers and Apaches followed.

Although neither Geronimo nor his followers had played any part in the Cibicu Creek ceremonies, large forces of cavalry began pursuing participants across the reservation, alarming the Chiricahuas. After their agent restricted the movements of Geronimo's people, some of them decided that life would be better in the old stronghold in the Sierra Madre of Mexico. And so in the autumn of 1881, for the second time, Geronimo and a few of his followers began slipping away from the reservation to seek freedom across the border.

The Geronimo legend was about to begin.

Geronimo had been only a few months in the Sierra Madre when he decided that all the Chiricahuas should be rescued from the semistarvation and sickness of the reservation and brought to Mexico.

Consequently, in April 1882, after careful planning, Geronimo and his warriors stealthily invaded San Carlos, cut the telegraph lines, and sought out all the Chiricahuas they could find for a flight to Mexico. Not all wanted to leave. According to Jason Betzinez, a cousin of Geronimo who was living on the reservation, they were given no time to find their horses and had to flee on foot. "We weren't allowed to snatch up anything but a handful of clothing and other belongings. There was no chance to eat breakfast. Geronimo . . . was out in front guiding us east along the foot of the hills north of the Gila River."

On their way out of the reservation they encountered a patrol of Apache police and killed the white leader, Albert Sterling. With about 100 warriors and 400 women and children, Geronimo now faced the difficult task of avoiding or outrunning several pursuing Army forces. Lieutenant Colonel George A. Forsyth of Beecher Island fame tried to intercept them with cavalry along the recently completed Southern Pacific Railroad, and came close enough for a sharp fight at Horseshoe Canyon on April 23, but he could not stop them.

"After we had crossed into Mexico," Jason Betzinez recalled, "we began to feel safe from attack by U.S. troops, not knowing that the troop commander, hot on our trail, intended to cross the border with or without permission of higher authorities."

Although Forsyth did pursue Geronimo's escaping band across the border, it was not the U.S. cavalry but that of the Mexican Army that was to deal them a deadly blow. In a dry stream bed within view of the Sierra Madre, the Mexicans struck the flank of the relaxed two-mile-long column of Apaches, shooting down men, women, and children. "As we ran," Betzinez said, "my mother and I heard Geronimo behind us, calling to the men to gather around him and make a stand to protect the women and children."

According to Geronimo's own account, told years afterward, the Mexican commander recognized him and ordered his soldiers to exterminate him and his band at any cost. "From all along the ditches arose the fierce war cry of my people," he said. "The columns wavered an instant and then swept on; they did not retreat until our fire had destroyed the front ranks. . . . That night before the firing had ceased a dozen Indians had crawled out of the ditches and set fire to the long prairie grass behind the Mexican troops. During the confusion that followed we escaped to the mountains." Geronimo failed to mention the severe losses suffered by his people — seventy-eight dead, thirty-three women and children made captive, and many wounded. One fourth of his fighting force of warriors was gone.

To obtain food supplies and horses, the Chiricahuas made lightning raids upon Mexican villages, taking cattle, horses, and mules, and capturing pack trains of supplies. Because they were unable to obtain ammunition that would fit their American-made rifles, Geronimo risked a foray into Arizona. He succeeded in bringing out large quantities of ammunition as well as saddles, bridles, and blankets. But at the same time his action generated headlines and lurid tales for the voracious American press. From that time until his final surrender, Geronimo would be blamed for almost every major or minor raid by Apaches anywhere in Arizona and New Mexico. This added to his notoriety, gave him a far more bloodthirsty image than he deserved, and made his capture or destruction the main objective of General George Crook when he returned to Arizona in September 1882.

In preparation for his campaign against Geronimo, Crook put San Carlos under military control and transformed the Apache police into scouts for tracking. He placed Captain Emmet Crawford in charge of the reservation and gave Lieutenant Britton Davis command of the scouts.

To stop the Apache raids Crook devised a plan for striking at Geronimo's base, the location of which he obtained from a Chiricahua who returned to the reservation. In order to avoid violating international law, he had to obtain permission from Mexican authorities to take his soldiers across the border. The slow process of completing these arrangements as well as making preparations for the expedition delayed the start until the spring of 1883.

With a force of 320, which included 76 civilian packers to handle the pack mules, 193 Apache scouts and a journalist-photographer, Crook crossed into Mexico early in May. When the mountainous country slowed the column's progress, he sent Captain Crawford with 150 scouts ahead of the pack train. On May 15, Crawford surrounded one of Geronimo's *rancherias* and captured the women and children. In a few days several warriors surrendered in order to join their families.

By this time Crook and his pack train had come up, and he learned from the warriors that Geronimo wanted to talk with him. Captain John Bourke, who was with Crook during the meetings that followed, described Geronimo and his warriors as a "fine-looking lot of pirates" all well-armed with breech-loading Winchesters. Geronimo told Crook that he had always wanted to be at peace, but that he had been ill-treated at San Carlos and driven away. He promised the general that if he would be allowed to go back to the reservation and guaranteed just treatment, he would gladly work for his living and follow the path of peace. Crook kept Geronimo in suspense for a few days, then consented to let him round up his scattered band for the long march back to San Carlos.

The column moved slowly northward, small groups of Chiricahuas joining it daily until there were more than 300 who had to be fed from the dwindling rations of the pack train. "All the old Chiricahuas were piled on mules, donkeys and ponies," Captain Bourke said. "So were the weak little children and feeble women. The great majority streamed along on foot, nearly all wearing garlands of cottonwood foliage to screen them from the sun." For most of the march Geronimo kept far to the rear, trying to convince reluctant members of his band to join the procession or searching for those who might have been away on hunts or on private raids.

Soon after the column crossed into Arizona on June 10, the territorial newspapers began clamoring for the heads of Geronimo and his warriors, demanding that they be executed and their women and children exiled to Indian Territory. Somehow the Chiricahuas learned of these threats — probably from officers who obtained the newspapers, repeated the stories within hearing of the Apache scouts who then told the Chiricahuas — and Geronimo and his lieutenants vanished again into the mountains.

The main column moved on to San Carlos, however, with the women and children, and months passed before the cautious warriors began coming in to join them. Crook sent Lieutenant Britton Davis with the Apache scouts down to the border to make searches for Geronimo and assure him that he would be safe at San Carlos. Not until late in February 1884 did Geronimo suddenly appear at the border crossing. He was riding on a white pony at the head of a herd of 350 beef cattle that he had stolen from Mexican ranchers for the purpose of starting livestock raising on the reservation.

To avoid difficulties with the Mexican Government, Crook ordered the cattle seized as soon as they reached San Carlos, and authorized payment of compensation to the Mexican ranchers from whom the animals had been stolen. Although Geronimo's anger was aroused by the seizure, in the end his people obtained their share of the beef, which was later issued to them as agency rations. But there was no longer a breeding herd.

As soon as he had settled down again at San Carlos, Geronimo petitioned Crook for a better location for his people, a place where there was plenty of grass and water for ranching and farming. He particularly wanted to move to Eagle Creek, but Crook could not help him. The Eagle Creek lands had been withdrawn from the reservation for settlement by whites. Eventually Geronimo was given an area along Turkey Creek that was suitable for small ranches, but Washington bureaucrats in the Indian Office refused to allow them any livestock, insisting that they adopt methods of farming suited to the East but that were impracticable in the arid Southwest. They were given wagons, plows, and harness that was too large for their wiry ponies. "The ponies, unaccustomed to a slow gait, preferred to trot or gallop," observed Lieutenant Davis, "and the plow-points were oftener above ground than in it."

Yet somehow the Chiricahuas managed to grow small crops of corn. Captain Crawford reported that the grain might make it possible to reduce government food allowances, but the Apaches had other plans. They used a considerable amount of their corn to secretly make *tiswin,* an alcoholic drink strictly forbidden by General Crook. The brewing process was fairly simple. After being soaked in moistened grass until it sprouted, the corn was then ground and boiled, the resulting liquid resembling beer that, as Geronimo said, "had the power of intoxication, and was very highly prized."

After one of the Chiricahua leaders named Kayatennae was caught making tiswin, he was arrested and sentenced to three years in irons at the federal prison at Alcatraz. Not long after he was taken away rumors began spreading that Kayatennae had been hanged by the Army and that Geronimo was next on the list of victims. This aroused all the old anxieties and fears of betrayal that lingered in Geronimo's mind, and by the late spring of 1885 he was also being resentful over the unfairness of reservation rules. He saw the Army officers relieving the tedium of their lives with whiskey and other forms of alcohol, and could not understand why they forbade his people to make and drink their favorite beverage.

On May 15, Geronimo's discontent came to a head when he joined several other tribal leaders in a demonstration outside Lieutenant Davis' tent. The Chiricahuas told Davis that they had agreed on a peace with the Americans, but that nothing had been said about their conduct among themselves. "They were not children to be taught how to live with their women and what they should eat or drink. All their lives they had eaten and drunk what seemed good to them. . . . They had complied with all they had promised to do when they had their talk with the General in Mexico; had kept the peace and harmed no one. Now they were being punished for things they had a right to do as long as they did no harm to others."

Lieutenant Davis told them that tiswin was forbidden because drunken Indians did not know what they were doing. Although Geronimo took little part in the discussion, Davis could see that he was angry, and as soon as the Apaches left he sent a warning telegram through channels to Crook. The message was pigeonholed by an inept superior officer, and Crook never received it. Forty-eight hours later Geronimo with 144 followers, including about a hundred women and children, left the reservation. This time Davis could not send a telegram because Geronimo and his warriors had cut the wires in several places, refastening the breaks with thin strips of buckskin so they could not easily be found and repaired.

This last breakaway of Geronimo started one of the longest and most publicized military campaigns of the Indian Wars, involving before it ended thousands of soldiers in pursuit of fewer than fifty warriors, and inspiring a multitude of blood-and-thunder newspaper stories.

"I did not leave of my own accord," Geronimo was to tell Crook afterward, explaining that he had been informed several times by friends that the Army was planning to arrest and hang him. "I want to know now who it was ordered me to be arrested. I was praying to the light and to the darkness, to God and to the sun, to let me live quietly there with my family. I don't know what the reason was that people should speak badly of me. . . . Very often there are stories put in the newspapers that I am to be hanged. I don't want that any more. When a man tries to do right, such stories ought not to be put in the newspapers."

With his usual ingenuity, Geronimo eluded pursuit by the cavalry, quickly crossed into Mexico, and reached his old refuge in the Sierra Madre. And once again Crook ordered Captain Crawford to go in pursuit of him. This time Crawford was accompanied by a hardbitten frontiersman, Tom Horn, serving as chief of the Apache scouts. (In an autobiography, which has the veracity of a dime novel, Horn exaggerated his importance in the campaign and added his name to the Geronimo legend.) While Crawford and Horn were tracking into Mexico, an Apache leader named Ulzana conducted bloody raids into New Mexico and Arizona, some of which were credited in the press to Geronimo.

Not until January 9, 1886, did Crawford find Geronimo's rancheria, and two days later Geronimo with his characteristic aplomb came in for a conference. After several long discussions he agreed to meet

Crook within two moons somewhere near the border. During the interval a large party of Mexican irregular troops in search of bounty scalps attacked the Apache scouts, killing Crawford and slightly wounding Horn. Geronimo nevertheless kept his promise and met with Crook on March 25.

The meetings just below the Arizona border at El Cañon de los Embudos were like scenes from a carefully staged drama. Every word of the rich dialogue of confrontation between Geronimo and Crook was set down by Captain Bourke, and the images of the participants were preserved for history by photographer Camillus S. Fly of Tombstone, Arizona.

In his speeches Geronimo tried to explain his past actions, but Crook responded by calling him a liar. When Geronimo spoke of returning to the reservation, the general bluntly told him that he had only two choices — surrender unconditionally or stay on the warpath, in which case he would be hunted down and killed. By the third day of the meetings, Geronimo knew that Crook meant to make prisoners of him and his warriors and send them to some distant place. One by one the warriors capitulated, and then Geronimo offered his hand to Crook. "I give myself up to you," he said. "Do with me what you please. Once I moved about like the wind. . . . That's all I have to say now, except a few words. I should like to have my wife and daughter come to meet me at Fort Bowie."

Crook promised Geronimo that his family would join him in imprisonment, and then left the meeting place to return to Fort Bowie ahead of the column of scouts and the surrendered Chiricahuas. He sent a telegram to the General of the Army, Philip Sheridan, announcing Geronimo's surrender. Three days later he had to send another message informing Sheridan that Geronimo and forty members of his band once again had fled to the Sierra Madre of Mexico. Sheridan was furious, condemning Crook for slackness of command and refusing to accept his explanations. Crook resigned, and on April 2 General Nelson Miles replaced him.

The villain in this last flight of Geronimo was a trader and whiskey runner to the Indians named Bob Tribolett, who had slipped across the border and unknown to the Army officers supplied the Apaches with mescal and other liquors. As soon as the Indians reached a state of intoxication, Tribolett began hinting to them that they would be hanged as soon as the Army got them to Fort Bowie, thus playing upon the suspicions that were always close to the surface in their minds.

"We were not under any guard at this time," Geronimo said afterward. "I feared treachery and decided to remain in Mexico." One of his lieutenants, Natchez, was more direct in his explanation of the flight: "I was afraid I was going to be taken off somewhere I didn't like, to some place I didn't know. I thought all who were taken away would die."

Many Army officers, including General Crook, suspected that Tribolett may have been sent by the "Indian Ring" of Arizona to frighten Geronimo into continuing the fighting. Civilian contractors and traders had profited from the long Apache wars, dealing with both sides, and they had a keen interest in the maintenance of the numerous forts and the continued presence of soldiers in the territories. Whether Tribolett's action was deliberately planned or not, it certainly resulted in a bonanza for the "Indian Ring."

Soon after he took command, the flamboyant and ambitious General Miles quickly put 5,000 soldiers (or about a third of the total combat strength of the U.S. Army) into the field. He also had 500 Apache scouts and many irregular civilian militia. For quick communication he organized an expensive system of heliographs to flash messages back and forth across Arizona and New Mexico. The enemy to be subdued by this powerful force consisted of Geronimo and twenty-four warriors who throughout that summer of 1886 were also under constant pursuit by thousands of Mexican soldiers.

On August 23, Geronimo finally chose to surrender to Lieutenant Charles Gatewood and two Apache scouts who found him in a Sierra Madre canyon. Geronimo laid his rifle down and shook hands with Gatewood, inquiring calmly about his health. He then asked about matters back in the United States. How were the Chiricahuas faring? Gatewood told that those who had surrendered had already been sent to Florida for imprisonment. If Geronimo would surrender to General Miles, he would be sent to Florida to join them.

Geronimo wanted to know what kind of man General Miles was. Was his voice harsh or agreeable to the ear? Was he cruel or kind-hearted? Did he look you in the eye or down at the ground when he talked? Would he keep his promises? Then he said to Gatewood: "Consider yourself one of us and not a white man . . . as an Apache, what would you advise me to do?"

"I would trust General Miles and take him at his word," Gatewood replied.

And so, for what was to be the last time in his life, Geronimo surrendered. Many Arizonians as well as President Grover Cleveland wanted to hang the old warrior, but Miles kept his promise to send him to Florida, and on September 8 put him on a railroad train at Bowie Station under heavy guard. Two days later Geronimo's enemies in the War Department in Washington ordered him hauled off the train at San Antonio while they debated whether or not he had surrendered or been captured. If it was the latter, they would hang him. While he awaited his fate in San Antonio a photographer posed him against a wall for a poignant portrait of a defeated 60-year-old Apache halfway into the white man's world, clad in a mixed costume of sack coat, hat, and boots over his native breechcloth.

After a month of bureaucratic haggling, the Army sent him on his way to Florida. For some time he was kept in a separate prison from that of his family and friends; at last in May 1888 they were all brought together at Mt. Vernon Barracks north of Mobile, Alabama. There the dying began in that warm humid land so unlike the high dry country of their birth. More than 100 died of a disease diagnosed as consumption, and when the Government took their children away to the Indian school at Carlisle, Pennsylvania, many more died there. Old friends and old enemies interceded for them. General Crook, Captain Bourke, General Howard, Surgeon Walter Reed, and Lieutenant Hugh Scott all came to offer their help, but the people of Arizona refused to permit Geronimo and his Chiricahuas to return to their homeland.

At last in 1894, the Kiowas and Comanches, after learning of their plight, offered these ancient Apache enemies a part of their reservation near Fort Sill in Oklahoma. There, nearby the fort, Geronimo and the other survivors built houses and plowed small farms. Geronimo began to enjoy life again with his wife and children, taking pride in his watermelon patch, growing enough melons to sell some at the fort. He adapted quickly to the white man's economic system, and because of his fame found it easy to sell his autograph, or bows and arrows, and even old hats to curious visitors. One visitor in 1905 described him as "a smiling, well-kept, well-dressed Indian about five feet nine inches tall . . . dressed in a well-fitting blue cloth suit of citizen's clothes."

It was at about this time that Stephen M. Barrett, a school superintendent in the nearby town of Lawton, asked Geronimo to dictate the story of his life, a task that he willingly undertook when he was assured that he would be paid for it. The result is a unique account of Indian life told from the viewpoint of a warrior-leader.

Although Geronimo was still technically a prisoner of war, the Army permitted him to attend, under guard, international fairs and expositions at Omaha, Buffalo, and St. Louis. He attracted large crowds, and profited from the sale of autographs, buttons, hats, and photographs of himself. One Sunday while in Omaha his guard took him out into the country for a buggy ride and they became lost in the fields of tall corn. Darkness fell before they could find their way back to the fairgrounds, and as they were returning through the city streets they could hear shouts of newsboys selling an extra edition of a local paper with headlines announcing that Geronimo had escaped and was on his way back to Arizona. He would always be a target for the sensational press, but such stories also helped sell more autographs and photos.

When President Theodore Roosevelt invited him to Washington for the inaugural parade, he was sent a check for $171 to cover his travel expenses. Geronimo took the check to his Lawton bank, deposited all but one dollar, and then boarded the train for Washington. At every stop along the way he sold autographs to crowds at the stations. When he rode down Pennsylvania Avenue with five other Indian "chiefs" he practically stole the show from Teddy Roosevelt, and then went home to Oklahoma with a trunkful of new clothes and his pockets full of money. He was no miser, however; he gave freely of his earnings to less fortunate tribespeople and sent needed goods to relatives and friends in Arizona.

In his last years Geronimo became fond of automobiles, although he never owned one. When he was allowed to attend rodeos and local fairs in Oklahoma, he would often ride in one of these new mobile inventions of the white man, preferring the bright red models with shiny brass trimmings. For a stunt at one Wild West show he shot a buffalo from the seat of a racing car. In one of his last public appearances, he was persuaded by a photographer to pose in a black top hat at the wheel of a resplendent open car — the perfect comic image of the American Indian as he was seen in the popular culture of the nation at the beginning of the 20th century.

It was a fall from a horse that finished the old Chiricahua. On a cold February night in 1909 he was returning home from Lawton, where he had sold some bows and arrows and obtained some whiskey. He fell from his saddle beside the bank of a creek, and lay exposed for several hours. Three days later, February 17, he was dead from pneumonia. His body was scarred with many wounds, but, as he had always boasted, no bullet killed him. At 80, or perhaps a year or two older, he had outlived most of his contemporaries of the Indian wars in the West.

23

The Ghost Dance and Battle of Wounded Knee

"To destroy the white man, bring back the buffalo, and restore their old way of life, all the Indians had to do was perform a magic dance . . . that was the message preached to the dispirited Western tribes in 1889 by a self-styled redeemer."

You may bury my body in Sussex grass,
You may bury my tongue at Champmedy.
I shall not be there. I shall rise and pass.
Bury my heart at Wounded Knee.

— Stephen Vincent Benet

---

*D*uring the decade following Custer's defeat on the Little Big Horn, the warring tribes of Indians in the American West were gradually shorn of their power and locked within reservations. Many of the great chiefs and mighty warriors were dead. The buffalo and antelope had almost vanished; the old ceremonies of the tribes were becoming rituals without meaning.

For the survivors it was a time without spirit, a time of despair. One might swap a few skins for the trader's crazy-water and dream of the old days, the days of the splendid hunts and fighting. One might make big talk for a little while but that was all.

In such times, defeated peoples search for redeemers, and soon on many reservations there were dreamers and swooning men to tell of approaching redemption. Most of them were great fakers, but some were sincere in their vagaries and their visions.

As early as 1870 the defeated Paiutes of Nevada had found a redeemer in Tavibo, a petty chief, who claimed to have talked with divine spirits in the mountains. All the people of the earth were to be swallowed up, the spirits told him, but at the end of three days the Indians would be resurrected in the flesh to live forever. They would enjoy the earth which was rightfully theirs. Once again there would be plenty of game, fish, and piñon nuts. Best of all, the white invaders would be destroyed forever.

When Tavibo first told his vision to the Paiutes, he attracted very few believers. But gradually he added other features to his story, and he went up into the mountains again for further revelations. It was necessary for the Indians to dance, everywhere; to keep on dancing. This would please the Great Spirit, who would come and destroy the white men and bring back the buffalo.

Tavibo died shortly after he told of these things, but his son, Wovoka, was considered the natural inheritor of his powers by those Paiutes who believed in the new religion of the dance. Wovoka, who was only 14 when his father died, was taken into the family of a white farmer, David Wilson, and was given the name of Jack Wilson. In his new home the boy's imagination was fired by Bible stories told to him; he was fascinated by the white man's God.

On New Year's Day of 1889, a vision came to Jack Wilson (Wovoka) while he lay ill with fever; he dreamed that he died and went to heaven. God spoke to him, commanding him to take a message back to earth. Wovoka was to tell the Indians that if they would follow God's commandment and perform a "ghost dance" at regular intervals their old days of happiness and prosperity would be returned to them.

In January 1889 on the Walker Lake Reservation, the first Ghost Dance was performed on a dancing ground selected by Wovoka. The ceremony was simple, the Paiutes forming into a large circle, dancing

The Ghost Dance by the Ogallala Sioux at Pine Ridge Agency, South Dakota. From a drawing by Frederic Remington made from sketches taken on the spot near the White River, Pine Ridge Agency and published in Supplement to Harper's Weekly, December 6, 1890.

and chanting as they constricted the circle, the circle widening and constricting again and again. The dancing continued for a day and a night, Wovoka sitting in the middle of the circle before a large fire with his head bowed. He wore a white striped coat, a pair of trousers, and moccasins. On the second day he stopped the dancing and described the visions that God had sent to him. Then the dancing commenced again and lasted for three more days.

When a second dance was held soon afterward, several Utes visited the ceremony out of curiosity. Returning to their reservation, the Utes told the neighboring Bannocks about what they had seen. The Bannocks sent emissaries to the next dance, and within a few weeks the Shoshones at Fort Hall Reservation saw a ritual staged by the Bannocks. They were so impressed they sent a delegation to Nevada to learn the new religion from Wovoka himself.

Perhaps more than any other of the tribes, the Cheyenne and Sioux felt the need for a messiah who could lead them back to their days of glory. After the story of Wovoka was carried swiftly to their reservations, several medicine men decided to make pilgrimages. It was a mark of prestige for them to travel by railroad, and as soon as they could raise enough money, they purchased tickets to Nevada. In the autumn of 1889, a Cheyenne named Porcupine made the journey, and a short time later Short Bull, Kicking Bear, and other Sioux leaders traveled all the way from Dakota.

The Sioux accepted the Ghost Dance religion with more fervor than any of the other tribes. On their return to the Dakota reservations, each delegate tried to outdo the others in describing the wonders of the messiah. Wovoka came down from heaven in a cloud, they said. He showed them a vision of all the nations of Indians coming home. The earth would be covered with dust and then a new earth would come upon the old. They must use the sacred red and white paint and the sacred grass to make the vanished buffalo return in great herds.

In the spring of 1890 the Sioux began dancing the Ghost Dance at Pine Ridge Reservation, adding new symbols to Wovoka's original ceremony. By June they were wearing ghost shirts made of cotton cloth painted blue around the necks, with bright-colored thunderbirds, bows and arrows, suns, moons, and stars emblazoned upon them.

To accompany the dancing they made ghost songs:

> *The whole world is coming,*
> *A nation is coming, a nation is coming,*
> *The Eagle has brought the message to the tribe.*
> *The father says so, the father says so.*
> *Over the whole earth they are coming,*
> *The buffalo are coming, the buffalo are coming.*

Mainly because they misunderstood the meaning of the Ghost Dance religion, the Government's policy makers who ran the reservations from Washington decided to stamp it out. If they had taken the trouble to examine its basic tenets, they would have found that in its original form the religion was opposed to all forms of violence, self-mutilation, theft, and falsehood. As one Army officer observed: "Wovoka has given these people a better religion than they ever had before."

The Ghost Dance might have died away under official pressure had not the greatest maker of medicine among the Sioux, Sitting Bull, chosen to come forth from his "retirement" near Standing Rock agency and join the new religion of the dance. Sitting Bull was the last of the great unreconciled chiefs. Since his return from Canada, where he had gone after the Custer battle, he had been carrying on a feud with the military as well as with civilian reservation agents.

When Kicking Bear, one of the early emissaries to Wovoka, visited Sitting Bull in late 1890 to teach him the Ghost Dance, Agent James McLaughlin ordered Kicking Bear escorted off the reservation. Sitting Bull may or may not have believed in the messiah, but he was always searching for opportunities to bedevil the authorities. Kicking Bear was hardly off the reservation before Sitting Bull set up a dance camp and started instructing his followers in the new religion. In a short time the peaceful ghost songs became warlike chants.

Sitting Bull. Engraving from A History of the American People *by Woodrow Wilson that originally appeared in* Harper's Weekly, *December 20, 1890, from a photograph by Barry, West Superior, Wisconsin.*

Efforts of authorities to put a stop to ghost dancing now led to resentment and increased belligerency from the Indians. Inevitably the Army was drawn into the controversy, and in the late autumn of 1890 General Nelson Miles ordered more troops into the plains area.

Suspecting that Sitting Bull was the leading trouble-maker, Miles arranged informally with Buffalo Bill Cody to act as intermediary. Cody had scouted with Miles in former years and had also employed Sitting Bull as a feature attraction with his Wild West show. "Sitting Bull might listen to you," Miles told Cody, "when under the same conditions he'd take a shot at one of my soldiers."

Buffalo Bill went at once to Fort Yates on the Standing Rock Reservation, but authorities there were dismayed when they read Miles's written instructions to Cody: "Secure the person of Sitting Bull and deliver him to the nearest commanding officer of U.S. troops." James McLaughlin, the reservation agent, and Lieutenant Colonel William Drum, the military commander, both feared that Cody's actions might precipitate a general outbreak throughout the area. The military authorities immediately took it upon themselves to get Buffalo Bill drunk, send a wire to Washington, and have his orders rescinded.

"All the officers were requested to assist in drinking Buffalo Bill under the table," Captain A. R. Chapin later recorded. "But his capacity was such that it took practically all of us in details of two or three at a time to keep him interested and busy throughout the day." Although the rugged Cody managed to keep a clear head through all this maneuvering, he had scarcely started out to Sitting Bull's encampment before a telegram came from Washington canceling his orders.

Meanwhile Agent McLaughlin had decided to take Sitting Bull into custody himself, hoping to prevent a dangerous disturbance which he felt would result if the military authorities forced the issue and tried to make an arrest. McLaughlin gave the necessary orders to his Indian police, instructing them not to permit the chief to escape under any circumstances.

Just before daybreak on December 15, 1890, forty-three Indian police surrounded Sitting Bull's log cabin. Lieutenant Bull Head, the Indian policeman in charge of the party, found Sitting Bull asleep on the floor. When he was awakened, the old war leader stared incredulously at Bull Head. "What do you want here?" he asked.

"You're my prisoner," said Bull Head calmly. "You must go to the agency."

Sitting Bull yawned and sat up. "All right," he said, "let me put on my clothes and I'll go with you." He called one of his wives and sent her to an adjoining cabin for his best clothing, and then asked the policeman to saddle his horse for him.

While these things were being done, his ardent followers who had been dancing the Ghost Dance every night for weeks, were gathering around the cabin. They outnumbered the police four to one, and soon had them pressed against the walls. As soon as Lieutenant Bull Head emerged with Sitting Bull, he must have sensed the explosive nature of the situation.

While they waited for Sitting Bull's horse, a fanatical ghost dancer named Catch-the-Bear appeared out of the mob. "You think you are going to take him," Catch-the-Bear shouted at the policemen. "You shall not do it!"

"Come now," Bull Head said quietly to his prisoner, "do not listen to anyone." But Sitting Bull held back, forcing Bull Head and Sergeant Red Tomahawk to pull him toward his horse.

Without warning, Catch-the-Bear suddenly threw off his blanket and brought up a rifle, firing point-blank at Bull Head, wounding him in the side. As Bull Head fell, he tried to shoot his assailant, but the bullet struck Sitting Bull instead. Almost simultaneously Red Tomahawk shot Sitting Bull through the head. A wild fight developed immediately, and only the timely arrival of a cavalry detachment saved the police from extinction.

———⟫●⟪———

News of Sitting Bull's death swept across the reservations, startling the Indians and the watchful military forces in the Dakotas. Most of the frightened followers of the great chief immediately came into Standing Rock agency and surrendered. Others fled toward the southwest.

Those who were fleeing knew exactly where they were going. They were seeking to join forces with a Ghost Dance believer, an aging chief named Big Foot. For some time, Big Foot had been gathering followers at a small village near the mouth of Deep Creek on Cheyenne River. As the Ghost Dance craze had increased, so had Big Foot's forces, and even before the fatal shooting of Sitting Bull, a small party of cavalrymen under Lieutenant Colonel Edwin V. Sumner, Jr. had been assigned to watch his movements.

As soon as news of Sitting Bull's death reached Big Foot, he began preparations to break camp. Lieutenant Colonel Sumner accepted the chief's explanation that the Indians were preparing to proceed eastward to the Cheyenne River agency where they would spend the winter. Big Foot was unusually friendly, and declared that the only reason he had permitted the fugitives from Sitting Bull's camp to join his people was that he felt sorry for them and wanted them to return to the reservation with him. Sumner was so convinced of Big Foot's sincerity that he permitted the band to keep their arms — a decision that was to precipitate the tragedy of Wounded Knee.

———⟫●⟪———

Before dawn the next day, December 23, Big Foot and his ever-increasing band were in rapid flight, moving in the opposite direction from the Cheyenne River agency. The question has never been settled as to whether they were heading for Pine Ridge agency, as Big Foot's followers later claimed, or for the Sioux recalcitrants' stronghold in the Badlands. But it is a fact that a few days earlier those two leaders, who had once visited the messiah in Nevada, were in the Badlands. And they had with them several hundred fanatical followers, keyed up to a high frenzy as a result of their continual dancing and chanting.

Learning of Big Foot's escape from Sumner's cavalry, General Miles ordered Major Samuel M. Whitside of the 7th Cavalry to intercept the Indians, disarm them, and return them to a reservation. On December 28, Whitside's scouts found the fugitives on Porcupine Creek and when the major sighted a white flag fluttering from a wagon, he rode out to meet it. He was surprised to find Big Foot lying in the bed of the wagon, swathed in blankets, suffering severely from pneumonia.

Whitside shook hands with the ailing chief, and told him that he must bring his people to the cavalry camp on Wounded Knee Creek. In a hoarse voice that was almost a whisper, Big Foot agreed to the order. Whitside, on the advice of one of his scouts, decided to wait until the band was assembled beside the cavalry camp before disarming them.

During the ensuing march, none of the cavalrymen suspected that anything was amiss. The Indians seemed to be in good humor; they talked and laughed with the soldiers, and smoked their cigarettes. Not one of the cavalrymen seemed to have been aware that almost all of these Indians were wearing sacred ghost shirts which they believed would protect them from the soldiers' weapons. And the soldiers seemed to be completely ignorant of the fact that their prisoners were obsessed with the belief that the day of the Indians' return to power was close at hand. One of the most fanatical members of the band was a medicine man, Yellow Bird, who all during the march was moving stealthily up and down the line, occasionally blowing on an eagle-bone whistle and muttering Ghost Dance chants.

When the column reached Wounded Knee, the Indians were assigned an area near the cavalry camps. They were carefully counted; 120 men and 230 women and children were present. Rations were issued, and they set up their shelters for the night. For additional cover, Major Whitside gave them several army tents. The troop surgeon, John van

R. Hoff, went to attend the ailing Big Foot, and a stove was set up in the chief's tent. Whitside, however, did not entirely trust Big Foot's band. He posted a battery of four Hotchkiss guns, training them directly on the Indians' camp.

It was a cold night. Ice was already an inch thick on the tree-bordered creek, and there was a hint of snow in the air. During the night, Colonel James W. Forsyth of the 7th Cavalry rode in and took command. Significantly there were now at Wounded Knee five troop commanders — Moylan, Varnum, Wallace, Godfrey, and Edgerly — who had been with Reno and Custer at the Little Big Horn. With Big Foot were warriors who had fought in the same battle. Much would be made of that in days to come.

In Forsyth's command was a young lieutenant, James D. Mann, who was to witness the opening shots of the approaching fight. "The next morning," Mann said afterwards, "we started to disarm them, the [men] being formed in a semi-circle in front of the tents. We went through the tents looking for arms, and while this was going on, every-one seemed to be good-natured, and we had no thought of trouble. The [women] were sitting on bundles concealing guns and other arms. We lifted them as tenderly and treated them as nicely as possible.

"While this was going on, the medicine man [Yellow Bird] who was in the center of the semi-circle of [men], had been going through the Ghost Dance, and making a speech, the substance of which was, as told me by an interpreter afterwards, 'I have made medicine of the white man's ammunition. It is good medicine, and his bullets can not harm you, as they will not go through your ghost shirts, while your bullets will kill.'

"It was then that I had a peculiar feeling come over me which I can not describe — some presentiment of trouble — and I told the men to 'be ready: there is going to be trouble.' We were only six or eight feet from the Indians and I ordered my men to fall back.

"In front of me were four [men] — three armed with rifles and one with bow and arrows. I drew my revolver and stepped through the line to my place with my detachment. The Indians raised their weapons over their heads to heaven as if in votive offering, then brought

Yellow Bird, the medicine man, throwing dust in the air as a signal to the Sioux to open fire, beginning the fight at Wounded Knee. From a drawing by Frederic Remington, in Harper's Weekly, *January 24, 1891.*

them down to bear on us, the one with the bow and arrow aiming directly at me. Then they seemed to wait an instant.

"The medicine man threw a handful of dust in the air, put on his war bonnet, and an instant later a gun was fired. This seemed to be the signal they had been waiting for, and the firing immediately began. I ordered my men to fire, and the reports were almost simultaneous."

Things happened fast after that first volley. The Hotchkiss guns opened fire and began pouring shells into the Indians at the rate of nearly fifty per minute. What survivors there were began a fierce hand-to-hand struggle, using revolvers, knives, and war clubs. The lack of rifles among the Indians made the fight more bloody because it brought the combatants to closer quarters. In a few minutes, 200 Indian men, women, and children and sixty soldiers were lying dead and wounded on the ground, the ripped tents blazing and smoking around them. Some of the surviving Indians fled to a nearby ravine, hiding among the rocks and scrub cedars. Others continued their flight up the slopes to the south.

Yellow Bird, the medicine man, concealed himself in a tent, and through a slit in the canvas began shooting at the soldiers. When one of the 7th Cavalry troopers ran forward to slash open the tent, Yellow Bird killed him by pumping bullets into his stomach. Angry cavalrymen responded with heavy fire, then piled hay around the tent and set it to blazing.

Big Foot died early in the fighting from a bullet through his head. Captain Edward Godfrey, who had survived the Little Bighorn (he was with Benteen), was shocked when he discovered he had ordered his men to fire on women and children hidden in a brush thicket. Captain George Wallace, who also had survived the Custer fight (with Reno's battalion), was shouting his first order to fire when a bullet carried away the top of his head.

On the bloody campground, Surgeon Hoff did what he could for the wounded. He disarmed a wounded Indian who was still trying to fire his rifle. The warrior staggered to his feet and looked down fixedly at the burned body of Yellow Bird. "If I could be taken to you," the wounded Indian muttered to the dead medicine man, "I would kill you again."

Disillusionment over the failure of the ghost shirts had already affected most of the other survivors. With blood flowing from her wounds, one of the [Indian women] tore off her brilliantly colored shirt and stamped upon it.

As it was apparent by the end of the day that a blizzard was approaching, the medical staff hastily gathered the wounded together to carry them to a field hospital at Pine Ridge. In the affair 146 Indians and 25 soldiers had been killed, but the full totals would not be known until several days afterward because of the snowstorm that blanketed the battlefield.

<hr>

After the blizzard, when a burial party went out to Wounded Knee, they found many of the bodies frozen grotesquely where they had fallen. They buried all the Indians together in a large pit. A few days later, relatives of the slain came and put up a wire fence around the mass grave; then they smeared the posts with sacred red medicine paint.

By this time the nation's press was having a field day with the new "Indian war." Some journalists pictured the Wounded Knee tragedy as a triumph of brave soldiers over treacherous Indians; others declared it was a slaughter of helpless Indians by a regiment searching for revenge since the Little Bighorn. The truth undoubtedly lay somewhere between these opposite points of view. Certainly it was a tragic accident of war.

At Wounded Knee, the vision of the peaceful Paiute dreamer, Wovoka, had come to an end. And so had all the long and bitter years of Indian resistance on the western plains.

Suggested Readings

CHAPTER 1 THE PIRATES OF THE OHIO

Baldwin, Leland Dewitt. *The Keelboat Age on Western Waters*. Pittsburgh: University of Pittsburgh Press, 1941.

Blair, Walter, and Franklin J. Meine, eds. *Half Horse, Half Alligator: The Growth of the Mike Fink Legend*. Chicago: University of Chicago Press, 1956.

Grayson, Frank Y. *Thrills of the Historic Ohio River*. Cincinnati: 1930(?).

Rothert, Otto A. *The Outlaws of Cave-in-Rock*. Carbondale, Ill.: Southern Illinois University Press, 1996.

CHAPTER 2 THE GREAT ADVENTURE

Ambrose, Stephen E. *Undaunted Courage: Meriwether Lewis, Thomas Jefferson, and the Opening of the American West*. New York: Charles Scribner's Sons, 1996.

Andrist, Ralph K. *To the Pacific with Lewis and Clark*. New York: American Heritage Publishing Co., 1967.

Bakeless, John. *Lewis and Clark, Partners in Discovery*. New York: William Morrow, 1947.

De Voto, Bernard, ed. *The Journals of Lewis and Clark*. Boston: Houghton, Mifflin, 1953.

Gass, Patrick. *Journals of Lewis and Clark Expedition*. Minneapolis: Ross & Haines, 1958.

Jackson, Donald, ed. *Letters of the Lewis and Clark Expedition—with Related Documents, 1783–1854*. 2 vols. Urbana: University of Illinois, 1978.

Lavender, David S. *The Way to the Western Sea: Lewis and Clark across the Continent*. New York: Harper & Row, 1988.

Lewis, Meriwether. *Original Journals of the Lewis and Clark Expedition 1804–1806*. Ed. Reuben Gold Thwaites. 8 vols. New York: Dodd, Mead & Co. 1904–1905.

Moulton, Gary, ed. *Atlas of the Lewis and Clark Expedition*. Vol. 1. Lincoln: University of Nebraska Press, 1983.

_____. *Journals of the Lewis and Clark Expedition*. Vols. 2–10. Lincoln: University of Nebraska Press, 1986–1996.

Salisbury, Albert, and Jane Salisbury. *Two Captains West*. New York: Bramhall House, 1950.

CHAPTER 3 INTRIGUE ON THE NATCHEZ TRACE

Dillon, Richard. *Meriwether Lewis*. New York: Coward-McCann, 1965.

Fisher, Vardis. *Suicide or Murder? The Strange Death of Governor Meriwether Lewis*. Denver: Alan Swallow, 1962.

Wilson, Charles M. *Meriwether Lewis of Lewis and Clark*. New York: Thomas Y. Crowell Co., 1934.

CHAPTER 4 THE TRAIL OF TEARS

Carter, Samuel III. *Cherokee Sunset: A Nation Betrayed. A Narrative of Travail and Triumph, Persecution and Exile*. New York: Doubleday & Co., 1976.

Ehle, John. *Trail of Tears: The Rise and Fall of the Cherokee Nation*. New York: Doubleday, 1988.

Jahoda, Gloria. *The Trail of Tears: The Story of the American Indian Removals 1813–1855*. New York: Holt, Rinehart & Winston, 1975.

Perdue, Theda, and Michael D. Green, eds. *The Cherokee Removal: A Brief History with Documents*. Boston: Bedford Books (St. Martin's Press), 1995.

Wilkins, Thurman. *Cherokee Tragedy: The Story of the Ridge Family and of the Decimation of a People*. New York: Macmillan Co., 1970.

CHAPTER 5 ALONG THE SANTA FE TRAIL

Brandon, William. *The Santa Fe Trail*. "American Trails Series." New York: McGraw-Hill, 1967.

Chalfant, William Y. *Dangerous Passage: The Santa Fe Trail and the Mexican War*. Norman: University of Oklahoma Press, 1994.

Crutchfield, James A. *The Santa Fe Trail*. Plano, Texas, Republic of Texas Press, 1996.

Duffus, Robert Luther. *The Santa Fe Trail*. New York: Longman's Green & Co., 1930.

Gregg, Josiah. *Commerce of the Prairies*. Ed. Max L. Moorhead. Norman: University of Oklahoma Press, 1958.

Inman, Col. Henry. *The Old Santa Fe Trail: The Story of a Great Highway*. Topeka: Crane & Co., 1916.

Magoffin, Susan Shelby. *Down the Santa Fe Trail and Into Mexico*. Ed. Stella M. Drumm. New Haven: Yale University Press, 1926.

Napton, William B. *Over the Santa Fe Trail—1857*. Santa Fe: Stagecoach Press, reprinted 1964.

Oliva, Leo E. *Soldiers on the Santa Fe Trail*. Norman: University of Oklahoma Press, 1967.

Porter, Clyde, and Mae Reed, eds. *Matt Field on the Santa Fe Trail*. Norman: University of Oklahoma Press, 1960.

Simmons, Marc, ed. *On the Santa Fe Trail*. Lawrence: University Press of
     Kansas, 1986.
_____. *The Old Trail to Santa Fe: Collected Essays*. Albuquerque: University
     of New Mexico Press, 1986.

CHAPTER 6 BRIDES BY THE BOATLOAD

Conant, Roger. *Mercer's Belles: The Journal of a Reporter*. Ed. Lenna A.
     Deutsch. Seattle: University of Washington Press, 1960.

CHAPTER 7 THE BELKNAP SCANDAL

Nevins, Allan. *Hamilton Fish: The Inner History of the Grant
     Administration*. New York: Frederick Ungar Publishing, 1936.

CHAPTER 8 JIM BRIDGER

Alter, J. Cecil. *Jim Bridger*. Norman: University of Oklahoma Press, 1962.
Chittenden, Hiram. *American Fur Trade of the Far West*. 2 vols. New York:
     Francis P. Harper, 1902.
Gowans, Fred R. *Fort Bridger: Island in the Wilderness*. Provo, Ut.: Brigham
     Young University Press, 1975.
Stewart, William Drummond. *Edward Warren*. Missoula, Mont.:
     Mountain Press, 1986.
Vestal, Stanley. *Jim Bridger, Mountain Man*. New York: William Morrow
     & Co., 1946.

CHAPTER 9 A GIRL WITH THE DONNER PASS PARTY

Croy, Homer. *Wheels West: The Story of the Donner Party*. New York:
     Hastings House Publishers, 1955.
McGlashan, C. F. *History of the Donner Party: A Tragedy of the Sierra*.
     Stanford, Calif.: Stanford University Press, 1947, rev. ed.
Stewart, George R. *Ordeal by Hunger: The Story of the Donner Party*.
     Lincoln: University of Nebraska Press, 1986.

CHAPTER 10 ELY S. PARKER

Armstrong, William H. *Warrior in Two Camps: Ely S. Parker Union General
     and Seneca Chief*. Syracuse, N.Y.: Syracuse University Press, 1978.
Hauptman, Laurence M. *Between Two Fires: American Indians in the Civil
     War*. New York: The Free Press, 1995.
Parker, Arthur C. *The Life of General Ely S. Parker*. "The Publications of
     the Buffalo Historical Society," vol. 23. Buffalo, N.Y.: Buffalo
     Historical Society, 1919.
Parker, Ely S. "General Parker's Autobiography." *The Publications of the
     Buffalo Historical Society*, 8: 527–36. Buffalo, N.Y.: Buffalo Historical
     Society, 1905.
U.S. Commissioner of Indian Affairs. Report of the Commissioner of
     Indian Affairs. Washington, D.C., 1869.
U. S. House of Representatives. "Affairs in the Indian Department."
     Report no. 39, Washington, D.C., 1871.

350

THE BEST OF DEE BROWN'S WEST

CHAPTER 11 THE ORDEAL OF SURGEON TAPPAN

Byrne, Dr. James. *Frontier Army Surgeon.* New York: Exposition Press, 1962.

Peterson, Dr. Edward S. "Abandoned Near Cottonwood Springs." *The Westerners Brand Book,* 32, no. 8 (December 1975).

CHAPTER 12 HOW STANDING BEAR BECAME A PERSON

Mathes, Valerie S. *Helen Hunt Jackson and Her Indian Reform Legacy.* Austin: University of Texas Press, 1990.

Tibbles, Thomas Henry. *The Ponca Chiefs: An Account of the Trial of Standing Bear.* Ed. Kay Graber. Lincoln: University of Nebraska Press, 1972.

CHAPTER 13 BUTCH CASSIDY AND THE SUNDANCE KID

Baker, Pearl. *The Wild Bunch at Robber's Roost.* New York: Abelard-Schuman, 1971.

Betenson, Lula Parker. *Butch Cassidy, My Brother.* Provo, Ut.: Brigham Young University Press, 1975.

Drago, Gail. *Etta Place: Her Life and Times with Butch Cassidy and the Sundance Kid.* Plano: Republic of Texas Press, 1995.

Frackleton, Will. *Sagebrush Dentist.* Chicago: McClurg, 1941.

Horan, James D. *The Wild Bunch.* New York: Signet Books (New American Library), 1958.

Kelly, Charles. *The Outlaw Trail: A History of Butch Cassidy and His Wild Bunch.* New York: Devin-Adair Co., 1959.

Meadows, Anne. *Digging Up Butch and Sundance.* New York: St. Martin's Press, 1994.

Pointer, Larry. *In Search of Butch Cassidy.* Norman: University of Oklahoma Press, 1977.

Redford, Robert. *The Outlaw Trail.* New York: Grosset & Dunlap, 1978.

CHAPTER 14 STORY OF THE PLAINS INDIANS

Brown, Dee. *Bury My Heart at Wounded Knee.* New York: Holt, Rinehart & Winston, 1970.

Grinnell, George Bird. *The Story of the Indian.* New York: D. Appleton, 1895.

____. *The Cheyenne Indians.* 2 vols. New Haven, Conn.: Yale University Press, 1923.

Jackson, Helen Hunt. *A Century of Dishonor.* Williamstown, Mass.: Corner House Publishers, 1973.

Koch, Ronald P. *Dress Clothing of the Plains Indian.* Norman: University of Oklahoma Press, 1977.

Mails, Thomas E. *The Mystic Warrior of the Plains.* Garden City, N.Y.: Doubleday, 1972.

____. *The Plains Indians: Dog Soldiers, Bear Men and Buffalo Women.* New York: Promontory Press, 1991.

Mishkin, Bernard. *Rank and Warfare Among the Plains Indians.* Lincoln: University of Nebraska Press, 1992.

Schultz, J. Willard. *My Life As an Indian.* Boston: Houghton Mifflin, 1910.

Utley, Robert M. *The Indian Frontier of the American West 1846–1890.* Albuquerque: University of New Mexico Press, 1984.

Wallace, Ernest, and E. Adamson Hoebel. *The Comanches: Lords of the South Plains.* Norman: University of Oklahoma Press, 1952.

CHAPTER 15 THE DAY OF THE BUFFALO

Branch, E. Douglas. *The Hunting of the Buffalo.* Lincoln: University of Nebraska Press, 1962.

Cook, John R. *The Border and the Buffalo.* Chicago: Lakeside Press, 1938.

Dary, David A. *The Buffalo Book.* Chicago: Sage Books, 1974.

Gard, Wayne. *The Great Buffalo Hunt.* New York: Alfred A. Knopf, 1960.

McHugh, Tom. *The Time of the Buffalo.* New York: Alfred A. Knopf, 1972.

Grinnell, George Bird. *When Buffalo Ran.* Norman: University of Oklahoma Press, 1966.

Sandoz, Mari. *The Buffalo Hunters.* New York: Hastings House, 1954.

CHAPTER 16 DAY OF THE LONGHORNS

Abbott, E. C. *We Pointed Them North.* New York: Farrar & Rinehart, 1939.

Adams, Andy. *The Log of a Cowboy.* New York: Houghton Mifflin, 1903.

Adams, Ramon. *The Rampaging Herd.* Norman: University of Oklahoma Press, 1959.

Brown, Dee, and Martin F. Schmitt. *Trail Driving Days.* New York: Charles Scribner's Sons, 1952.

Chrisman, Harry E. *Lost Trails of the Cimarron.* Denver: Sage Books, 1961.

Dale, Edward Everett. *The Range Cattle Industry.* Norman: University of Oklahoma Press, 1960.

Dobie, J. Frank. *Cow People.* Boston: Little, Brown, 1964.

_____. *The Longhorns.* Boston: Little, Brown, 1941.

Dykstra, Robert R. *The Cattle Towns.* New York: Alfred A. Knopf, 1968.

Haley, J. Evetts. *Charles Goodnight.* Norman: University of Oklahoma Press, 1949.

Hamner, Laura V. *Short Grass and Longhorns.* Norman: University of Oklahoma Press, 1943.

Ridings, Sam. *The Chisholm Trail.* Guthrie, Okla.: Co-Operative Publishing House, 1936.

Rollins, Philip A. *The Cowboy.* Rev. ed. New York: Charles Scribner's Sons, 1936.

_____. *Jinglebob.* New York: Charles Scribner's Sons, 1927.

Sandoz, Mari. *The Cattlemen.* New York: Hastings House, 1958.

Wellman, Paul I. *The Trampling Herd.* New York: Carrick & Evans, 1939.

CHAPTER 17 THE PONY EXPRESS

Bloss, Roy S. *Pony Express: The Great Gamble*. Berkeley, Calif.: Howell-North, 1959.

Chapman, Arthur. *The Pony Express*. New York: G. P. Putnam's Sons, 1932.

De Wolff, J. H. *Pawnee Bill (Major Gordon W. Lillie): His Experiences and Adventures*. Pawnee Bill's Historic Wild West Company, 1902.

Majors, Alexander. *Seventy Years on the Frontier*. Minneapolis: Ross & Haines, Inc., 1965.

Reinfeld, Fred. *Pony Express*. New York: Collier Books, 1966.

Settle, Raymond W., and Mary Lund Settle. *Saddles and Spurs: The Pony Express Saga*. Harrisburg, Stackpole, 1955.

Visscher, William Lightfoot. *The Pony Express: A Thrilling and Truthful History*. Golden, Colo.: Outbooks, 1980.

CHAPTER 18 THE SETTLEMENT OF THE GREAT PLAINS

Emmons, David M. *Garden in the Grasslands: Boomer Literature of the Central Great Plains*. Lincoln: University of Nebraska Press, 1971.

Holmes, Kenneth L., ed. *Covered Wagon Women: Diaries and Letters from the Western Trails, 1840–1849*. Lincoln: University of Nebraska Press, 1995.

Schmitt, Martin F., and Dee Brown. *The Settlers' West*. New York: Charles Scribner's Sons, 1955.

Unruh, Jr., John D. *The Plains Across: The Overland Emigrants and the Trans-Mississippi West, 1840–60*. Champaign: University of Illinois Press, 1993.

Webb, Walter Prescott. *The Great Plains*. Boston: Ginn & Co., 1931.

CHAPTER 19 IN PURSUIT OF REVENGE

Anderson, Gary Clayton. *Little Crow: Spokesman for the Sioux*. St. Paul: Minnesota Historical Society Press, 1986.

Berghold, Rev. Alexander. *The Indians' Revenge: Or Days of Horror*. San Francisco: P. J. Thomas, 1891.

Buck, Daniel. *Indian Outbreak*. Minneapolis: Ross & Haines, Inc. 1965.

Carley, Kenneth. *The Sioux Uprising of 1862*. St. Paul: The Minnesota Historical Society, 1961.

Oehler, C. M. *The Great Sioux Uprising*. New York: Oxford University Press, 1959.

CHAPTER 20 GALVANIZED YANKEES

Brown, D. Alexander. *The Galvanized Yankees*. Urbana: University of Illinois Press, 1963.

CHAPTER 21 BEECHER'S ISLAND

Criqui, Orvel A. *Fifty Fearless Men: The Forsyth Scouts & Beecher Island*. Marceline, Walsworth Publishing Co., 1993.

Dixon, David. *Hero of Beecher Island: The Life and Military Career of George A. Forsyth.* Lincoln: University of Nebraska Press, 1994.

Monnett, John H. *The Battle of Beecher Island and the Indian War of 1867–1869.* Niwot, Colo.: University Press of Colorado, 1992.

CHAPTER 22 GERONIMO

Betzinez, Jason, and W. S. Nye. *I Fought with Geronimo.* Harrisburg, Penn.: Stackpole, 1960.

Bigelow, Lt. John. *On the Bloody Trail of Geronimo.* Los Angeles: Westernlore Press, 1968.

Davis, Britton. *The Truth about Geronimo.* Chicago: Lakeside Press, 1951.

Debo, Angie. *Geronimo: The Man, His Time, His Place.* Norman: University of Oklahoma Press, 1976.

Faulk, Odie B. *The Geronimo Campaign.* New York: Oxford University Press, 1969.

Haley, James L. *Apaches: A History and Cultural Portrait.* Garden City, N.Y.: Doubleday, 1981.

Lockwood, Frank C. *The Apache Indians.* New York: Macmillan, 1938.

Lummis, Charles F. *General Crook and the Apache Wars.* Ed. Turbese Lummis Fiske. Flagstaff, Ariz.: Northland Press, 1966.

Mazzanovich, Anton. *Trailing Geronimo.* Hollywood: A. Mazzanovich, 1931.

Thrapp, Dan L. *Dateline Fort Bowie—Charles Fletcher Lummis Reports on an Apache War.* Norman: University of Oklahoma Press, 1979.

CHAPTER 23 THE GHOST DANCE AND BATTLE OF WOUNDED KNEE

Bailey, Paul. *Wovoka, The Indian Messiah.* Los Angeles: Westernlore Press, 1957.

McLerran, Alice. *The Ghost Dance.* New York: Clarion Books, 1995.

Marshall, S. L. A. *Crimsoned Prairie.* New York: Charles Scribner's Sons, 1972.

Miller, David Humphreys. *Ghost Dance.* New York: Duell, Sloan, & Pearce, 1959.

Mooney, James. *The Ghost Dance Religion and the Sioux Outbreak of 1890.* Lincoln: University of Nebraska Press, 1991.

Credits

"On Writing Western," *Roundup Magazine*, December 1995; "The Pirates of the Ohio," *American History Illustrated* 7, no. 4; "The Great Adventure," *American History Illustrated* 4, no. 8, and 4, no. 9; "Intrigue on the Natchez Trace," *Southern Magazine* 1, no. 2; "The Trail of Tears," *American History Illustrated* 7, no. 3; "Along the Santa Fe Trail," *American History Illustrated* 15, no. 6; "Brides by the Boatload," *American History Illustrated* 1, no. 1; "The Belknap Scandal," *American History Illustrated* 4, no. 2; "Jim Bridger," *American History Illustrated* 3, no. 4; "A Girl with the Donner Pass Party," *American History Illustrated* 1, no. 6; "Ely S. Parker — 'One Real American,'" *American History Illustrated* 4, no. 7; "The Ordeal of Surgeon Tappan," *True West* 10, no. 2; "How Standing Bear became a Person," *American History Illustrated* 6, no. 1; "Butch Cassidy and the Sundance Kid," *American History Illustrated* 17, no. 4; "Story of the Plains Indians," *American History Illustrated* 8, no. 5; "The Day of the Buffalo," *American History Illustrated* 11, no. 4; "Day of the Longhorns," *American History Illustrated* 9, no. 9; "The Pony Express," *American History Illustrated* 11, no. 7; "The Settlement of the Great Plains," *American History Illustrated* 9, no. 3; "Sailing over the Plains," *American History Illustrated* 1, no. 6; "In Pursuit of Revenge," *American History Illustrated* 16, no. 5; "Galvanized Yankees," *Civil War Times Illustrated* 4, no. 10; "Beecher's Island," *American History Illustrated* 2, no. 8; "Geronimo," *American History Illustrated* 15, no. 3, and 15, no. 4; "The Ghost Dance and Battle of Wounded Knee," *American History Illustrated* 1, no. 8.

Index

Standing Bear *versus* Crook, 160
Standing Rock, 230
Standing Rock Reservation, 339–40
Stanley, Henry M., 292
Stansbury, Captain Howard, 118
Stanton, Secretary of War Edwin M.,
  293–95
Stanton, T. C., 134
starvation, 135
Steck, Dr. Michael, 318
Sterling, Albert, 322
Stevens, Annie, 92, 95
Stewart, William Drummond, 116
Stillwell, Jack, 304, 309–11
stockades, 25
Stowe, Harriet Beecher, 87
Sublette, Bill, 114
Sublette, Milt, 116
Sully, Brigadier-General Alfred, 296–97
Sumner, Lieutenant Colonel Edwin V., Jr.,
  341–42
Sumner, Stevens, 152–53, 156
Sun Dance, 187, 204, 209–12
Sundance Kid. *See* Longabaugh, Harry
  (Sundance Kid)
survival, 36
Sutter's Fort, 134, 136
Swift Running Water. *See* Niobrara River

tall tales, 125–27, 269
Tanner, 94
Taoyateduta. *See* Little Crow (Sioux)
Tappan, Assistant Surgeon Benjamin,
  152–56
  Apache attack on, 152–54
  heroism of, 155–56
Tavibo (Paiute), 334
teachers, 89–90
Tennessee
  Chattanooga, 67
  McMinnville, 73
  Memphis. *See* Chickasaw Bluffs
  Nashville, 51
Tennessee River, 9, 49, 67–68
territorial borders, 36
Texas
  El Paso, 249
  Fort Worth, 168, 228
  San Antonio, 167, 170, 330
Tibbles, Thomas Henry, 160
Tiffany's, 170
Tilden, Samuel, 109
Timber Culture Act, 262

Timberlake, Henry, 60
tobacco, 21, 23, 207–8
Tomlinson, Amanda. *See* Belknap,
  Amanda (Puss) Tomlinson Bower
Tomlinson, Carita. *See* Belknap, Carita
  (Carrie)
Tomlinson, James, 102
Tongue River, Battle of, 122
Townsend, J. K., 220
Trail of Tears, 66–73
  background of, 59–62
  division among indians, 62–67
  terrors along the trail, 67–74
trans-Allegheny west, 3
transportation. *See also* animals, horses
  bull-boat, 114–15
  canoes, 25, 37
  covered wagons, 4, 70–73, 76, 81, 130
  flatboats, 4–5
  keelboats, 5, 17, 19
  pirogues, 17, 21–22
  railroads, 86, 124, 167–69, 224–28,
    259, 262–64, 276
  sailing ships, 50
  stagecoaches, 85, 292
  steamships, 91–94
  travois poles, 175, 181–83
  wagons, 31. *See also* transportation,
    covered wagons
trapping beaver, 114–16
Travelers' Rest, 44
Tribolett, Bob, 328–29
Truckee River, 134
Trudeau, Pierre (Pete), 309–11
Tsali (Cherokee), 68–69, 72
Turkey Creek, 325
Twain, Mark, 247, 254

Ulzana (Apache), 327
Union Pacific Railroad, 124, 160, 224,
  227, 268, 292
Utah
  Beaver, 163
  Castle Gate, 167
  Salt Lake City, 121, 251–52, 292
Utah Territory, 120
Utah War, 121
Utsala, Chief (Cherokee), 69

Vann, Joseph (Cherokee), 62
vaquero, 233
Virginia
  Charlottesville, 16